W9-BFF-687

DELICIOUS DIABETIC RECIPES

www.penn.co.il

Created by Penn Publishing Ltd.

An Imagine Book
Published by Charlesbridge
85 Main Street, Watertown, MA 02472
(617) 926-0329
www.charlesbridge.com

Text © 2009 by Rani Polak

ISBN 978-1-62354-032-6 (Special Edition for Barnes & Noble)
Library of Congress Control Number: 2009922014

2 4 6 8 10 9 7 5 3 1

Printed in China, May 2013.

For information about custom editions, special sales, premium and corporate purchases, please contact Charlesbridge Publishing at specialsales@charlesbridge.com

This publication contains the opinions and ideas of the author. It is intended to provide helpful and informative material on the subjects addressed in the publication. It is sold with the understanding that the author and publishers are not engaged in rendering medical, health, or any other kind of personal professional services in the book. The reader should consult his or her medical, health, or other competent professional before adopting any of the suggestions in this book or drawing inferences from it. The author and publishers specifically disclaim all responsibility for any liability, loss or risk, personal or otherwise, which is incurred as a consequence, directly or indirectly, of the use and application of any of the contents of this book.

DELICIOUS DIABETIC RECIPES

The Gourmet Cookbook for a Healthy Life

Rani Polak, MD, Le Cordon Bleu Chef

Photography by Danya Weiner

imagine!
Publishing

Table of Contents

Part 1

How to Use this Book

This book is written so that it can be used in two manners: as a regular cookbook and as a textbook. To use it as a regular cookbook, simply flip through the book when you're planning a meal and stop at a recipe that looks tasty, or use the index to find recipes that contain ingredients you'd like to use. If you follow this method, you'll find that every recipe contains tips that explain essential points about the manner of preparation, or ideas for possible variations of the basic recipe.

As a textbook, this book is organized in a sequential manner, and I warmly recommend reading it this way, and not necessarily while you are working in the kitchen. The paragraphs of text between the recipes, in combination with the recipes themselves, make up a comprehensive guidebook on the basic principles of healthy cooking. Reading the book in this manner will allow you to extract the most from it, beyond learning specific recipes, to gain a deeper understanding of recommended ingredients, healthy cooking techniques, and the equipment needed to help manage your kitchen in a time- and cost-efficient manner.

I hope that this understanding helps improve your confidence in the kitchen, and makes you feel freer to create, cook, and alter foods to suit your desires. Try to vary the recipes yourself to make new dishes with ingredients you particularly like. If you have read this entire book, you'll be able to succeed. The kitchen can be a friendly place because the possibilities before you, in spite of (or perhaps thanks to) your desire to prepare healthy foods, are practically endless!

* The Nutritional Calculations
You'll find detailed nutrition information at the end of each recipe. For diabetics who have personalized nutritional recommendations, each recipe provides the exchanges, based on the American Dietetic Association and American Diabetes Associations' exchange lists, as well as the carbohydrates choice if you use the 'counting carbohydrates' method. Use the method recommended by your dietitian in order to know how much of each food you should eat.

Introduction

This book is for people with diabetes and for people who are healthy and want to eat right. Many people ask themselves: What is healthy cooking? What foods are good for us to eat? Finding clear guidelines on this issue is difficult, and people are often confused since there are so many recommendations that sometimes contradict each other and often change. This book doesn't suggest a single method of eating, nor does it recommend one food or another that works like magic. It also doesn't tell you how much fat or carbohydrates you should eat daily.

The primary and founding principle of this book is simple: to return pleasure to cooking, and to make good food easy and accessible for everyone, especially for people living with diabetes.

Sometimes, I feel that an unnecessary word sneaks into the expression "Healthy Cooking," and that word is "healthy." Almost every time you cook, you will prepare food that is tastier and healthier than prepared and prepackaged frozen food, or food served at fast-food outlets.

Nutritional research is important and definitely guides the contents of this book. However, sometimes too much information causes us to miss the main point: the pleasure of cooking and in eating good food. Prepare family meals, eat reasonable amounts of food, use healthy cooking methods, integrate tasty ingredients, sit with your children to eat together, and simply enjoy. The recipes in this book will make everyone happy, not just people living with diabetes.

For years, researchers have tried to identify specific nutritional elements that contribute to good health. Almost every time someone claims to have found the right element, whether it is a vitamin or an antioxidant, and tried to isolate that element in a controlled manner, they have found that the element's benefits were smaller, or even rendered harmful, when taken out of the food source in which it was naturally found. Indeed, despite so much research, no one has yet found a substitute for simple and enjoyable good food.

In this book, I combine the culinary skills I acquired while studying at the Cordon Bleu with the medical and nutritional considerations I learned during my medical studies. The book is a culmination of years of work and hands-on experience at the Center for Healthy Cooking that I founded. Most of my time at this center has been devoted to developing recipes and learning from people who live with diabetes about how to help them. Though many of the students are diabetics, there are also students who come to the Center to learn healthy cooking habits.

This book contains almost 100 recipes; when combined with suggestions made for substitutions and alterations, you'll find more than 300 ideas for using delicious high-quality ingredients that are increasingly easy to find. Even the more complicated recipes in this book don't require a lot of preparation time. I hope you enjoy preparing these recipes as much I did, and that they add pleasure, flavor, and good health to your life.

Rani Polak, MD, Le Cordon Bleu Chef

Part 1

Basic Ingredients and Techniques

Starches

Starches, such as grains, breads, and legumes, are foods that contain mainly carbohydrate. Two goals of this book are to teach you cooking strategies to help you consume the appropriate amount of carbohydrate, and to increase your consumption of carbohydrate-containing foods made with whole grains and legumes. Many tips to help you consume the recommended amount of carbohydrate are found in the Lots of Vegetables chapter (pages 88–109). In the current chapter, you'll find recipes and cooking techniques using healthier starches to make a variety of delicious and nutritious foods.

Whole grains such as brown rice and whole-wheat pasta are considered healthier than foods made with refined grains, but making the transition to these foods can be difficult. For example, it may seem that brown rice is less tasty than white rice, or that whole-wheat pasta takes too long to cook.

One reason why preparing tasty foods that contain whole grains may be difficult is because these foods often require different preparation techniques than those used for refined grains. Another reason is that whole grains have a different texture than refined grains, and integrating them into recipes may require a different combination of ingredients. For example, substituting whole-wheat pasta in a recipe that calls for pasta made with refined flour won't always taste good unless other ingredients are adjusted as well.

In this chapter, you'll find explanations on how to cook whole grains, and recipes for diverse dishes that contain them. You'll also find guidelines for choosing ingredients to make simple combinations that are delicious with whole grains. Adopt these principles when you cook, and you'll find it easy to make delicious and nutritious gourmet foods.

Another issue relating to foods that contain carbohydrate is the question of which starch is the healthiest to consume. People often ask me if rye bread is better than whole-wheat bread or if "buckwheat is the best starch". I encourage people to think about variety as an important element of food choices. Every whole grain and legume has its unique advantage. One may contain a lot of Vitamin E while another is particularly rich in protein. The important thing is to use diverse healthy ingredients that provide balanced nutrition, increase your choices, and help you prepare interesting and attractive dishes.

In the next few pages, you'll become familiar with a wide selection of recipes for foods that contain whole grains, legumes, and starchy vegetable. This variety continues and expands throughout the book, providing you with an almost endless range of possibilities. Try them all, experiment a bit, and enjoy.

WHOLE-WHEAT PASTA

Pasta is a great whole-grain to start with, since it allows me to refute one of the claims many people make against whole grains: that cooking them is more complicated than cooking refined grains. In fact, achieving excellent results when cooking whole-wheat pasta is actually easier than when cooking regular pasta, for a number of reasons. The proper way to cook pasta is al dente, or until the texture of the pasta is still a bit hard. In order to reach this texture, the cooking time for pasta made with white flour is usually quite precise. If you missed the moment when your pasta was al dente and cooked it for a few extra minutes, the pasta will likely be soft, mushy, and not the right texture for eating.

An advantage of whole-wheat pasta is the presence of the wheat kernel, which retains its essential hardness, even when the pasta is cooked. As a result, it is easier to achieve the al dente texture with whole-wheat pasta than with pasta made from white flour, because even if you miss by a minute or two, its texture will still be a bit hard.

It is easier to achieve excellent results using whole-wheat pasta
Another benefit whole-wheat pasta has over regular pasta relates to the issue of stickiness. Whole-wheat pasta is naturally less sticky than pasta made from white flour because it has much less starch, and starch is what makes pasta sticky. In other words, you don't need to do anything to prevent whole-wheat pasta pieces from sticking to each other. Simply cook the pasta in a large pot of boiling salted water, then drain it when it is ready. If you do not plan on serving the pasta immediately after draining it, mix 1 tablespoon of olive oil into every pound of cooked pasta to keep the pasta pieces from sticking together until it is served.

When cooking, I often measure the level of difficulty in a recipe according to the amount of attention it demands. Making whole-wheat pasta requires less attention than making pasta made from white flour, since the cooking time is not strict. Dishes that don't require too much attention have an advantage over dishes that require precise measurements, especially if you want to do other things while your food is cooking.

If people in your household are reluctant to make the transition to whole-grain pasta due to its different color or texture, try making the transition gradual by combining pasta made with white flour and whole-wheat pasta in the same dish. It's true that you'll have to prepare the pastas in two different pots, but the results will be attractive and tasty, and you'll be making the transition to healthier cooking a transition to gourmet cooking as well.

There are two ways of preparing pasta dishes: in the recipe on the next page, vegetables are first stir-fried, then the pasta is added. Another way of making pasta dishes is by preparing the pasta and sauce separately, and combining them when the dish is served (see the Whole-Wheat Spaghetti with Roasted Vegetable Bolognaise on page 196). Whole-wheat pasta is also delicious in cold salads, and can be used for example, instead of wild rice in the Wild Rice and Beet Salad (page 26).

Whole-Wheat Pasta with Zucchini, Basil, and Cheese

With lemon juice and lemon rind, this sauce has a delicately tangy flavor that is a perfect complement for the nutty taste of whole-wheat pasta. It is a lovely alternative to traditional tomato, olive oil, cream, or herb-based sauces. Try substituting the zucchini with cubed kohlrabi or slices of Swiss chard or fennel. The cheese can be replaced with strips of grilled chicken breast or cubes of tofu that are sautéed before the rest of the vegetables, then added at the end of the cooking process.

INGREDIENTS

Serves 8 / Serving size: 1 cup

- ½ pound whole-wheat durum penne pasta
- 3 tablespoons extra-virgin olive oil
- 4 cloves garlic, crushed
- 6 medium zucchini, thinly sliced into rounds
- Pinch Atlantic sea salt
- ¼ teaspoon ground black pepper
- 3 tablespoons fresh lemon juice
- 1 tablespoon grated lemon rind
- 3 tablespoons chopped fresh basil
- 3½ ounces low-fat, semi-soft, white goat cheese, cut into ½-inch cubes
- 1 teaspoon sumac, for garnish

Calories	192
Total fat	8 g
Calories as fat	37%
Saturated fat	3 g
Cholesterol	6 mg
Carbohydrates	24 g
Dietary fiber	4 g
Sodium	62 mg
Protein	8 g
Carbohydrate choices	**2**

Exchanges:
½ starch, 1 vegetable, 1½ fat

PREPARATION

1. Prepare pasta according to instructions on bag, and drain. Toss with 1 tablespoon olive oil, and set aside.

2. In a large frying pan over medium heat, heat remaining 2 tablespoons oil. Add garlic and sauté for 3 minutes, until brown. Add zucchini, salt, and pepper, and sauté until brown. Add lemon juice and lemon rind, and sauté for 1 minute, while stirring.

3. Transfer pasta to frying pan, mix in basil, and cook for another minute. Add salt and pepper to taste. Top with cheese and sprinkle with sumac before serving.

Whole-Wheat Pasta with Zucchini, Basil, and Cheese

QUINOA

With its high protein content, crunchy texture, and nutty flavor, quinoa is one of today's trendiest starches. People who think whole-grain starches require longer cooking time will be delighted to discover that this isn't true of quinoa. It actually requires a relatively short cooking time and doesn't need to be soaked in advance. To prepare quinoa, simply put it in a pot at a ratio of 1 cup quinoa to 1¾ cups water and 1 or 2 tablespoons vegetable stock (page 63). Add a bit of salt and bring to a boil over high heat. Cover, reduce heat to low, and cook for about 7 minutes, or until half of the water has been absorbed. Turn off the heat and let the quinoa rest, covered, for 5 to 10 minutes, until the remaining liquid is absorbed and the quinoa is fluffy.

Frying quinoa before cooking it is unnecessary. In fact, there isn't any whole grain that requires frying. The reason for this is simple. People fry starches to create an artificial seal on each grain that prevents the grains from sticking. White rice, for example, is sometimes fried before cooking to prevent the starch from causing stickiness. However, whole-grain starches don't require frying to seal each grain, because the grains are already sealed in their natural shell.

In the following recipe the quinoa is cooked with salt, vegetable stock, and water, then mixed with vegetables that were prepared separately. You can also add quinoa while the vegetables are being cooked, as in the pasta dish on the previous page, or cook the quinoa with herbs and spices, like the bulgur that is prepared on page 21. Quinoa looks lovely mixed into cold salads, and it can be used as a substitute for brown rice in the Stuffed Peppers with Brown Rice and Tomato Sauce (page 30).

Quinoa with Sautéed Cherry Tomatoes and Asparagus

This recipe is a favorite among my students since it's easy to prepare, attractive, and features an interesting and delicious combination of textures—soft cherry tomatoes and crunchy asparagus. If you want to try some variations, substitute the cherry tomatoes with soft vegetables such as cooked pumpkin cubes or mushroom halves. The asparagus can be replaced with crunchy broccoli or cauliflower florets, or cubes of zucchini.

INGREDIENTS

Serves 10 / Serving size: ⅓ cup quinoa + 1 cup vegetables

- 1 cup quinoa
- 1¾ cups water
- 2 tablespoons vegetable stock (page 63), optional
- 2 pinches of Atlantic sea salt
- 20 asparagus spears, trimmed, cut into 2-inch pieces, and blanched (page 88)
- 4 tablespoons extra-virgin olive oil
- 8 cloves crushed garlic
- 1¾ pounds cherry tomatoes
- 2 tablespoons chopped fresh parsley
- 1 tablespoon chopped fresh cilantro
- 1 tablespoon chopped fresh basil
- 2 tablespoons chopped fresh mint
- 4 tablespoons chopped fresh chives
- 1 tablespoon chopped fresh thyme
- Pinch ground black pepper

Calories	130
Total fat	7 g
Calories as fat	48%
Saturated fat	1 g
Cholesterol	0 mg
Carbohydrates	15 g
Dietary fiber	2 g
Sodium	63 mg
Protein	4 g
Carbohydrate choices	**1**

Exchanges:
½ starch, 1 vegetable, 1½ fat

PREPARATION

1. In a medium pot, bring water, stock, quinoa, and a pinch of salt to a boil over high heat. Reduce heat to medium, cover, and cook for about 7 minutes, or until half the liquid is absorbed. Remove from heat and set aside covered for 10 minutes.

2. Separately, place wok over medium-high heat and add oil, swirling to coat. When oil is hot, add garlic and sauté for 3 minutes, until brown.

3. Add cherry tomatoes and asparagus and sauté for 3 minutes, stirring occasionally. Add parsley, cilantro, basil, mint, chives, and thyme, and sauté for 3 minutes, until cherry tomatoes begin to soften. Add salt and pepper to taste. To serve, place quinoa on individual plates and top with sautéed vegetables.

BULGUR

If you are really short on time, you may want to cook bulgur. This delicate version of wheat seeds is a staple in Mediterranean cooking. It is produced by parboiling whole wheat, breaking it, then drying it and sifting it into particles. Bulgur comes in various sizes, and each size is used for a different purpose. I recommend using coarse bulgur in the following recipes. The wheat husk is present, but broken, in bulgur. Water penetrates to the seed quickly, much like in white starches, so the preparation time is very short.

Preparing bulgur is simple. Just place equal parts of bulgur and water in a pot, add stock and a pinch of salt, and bring to a boil. Cover, reduce heat to low, and cook for 3 to 5 minutes. Bulgur can also be prepared without any cooking at all. Simply mix equal parts bulgur and boiling water in a bowl, cover, and let sit for 5 to 10 minutes. When all the water has been absorbed, the bulgur will be soft and ready to eat. Bulgur prepared in this manner can be served with vegetable dishes such as ratatouille (see Mediterranean Ratatouille with Millet, page 177) or with meat dishes such as the Persian Beef Stew with Quince and Pomegranate Seeds (page 167). If you serve bulgur alongside a dish that has been frozen, you can prepare a wholesome meal without using a single pot. Bulgur is an excellent food for keeping at the office. Bring a frozen stew with you in the morning, and heat it in the microwave at lunchtime. To prepare the bulgur, you just need boiling water and a covered bowl. Within minutes, you'll have a hot, healthy, and filling meal ready at work.

In the Mediterranean kitchen, bulgur is often used to make cold salads. See the Taboule Salad (page 22) for a delicious salad that can be eaten at home, or prepared in advance and brought to work in an airtight container. To make a delicious and satisfying salad, just prepare the bulgur, then add olive oil, lemon juice, fresh herbs, and vegetables.

Bulgur with Fresh Figs and Pistachios

This recipe is aromatic and flavorful, thanks to its inclusion of nuts and fruit. People who are watching what they eat are often wary of these ingredients, since nuts have a high fat content and fruits are rich in carbohydrate, but using these ingredients in moderation can really enhance the flavor of a dish without increasing its calories too much. Try preparing other whole grains, such as quinoa and brown rice with a few nuts and cubed fruits that you like, to create a starch that is attractive and delicious.

Calories	134
Total fat	4 g
Calories as fat	27%
Saturated fat	1 g
Cholesterol	0 mg
Carbohydrates	24 g
Dietary fiber	5 g
Sodium	103 g
Protein	4 g
Carbohydrate choices	**1½**

Exchanges:
1½ starch, 1 vegetable, ½ fat

INGREDIENTS

Serves 12 / Serving size: ½ cup

- **2 tablespoons extra-virgin olive oil**
- **1 medium onion, finely chopped**
- **½ leek, sliced**
- **2 cups coarse bulgur**
- **2 tablespoons vegetable stock (page 63), optional**
- **2 cups water**
- **1¾ ounces raw pistachios**
- **4 medium fresh figs, cut into ½-inch chunks**
- **½ teaspoon Atlantic sea salt**
- **½ teaspoon ground black pepper**

PREPARATION

1. In a medium pot, heat oil over medium-high heat. Add onion and leek, and sauté for about 3 minutes, until onion is golden brown. Add bulgur, stock, water, pistachios, and figs.

2. Cover, increase heat to high, and bring to a boil. Reduce heat to low and cook until liquids are absorbed, about 7 minutes. Add salt and pepper to taste, and serve.

Taboule Salad

This bright salad is tangy, colorful, and easy to make. I start by making the bulgur and then mixing it with fresh herbs, lemon juice, and olive oil. All these flavors blend while I chop the vegetables. For variation, try replacing the bulgur with quinoa, millet, or brown rice. You can also vary the vegetables by using roasted cauliflower florets or cubed root vegetable. If adding root vegetables, serve with a tablespoon of low-fat yogurt.

INGREDIENTS

Serves 6 / Serving size: ¾ cup

- ½ cup coarse bulgur
- ½ cup boiling water
- 3 tablespoons extra-virgin olive oil
- 6 tablespoons fresh lemon juice
- 8 tablespoons chopped fresh parsley
- 4 tablespoons chopped fresh mint
- 8 tablespoons chopped scallions
- 4 tablespoons chopped fresh thyme
- 1 medium Lebanese cucumber, cut into small cubes
- 2 romaine lettuce leaves, finely chopped
- 1 medium tomato, cut into small cubes
- ¼ teaspoon Atlantic sea salt
- ½ teaspoon ground black pepper

Calories	114
Total fat	7 g
Calories as fat	55%
Saturated fat	1 g
Cholesterol	0 mg
Carbohydrates	12 g
Dietary fiber	3 g
Sodium	102 mg
Protein	2 g
Carbohydrate choices	**1**

Exchanges:
½ starch, 1 vegetable, 1½ fat

PREPARATION

1. In a small heat-proof bowl, mix together bulgur and boiling water. Cover and let sit for 5 minutes, until water is absorbed.

2. Mix oil, lemon juice, parsley, mint, scallions, thyme, cucumber, and lettuce into bulgur, and let sit for 30 minutes. Mix tomato and stir until combined. Add salt and pepper to taste.

Taboule Salad

WILD RICE

Attractive both in flavor and appearance, wild rice is ideal for mixing with another starchy food. Besides being relatively expensive, wild rice alone usually does not make for a truly satisfying dish. The classic combination is wild rice mixed with brown rice, but wild rice can be combined with many other starchy foods, or with hard vegetables, as demonstrated in the following recipe. Beets are a hard vegetable traditionally eaten cooked, although they are beginning to appear more often as a raw ingredient as well. When cooking hard vegetables such as beets, I recommend roasting them in the oven at 350°F to 400°F. Although this can take a relatively long time, the result is much tastier than boiling, since vegetables lose some of their flavor, as well as some of their nutrients, when cooked in water. Think about the red color of water that has been used to cook beets. This color comes from elements in the beets that were transferred to the water during the boiling process. When vegetables are roasted in the oven, their nutrients and flavors stay inside. This results in a beet that is much tastier and healthier.

Combine starches with hard vegetables in a single dish

A dish that combines hard vegetables with whole grains or legumes can be very attractive, texturally interesting, and rich in taste, besides increasing the amount of vegetables you consume. The combination is excellent for cold salads but can also upgrade warm dishes. The next time you prepare brown rice, try adding some coarsely grated pumpkin to the rice. Mix 5 ounces of pumpkin into every 1 pound of rice at the beginning of the cooking process, and cook as usual (see page 28).

How to prepare wild rice

To prepare wild rice, rinse it with tap water until the water runs clear. Put rinsed rice in a pot, and add stock with salted water until rice is covered with ½ inch of liquid. Cover and bring to a boil over high heat. Reduce heat to low, and cook for 30 minutes, or until liquid is absorbed.

Wild Rice and Beet Salad

Whole grains and legumes are excellent in cold salads, thanks to their naturally crunchy texture. The next time you prepare a pasta salad, for example, try making it with whole-wheat pasta. The result will be of a much higher culinary quality. Let the salad sit for a few minutes after all the ingredients have been mixed so that the pasta has a chance to absorb all of the flavors. Borrow ideas for interesting salads with starch from international cuisines. Think about the legume salads in Central America, the whole-grain salads of the Mediterranean, and the soba noodle salads from Asia.

INGREDIENTS

Serves 10 / Serving size: ¾ cup

- 1 cup wild rice
- 3 tablespoons vegetable stock (page 63), optional
- Water, boiling
- 2 medium beets, roasted (page 25) and cut into ½-inch cubes
- 2 tablespoons chopped fresh cilantro
- 4 tablespoons chopped fresh mint
- 1⅖ ounces raw hazelnuts, coarsely chopped
- 2 tablespoons fresh lemon juice
- 4 tablespoons extra-virgin olive oil
- ½ teaspoon ground black pepper
- ½ teaspoon Atlantic sea salt
- ½ cup plain low-fat yogurt, for garnish

Calories	160
Total fat	8 g
Calories as fat	45%
Saturated fat	1 g
Cholesterol	0 mg
Carbohydrates	19 g
Dietary fiber	2 g
Sodium	147 mg
Protein	3 g
Carbohydrate choices	**1**

Exchanges:
1 starch, 1 vegetable, 1½ fat

PREPARATION

1. Rinse wild rice in cold water until water runs clear; then transfer to a small pot. Add stock and enough boiling water to cover rice with ½ inch of liquid. Cover pot and bring to a boil over high heat; then reduce heat to low and cook for 30 minutes, or until liquid is absorbed. Set aside to cool.

2. In a medium bowl, combine beets, cilantro, mint, hazelnuts, lemon juice, and oil. Mix in rice, then let sit for about 30 minutes. Add salt and pepper to taste. Serve with yogurt.

Wild Rice and Beet Salad

BROWN RICE

A chapter on starches wouldn't be complete if it didn't discuss brown rice, the whole-grain version of one of the world's most widely consumed starches, rice. Many people would like to consume more brown rice but find it difficult to prepare. From my experience, one of the challenges people face when trying to make their kitchen healthier is learning how to incorporate brown rice.

Soak brown rice for a day in advance

For best results, I recommend starting with high-quality ingredients. In the case of brown rice, I recommend using round basmati brown rice. The best way to prepare any type of brown rice is to soak it in water at room temperature for 3 to 24 hours. This gives the rice a chance to absorb liquid slowly, increasing its softness. Ideally, brown rice should soak for a full 24 hours before it is prepared, but if you don't have enough time, soak it for at least 3 hours in advance. You can also shorten the soaking period by using warm rather than room-temperature water, although this can damage the taste and quality of the dish.

Keep cooking spontaneous—store soaked brown rice in the refrigerator

Brown rice can be soaked, drained, transferred to an airtight container, and refrigerated for up to five days. You can soak a large quantity of rice at a convenient time and refrigerate it until you are ready to cook.

To prepare brown rice, put it in a pot, and add enough stock and water to cover rice with about ½ inch of liquid. Cover pot and bring to a boil over high heat, then reduce heat to low and cook for about 30 minutes, or until liquid is absorbed. Remove pot from heat and let sit, covered, for about 10 minutes before serving. Add salt at the end of the cooking process, rather than the beginning; otherwise, the cooked rice will probably be harder. (The same principle applies when cooking most legumes.)

Brown rice looks different than white rice, and has a different texture. Sometimes, this causes people to reject brown rice before they have a chance to get used to it. A good way to overcome this is by dressing it up a bit, so that people don't judge it before tasting it. An excellent disguise for brown rice (or for any other whole-grain starch you want to integrate into your kitchen) comes from the Mediterranean kitchen, where people often stuff fresh vegetables. For a delicious example of this technique, see the recipe on page 30.

Another way of concealing brown rice is by mixing it with white rice. Start by serving ¼ cup of brown rice with every ¾ cup of white rice, and gradually increase the quantity of brown rice. It's true you'll need to use two pots for cooking, but this method will help your family adapt to the taste, texture, and appearance of brown rice. Once people are familiar with the taste of the brown rice—or any other whole-grain starch that may be new to them—you won't need to conceal it any more.

Stuffed Peppers with Brown Rice in Tomato Sauce

In the Mediterranean region, grains are used to fill a wide variety of vegetables, including peppers, zucchini, tomatoes, onions, eggplants, kohlrabi, and fennel. Vegetables such as peppers are hollow to begin with, but you can stuff any seasonal vegetable you like just by hollowing out the center. Chop the pieces you remove from the center and add them to the filling.

INGREDIENTS

Serves 8 / Serving size: 1 stuffed pepper + 2 tablespoons sauce

Stuffed peppers

- 1 pound lean beef round, ground
- 2 medium zucchini, grated
- 1 medium onion, chopped
- 1 medium tomato, seeded and grated
- 2 tablespoons chopped fresh parsley
- 1 cup brown rice, soaked overnight and drained
- 1 teaspoon ground allspice
- ½ teaspoon ground cinnamon
- 1 teaspoon ground cumin
- ¼ teaspoon Atlantic sea salt
- ¼ teaspoon ground black pepper
- 8 medium red bell peppers, tops, stems, and seeds removed

Sauce

- 8 medium tomatoes, halved and seeded
- 1 tablespoon extra-virgin olive oil
- 4 cloves chopped garlic
- 1 cup water
- 1 tablespoon vegetable stock (page 63), optional
- ½ teaspoon Atlantic sea salt
- ½ teaspoon ground black pepper

Calories	274
Total fat	8 g
Calories as fat	26%
Saturated fat	3 g
Cholesterol	39 mg
Carbohydrates	34 g
Dietary fiber	6 g
Sodium	194 mg
Protein	17 g
Carbohydrate choices	**2**

Exchanges: 2 lean meat, 1 starch, 3 vegetable, ½ fat

PREPARATION

1. Prepare stuffed peppers: In a medium bowl, mix together ground round, zucchini, onion, tomato, parsley, rice, allspice, cinnamon, cumin, salt, and pepper. Stuff peppers with mixture until they are three-quarters full. Set aside.

2. Prepare sauce: Place tomatoes in a food processor, and process until smooth. In a wide-based pan, heat olive oil over medium-high heat. Add garlic and sauté for 3 minutes, until brown. Add tomatoes, water, and stock and bring to a boil over medium-high heat. Reduce heat to low, and cook for 20 minutes, until sauce thickens.

3. Add stuffed peppers, cover, and cook over low heat for 40 minutes, until rice is soft. Remove from heat and set aside, covered, for about 1 hour, to let flavors blend. Reheat before serving, and season with salt and pepper.

Stuffed Peppers with Brown Rice in Tomato Sauce

Tip *You can also replace the tomato-based sauce with the following green sauce: Sauté 1 chopped garlic clove in a wide-base pan with 1 tablespoon canola oil for about 3 minutes. Chop 1¼ pounds Swiss chard, and sauté it for 5 minutes. Add 1 cup water, and cook for 5 minutes. Transfer Swiss chard and liquid to a food processor, add juice from 1 lemon, salt and pepper, and process until smooth. Transfer the sauce back into the pan and cook as instructed on previous page.*

LEGUMES

There are many myths about alleged difficulties in preparing legumes. Some people imagine long soaking periods, others dread complicated preparation techniques. The truth is, legumes are very friendly to use, especially when you know some tips about preparing them.

Let's start with lentils, which come in a variety of colors including orange, green, and black. Not only do many lentils have relatively short cooking times, but they don't require advance soaking. Even lentils that are relatively slow to cook require just 20 minutes (see Aromatic Mixed Rice and Lentils, page 66). Furthermore, you can always prepare a double batch of lentils when cooking them. Cooked lentils can be stored in the refrigerator up to five days.

Split orange lentils are particularly easy to prepare. All you do is rinse them, put them in a pot with cold water and salt, and bring to a boil. When the water boils, the lentils are ready. Rinse them in cold water to stop the cooking process, then use them in your recipe. In the recipe on page 34, you'll see how these lentils can contribute to a delicious salad. You can also use split orange lentils to enrich the color and texture of brown rice or quinoa by adding 1 tablespoon of cooked lentils for every cup of prepared rice or quinoa. Lentils are also suitable for adding to meat.

The texture of quickly cooked lentils is a bit crunchy; if you want them softer, cook them for a few seconds longer. If you cook lentils for quite a long time, their texture becomes very soft, and they may almost seem pureed. Lentils cooked in this manner can be made into thick, Indian-style sauce by adding spices such as curry, turmeric, cumin, and garam masala, and served on brown rice. Another excellent use for legumes, in general, and for lentils, in particular, is adding them to soup. Legumes are an excellent soup base, as in the Pea Soup with Fresh Mint (page 72), and can also be added to make soup thicker, as in the Fennel, Lentil, and Lemon Soup (page 33).

Prepare slow cooking legumes in advance and store them in the freezer

Another easy way of enriching your cooking is by freezing cooked legumes. The next time you prepare slow cooking legumes such as chickpeas or white beans, prepare a double batch, and freeze the portion you're not using immediately in freezer-safe storage bags. See the Sautéed Sea Bass with Seasonal Vegetables and Chickpeas (page 36) for instructions on how to cook chickpeas, and use this technique for cooking similar legumes. Defrost the frozen chickpeas, and use them to make a healthy snack by adding a bit of salt and pepper, sprinkling them with cumin or lemon juice, or sautéing them lightly with Indian spices. Chickpeas can be served with sauce, such as the Red Pepper and Basil Sauce (page 83), or alongside chicken or fish. They can also be served with other starches; for example, as a replacement for the lentils in the Aromatic Mixed Rice and Lentils (page 66). Chickpeas are also an excellent addition to any salad. They can replace the beets in the Wild Rice and Beet Salad (page 26), or be added to the Cucumber and Parsley Root Salad (page 158).

Fennel, Lentil, and Lemon Soup

Whole grains and legumes are excellent in soups. Since soups naturally require longer cooking times, you won't be bothered by the time required to cook the grains. Try using brown rice in a traditional tomato and rice soup recipe and you'll achieve an excellent, healthier result. Another use for legumes in soup is for thickening; in the following recipe, the lentils break down completely and really thicken the soup. If you prefer your lentils whole, cook them for just 2 minutes before adding the rest of the ingredients and they won't break down. For variety, replace the fennel in this recipe with vegetables that complement the dish's slightly tangy flavor.

INGREDIENTS

Serves 8 / Serving size: 1 cup

- 1 cup split orange lentils, rinsed and drained
- 6 cups water
- 6 tablespoons vegetable stock (page 63), optional
- ½ teaspoon Atlantic sea salt, or to taste
- 2 tablespoons extra-virgin olive oil
- 2 celery stalks, sliced widthwise
- 6 cloves garlic, crushed
- ¾ ounce (½ bunch) fresh cilantro, chopped, plus more for garnish
- 4 medium fennel bulbs, sliced
- ½ teaspoon black ground pepper
- 3 tablespoons fresh lemon juice
- ½ lemon, with peel, thinly sliced

Calories	125
Total fat	6 g
Calories as fat	43%
Saturated fat	1 g
Cholesterol	0 mg
Carbohydrates	17 g
Dietary fiber	1 g
Sodium	447 mg
Protein	4 g
Carbohydrate choices	**1**

Exchanges: 1 starch, 1 fat

PREPARATION

1. In a large pot, bring lentils, water, stock, and a pinch of salt to a boil over high heat. Reduce heat to low, and cook uncovered for 30 minutes, until lentils break down. Periodically remove foam that forms on top.

2. In the meantime, heat oil in a large frying pan over medium heat. Add celery and garlic, and sauté for 2 minutes, until brown. Add cilantro, fennel, and cook for 2 minutes. Add salt and pepper to taste.

3. Add fennel mixture to lentils, and cook for 20 minutes. Mix in lemon juice and lemon slices, and cook for 3 minutes. Add salt and pepper to taste, and distribute into individual serving bowls. Top each bowl with cilantro.

Orange Lentil Salad with Feta and Fresh Herbs

This salad can be prepared a full day in advance if you leave out the cubes of cheese until just before serving. Simply mix together the rest of the ingredients and let the salad sit covered at room temperature. Despite the cooking, some lentils may sprout while the salad is marinating, giving the salad a softer texture and more interesting appearance (see page 168 for information on seed sprouts). For variety, try adding walnuts, tomato cubes, celery slices, sliced chicken breast, or a combination of these ingredients. You can also replace the orange lentils with cooked green lentils, chickpeas, or white beans.

Calories	125
Total fat	5 g
Calories as fat	36%
Saturated fat	1 g
Cholesterol	3 mg
Carbohydrates	15 g
Dietary fiber	3 g
Sodium	114 mg
Protein	6 g
Carbohydrate choices	**1**
Exchanges: 1 starch, 1 fat	

INGREDIENTS

Serves 8 / Serving size: ½ cup

- **7 ounces split orange lentils, rinsed and drained**
- **2 pinches Atlantic sea salt**
- **3 tablespoons fresh lemon juice**
- **2 tablespoons extra-virgin olive oil**
- **1 clove crushed garlic**
- **1 tablespoon chopped fresh mint**
- **2 tablespoons chopped fresh parsley**
- **1 ounce low-fat semi-soft white goat cheese, such as feta**
- **Pinch ground black pepper**

PREPARATION

1. Place lentils in a small pot, and add water with a pinch of salt to cover. Bring to a boil over medium heat; then immediately remove from heat and drain. Rinse lentils in cold water and drain in a colander.

2. Transfer lentils to a salad bowl. Add lemon juice, oil, garlic, mint, and parsley. Let sit for at least 30 minutes at room temperature for flavors to blend. Add cheese, salt, and pepper before serving.

Orange Lentil Salad with Feta and Fresh Herbs

Sautéed Sea Bass with Seasonal Vegetables and Chickpeas

This attractive dish is simple to prepare if you use frozen chickpeas. If you want to vary the recipe, replace the chickpeas with black or white beans, or with any other legume whose color goes well with the other ingredients. As for the fish, you can replace the sea bass with another type of low-fat white fish such as sea bream. Replacing the tomatoes with small cubes of raw beets is a delicious alteration that suits the dish's tangy flavor and maintains its colorful appearance.

INGREDIENTS

Serves 4 / Serving size:
1 fillet + ½ cup vegetables

Chickpeas

- 2 pounds dry chickpeas, soaked overnight and drained (½ cup for use in this recipe, the rest for freezing)
- 5 quarts water
- 1 tablespoon baking soda
- ½ teaspoon Atlantic sea salt
- ½ teaspoon ground black pepper

Calories	282
Total fat	10 g
Calories as fat	32%
Saturated fat	2 g
Cholesterol	45 mg
Carbohydrates	15 g
Dietary fiber	4 g
Sodium	682 mg
Protein	25 g
Carbohydrate choices	**1**

Exchanges:
3 lean meat, ½ starch, 2 vegetable

Fish

- 2 tablespoons extra-virgin olive oil
- 4 cloves garlic, finely chopped
- 1½ pounds (1 bunch) Swiss chard, stalks removed and thinly sliced
- Pinch Atlantic sea salt
- Pinch ground black pepper
- 2 cups dry white wine
- Four 4-ounce sea bass fillets
- 4 tablespoons fresh lemon juice
- 2 medium tomatoes, cut into ¼-inch cubes

PREPARATION

1. Prepare chickpeas: In a large pot, combine chickpeas, water, and baking soda, and bring to a boil over high heat. Reduce heat to medium and cook, uncovered, for about 2 hours, until chickpeas are soft. Periodically remove foam that forms on top. Drain chickpeas, season with salt and pepper, and set aside to cool.

Reserve ½ cup chickpeas for this recipe, and transfer the rest to freezer-safe storage bags or containers. Freeze for up to 4 months.

2. Prepare fish: Place wok over medium-high heat and add oil, swirling to coat. When oil is hot, add garlic and sauté gently for 3 minutes, until brown. Add Swiss

Sautéed Sea Bass with Seasonal Vegetables and Chickpeas

chard and sauté until chard wilts about 3 minutes. Add salt and pepper to taste. Remove chard from pan and transfer to a plate.

3. Add wine to pan and bring to a boil over medium-high heat. Add fish and cook for 5 minutes on low heat, until fish is opaque. Add chickpeas, lemon juice, tomatoes, and chard, and cook for 3 minutes. Add salt and pepper to taste.

Cooking with Fats

I have been trying to solve a mystery about fats and taste for years. How is it that, on the one hand, people think fats make food taste good and, on the other hand, when food critics rate restaurants, a common criticism is that the food is too fatty. How come people often pale at the suggestion of making low-fat sauces, but the teacher at the French cooking school I attended was immediately able to detect a drop too much of oil in a sauce I prepared.

The only solution I can imagine for this conundrum is the following: cooking with fat gives relatively good results, with relatively little effort. After all, how many people will complain about the taste of deep-fried fish sticks or a luscious cream sauce? It's hard to ruin such recipes, and fairly easy to get them right. Using low-fat techniques requires practice and precision, but the results can be excellent. In this chapter, you'll discover ingredients, techniques, and tips that can help you make lower fat dishes that are higher in quality and taste.

When it comes to fats, one of the goals in healthy cooking is to reduce the amount of fat that is consumed. To reduce the amount of fat in the foods you cook, it's important to understand two ways in which fats are present. Some fats are used in the cooking process, as when frying in oil or thickening sauces with cream. Other fats are an integral part of food, such as high-fat cheeses and meats.

An excellent way of reducing the amount of fat in a dish that contains high-fat ingredients is by choosing high-quality low-fat alternatives, and by using the right techniques for cooking with them. In fact, the secret to success when cooking low-fat foods really lies in the techniques you use to prepare them, since these often differ from the techniques used to cook high-fat ingredients. You'll find tips on these cooking techniques throughout this chapter.

The common advice, beyond reducing fat consumption, is to make a transition to healthier fats. For example, although a serving of olive oil and margarine may have similar amounts of fat and calories, olive oil is considered much healthier than margarine, since it is rich in monounsaturated fats while margarine may contain trans fats. In this chapter, you'll find tips on using products that contain healthier fats for healthier cooking. For more tips and recipes, see the Baked Goods chapter (pages 129–145).

When it comes to choosing healthy fats, as with starches, the goal isn't to find the healthiest fat and use only that, but to choose from a variety of healthy fats, and use the best one for each purpose. For example, olive oil and walnut oil are both considered healthy fats, but they are suitable for different foods, since they have different tastes. A combination of healthy fats is what makes food interesting and flavorful, and contributes to balanced nutrition.

IN THE OVEN

Baking and roasting foods in the oven is an excellent substitute for frying. In fact, items that are usually fried can be prepared in the oven and turn out crispy and tasty. Besides saving the calories added in frying, baking has culinary benefits as well. For example, it is faster to prepare large quantities of food when baking rather than frying, and the process requires much less attention.

When preparing food in the oven, there are a few challenges to overcome. For example, food baked in the oven, even if just a bit too long, can dry out. One solution to this problem is to ensure precise baking times. Use a timer if you have one, and check the food as the end of the baking time nears to make sure it is still moist.

Roast with a protective layer
Some ingredients have a natural layer that protects them from drying out in the oven. For example, potatoes, sweet potatoes, and beets all have peels that can protect them naturally while they are in the oven. To oven-cook these vegetables, place them whole on a baking sheet and roast at 350°F to 400°F until soft. When the vegetables are cool to the touch, remove the peels and prepare as desired. When making roasted peppers, transfer the peppers to a bowl immediately after roasting, and cover the bowl with plastic wrap. Let the peppers sit for about 15 minutes, or until they are cool enough to touch, then peel the peppers and discard skins, seeds, and stems.

To protect foods that don't have a natural protective layer, such as chicken breasts, simply brush a bit of oil on them before roasting. Make sure the oil is spread evenly and thinly, since you don't need it for the flavor, but simply to protect the food. Another way of preserving moisture in foods that don't have a natural peel is by wrapping them with aluminum foil. To avoid direct contact between the foil and the food you are cooking, add a parchment paper lining to the aluminum foil wrapper as described on the next page.

Create moisture in the oven
Prevent food from drying out in the oven by placing a bowl of water in the oven while you roast. This method replicates the water systems used in industrial ovens and in combi-steam ovens.

Chicken Medallions Stuffed with Pumpkin and Spinach with Tomato and Basil Sauce

The tomato sauce in this recipe is easy to prepare, since the tomatoes aren't peeled in advance. Pouring the sauce through a strainer after it is cooked removes chunks and creates a smooth texture. Want to improvise? Try using different spreads on the chicken breasts; just make sure the colors harmonize. For example, try spreading Dried Tomato and Thyme Spread (page 109), Pistachio Pesto Sauce (page 56), or roasted zucchini. If you decide to use a tomato-based spread, remember to use a sauce with a contrasting color, such as Thick Mushroom Sauce (page 52).

Calories	122
Total fat	4 g
Calories as fat	30%
Saturated fat	1 g
Cholesterol	43 mg
Carbohydrates	4 g
Dietary fiber	1 g
Sodium	241 mg
Protein	17 g
Carbohydrate choices	**None**

Exchanges: 2 lean meat, 1 vegetable

INGREDIENTS

Serves 12 / Serving size: 3 chicken medallions + 2 tablespoons sauce

Chicken medallions

- 3½ ounces fresh pumpkin, peeled, seeded, and cut into ½-inch cubes
- ½ teaspoon ground black pepper, or to taste
- ½ teaspoon Atlantic sea salt, or to taste
- 1 tablespoon extra-virgin olive oil
- 7 ounces fresh spinach
- Six 4-ounce chicken breasts

Sauce

- 8 medium tomatoes, halved and seeded
- 1 tablespoon extra-virgin olive oil
- 2 cloves garlic, peeled and sliced
- ¼ cup water
- 1 tablespoon vegetable stock (page 63), optional
- ½ cup fresh basil leaves, sliced into strips
- ½ teaspoon Atlantic sea salt
- ½ teaspoon ground black pepper

PREPARATION

1. Prepare chicken medallions: Preheat the oven to 350°F. Place pumpkin cubes in a shallow baking dish, and season with salt and pepper. Add oil and mix to coat. Roast for 45 minutes, or until soft. Mash with a fork until smooth.

2. In a medium frying pan, heat water over low heat. Add spinach and steam for 10 minutes, until soft. Transfer to a cutting board, and finely chop.

3. Pound chicken breasts with a kitchen hammer until ½-inch thick, and season with salt and pepper.

4. Lay a piece of aluminum foil on your work surface, and place a sheet of parchment paper on top. Place 1 chicken breast on the parchment paper, and spread ⅓ of mashed pumpkin on top. Roll chicken breast into a cylinder, then wrap with foil and parchment paper, so that chicken resembles a large candy. Repeat process to spread 2 more chicken breasts with mashed pumpkin, then repeat with remaining 3 chicken breasts and chopped spinach, spreading ⅓ of chopped spinach on each breast. Place wrapped chicken breasts on a baking sheet

and bake for 15 minutes, or until chicken is cooked through.

5. In the meantime, prepare sauce: Place tomatoes in a food processor and process until smooth. In a small saucepan, heat oil over medium heat. Add garlic and sauté for 3 minutes, until brown. Add tomatoes, water, and stock, and bring to a boil, then reduce heat to low and simmer for 30 minutes, until thick. Pour sauce through a fine-mesh strainer into a heatproof bowl; then return to saucepan. Add basil and heat for 30 seconds, then add salt and pepper to taste.

6. To serve, remove foil wrapping from chicken, and slice each chicken breast into 6 medallions. Serve with tomato sauce on top.

STEAMING

Steaming is a cooking technique that is particularly popular in Southeast Asian cuisine. A variety of steamers can be found these days, but I recommend using bamboo steamers that are placed on top of pots. These steamers add excellent aroma to food, but since the scent of the food can remain on the steamer even after it has been cleaned, I recommend having several: one for vegetables, one for poultry, and one for fish.

How to steam

Place the food you want to steam in the steamer basket, and place basket on a pot that contains a small quantity of liquid (see photo page 105). This liquid may be water, soup, wine, or even jasmine tea. Heat the pot over medium heat. The steam emanating from the heated liquid will warm or cook the food in the steamer. Replenish the liquid in the pot as required.

There are many nutritional benefits to steaming, including the fact that no nutrients are lost to water. There are many culinary benefits as well. One benefit is that the food stays moist as it is heated. Another is that the food does not come in direct contact with the steaming liquid and become diluted. With steaming, you can enjoy food that is juicy, flavorful, and doesn't contain a drop of oil.

What can be steamed?

One of my favorite types of steamed food is dim sum, the famed Asian dishes made with various types of dough that are filled with an even wider variety of fillings. Rice paper wrappers, also known as spring roll wrappers, are excellent for using as dough in dim sum. These wrappers are quick and simple to use, and make cooking at home very easy. Rice paper wrappers are sold in Asian food markets and many supermarkets. They become soft after being dipped in warm water for a few seconds.

Although rice paper wrappers are made from white rice, a single 8½-inch wrapper is equal to just ½ of a carbohydrate serving. This means you can have a relatively large quantity of dim sum, filled with lots of fresh vegetables (see recipe on facing page), and still consume your appropriate amount of carbohydrate choices.

In addition to dim sum, steamers can be used to prepare entire meals. For example, place a selection of vegetables and fish in a steamer basket, place the basket on a pot with liquid, and cook over medium heat for about 10 minutes, or until the food is cooked through. Serve this with a whole-grain and you have a complete meal. If all the food you want to prepare doesn't fit into one steamer basket, invest in a larger steamer, or stack two or three steamer baskets on top of each other. The recipe on page 46 demonstrates how to steam tilapia and mushrooms, but you can steam any type of fish you like. When it comes to choosing the vegetables, any vegetable that is usually blanched or roasted can be steamed.

Broccoli, Tofu, and Leek Dim Sum with Asian Salsa

Dim sum fillings and sauces are great for expressing creativity. Just keep one guideline in mind: If the filling has a delicate flavor, serve it with a strongly flavored sauce, and vice versa. Note that the sauce in this recipe contains a ratio of 1 tablespoon oil to ¼ cup vinegar. Try using a similar ratio of oil to vinegar when making other dressings, and you'll reduce the amount of fat. Replace part of the vinegar with water if the dressing is too sour.

INGREDIENTS

Serves 8 / Serving size: 1 whole dim sum + 2 tablespoons salsa

Salsa

- ¼ cup low-sodium soy sauce
- ¼ cup rice vinegar
- 1 tablespoon mirin
- 1 tablespoon unrefined sesame oil
- 1 tablespoon chopped fresh cilantro
- 4 small radishes, grated
- 2 medium Lebanese cucumbers, seeded and cut into ¼-inch cubes
- ¼ cup chopped scallions
- 2 cloves garlic, crushed
- 1 teaspoon chopped seeded hot red chili pepper

- 1½ ounces raw cashews
- Eight 8½-inch rice paper wrappers
- Wilted lettuce or cabbage leaves, for lining steamer

Calories	119
Total fat	6 g
Calories as fat	45%
Saturated fat	1 g
Cholesterol	0 mg
Carbohydrates	14 g
Dietary fiber	2 g
Sodium	456 mg
Protein	4 g
Carbohydrate choices	**1**

Exchanges:
½ starch, 1 vegetable, 1 fat

Dim Sum

- 1 tablespoon unrefined canola oil
- 2 leeks, cut into thin slices
- 10 ounces broccoli florets, blanched (page 88)
- ½ teaspoon Atlantic sea salt
- ½ teaspoon ground black pepper
- 1¾ ounces firm tofu, grated

PREPARATION

1. Prepare salsa: In a medium bowl, mix together soy sauce, vinegar, mirin, and oil until blended. Add cilantro, radishes, cucumbers, scallions, garlic, and hot pepper, stirring until evenly combined. Set aside.

2. Prepare dim sum: Place wok over high heat and add oil, swirling to coat. When oil is hot, add leeks and sauté for 5 minutes, until soft. Add broccoli and stir fry for 2 minutes. Mix in tofu and cashews, and stir fry for ½ minute, then add salt and pepper to taste.

3. Partially fill a large heatproof bowl with warm water by mixing together boiling water and tap water.

(continued on page 44)

(continued from page 43)

Soak 1 wrapper for 10 to 20 seconds, until it softens. Remove wrapper, gently shake off excess water, and lay on work surface. Place another wrapper to soak.

4. Arrange ⅛ of leek mixture in a horizontal mound below center of wrapper. Leave left and right sides of wrapper bare. Fold sides over filling and roll up wrapper, using your fingers to press filling firmly inside, to form a tight cylinder (see photos). Repeat process with remaining wrappers and leek mixture.

5. Line steamer basket with lettuce leaves, and arrange dim sum on top. Make sure dim sum don't touch each other. Heat a bit of water in a pot the size of the steamer basket, and place steamer basket on pot. Cover steamer basket and heat just until dim sum are warm, about 1 minute. Serve whole, or cut in half on a diagonal, with salsa on the side.

Broccoli, Tofu, and Leek Dim Sum with Asian Salsa

Steamed Tilapia and Mushrooms

I recommend using low-sodium soy sauce rather than ordinary soy sauce, for the taste. Not only does low-sodium soy sauce have less sodium, but it actually has more soy flavor due to the technique used to extract the liquid from the soy bean. Serve this attractive dish with brown rice or noodles for an easy and impressive dinner. Replace the tilapia with another type of white fish if you like, such as sea bream, sea bass, or corvina.

INGREDIENTS

Serves 2 / Serving size: 1 fillet +
½ cup sauce

Fish
- **6 shiitake mushrooms**
- **1½ cups lukewarm water**
- **6 button mushrooms, sliced**
- **2 medium Portobello mushrooms, sliced**
- **Two 4-ounce tilapia fillets, with or without skin**
- **Pinch Atlantic sea salt**
- **Pinch ground black pepper**
- **Water, for steaming**

Sauce
- **3 tablespoons low-sodium soy sauce**
- **5 tablespoons dry white wine**
- **3 tablespoons chopped scallions**
- **1 tablespoon peeled and grated fresh ginger**
- **1 teaspoon seeded and chopped red hot chili pepper**
- **1 tablespoon chopped fresh cilantro, for garnish**

PREPARATION

1. Prepare fish: In a small bowl, soak shiitake mushrooms in water for 7 minutes, until soft. Remove mushrooms, and slice. Discard soaking liquid.

2. In a medium bowl, mix together shiitake mushrooms, button mushrooms, and Portobello mushrooms. Transfer to a steamer basket.

3. Score skinless side of fillets with 3 or 4 diagonally cuts, and season with salt and pepper. Arrange fillets on mushrooms, skin-side down.

4. Prepare sauce: In a small bowl, mix together soy sauce and wine. Mix in scallions, ginger, and chili pepper until combined.

5. Boil 2 inches of water in a pot, the size of the steamer basket, and place steamer basket on pot. Pour half of the sauce over fish and mushrooms. Cover steamer basket and steam for 5 minutes.

Pour remaining sauce over fish, and steam for another 5 minutes, until fish is soft. Transfer to serving dish, garnish with cilantro, and serve.

Calories	213
Total fat	2 g
Calories as fat	8%
Saturated fat	1 g
Cholesterol	57 mg
Carbohydrates	17 g
Dietary fiber	3 g
Sodium	471 mg
Protein	28 g
Carbohydrate choices	**1**
Exchanges: 3 lean meat, 3 vegetable	

GRILLING

Another way to make high-quality food is to grill ingredients on a lined grill pan. Grilling with this type of pan results in an attractive, crispy texture. The raised lines on the pan separate the food from the base and allow you to grill without adding any oil. Food cooked on a lined grill pan should not stick to the pan; if it does, it likely means the raised lines are worn and it's time to get a new pan.

What can be grilled on a lined grill pan?

This type of pan is excellent for grilling thin types of protein-rich ingredients that require a relatively short cooking time, such as fish fillets or marinated tofu slices. If you want to cook something a bit thicker such as chicken breasts, pound the chicken to a thickness of about 1 inch before grilling. The chicken can then be grilled without any oil, over medium heat, in about 5 minutes. Try this as an alternative to the shrimp in the Vietnamese Shrimp Dim Sum in Ginger and Lemon Sauce (page 210).

Lined grill pans have many other uses as well. You can use them to sear meat, or to grill thinly sliced vegetables that don't contain a lot of liquid. For example, try using one when you make the Grilled Zucchini in Mint Vinaigrette (page 230) or the Grilled Eggplant with Tomato Stew (page 65). You can also make desserts with a lined grill pan. For example, core an apple and then slice it into very thin rounds. Marinate the slices in ½ cup red wine and a handful of mint leaves for about 30 minutes. Grill the apple slices on a lined grill pan over medium heat for about 10 seconds on each side, then serve with reduced balsamic vinegar (see page 119) or pomegranate and red wine sauce (page 143).

Grilled Marinated Bass Fingers Wrapped in Swiss Chard

Large and attractive, Swiss chard leaves become pliable after a short period of soaking in boiling water, making them excellent for wrapping food. In this recipe, make sure to roll each strip of fish no more than twice in the Swiss chard, and allow a bit of fish to poke out on either side of the Swiss chard wrapper. For a Mediterranean twist, roll the fish in finely chopped herbs rather than soaking it in marinade and replace the sauce with Red Tahini Spread (page 108) or Fresh Herb and Yogurt Sauce (page 82).

Calories	69
Total fat	2 g
Calories as fat	26%
Saturated fat	1 g
Cholesterol	23 mg
Carbohydrates	2 g
Dietary fiber	1 g
Sodium	171 mg
Protein	11 g
Carbohydrate choices	**None**
Exchanges: 1 lean meat	

INGREDIENTS

Serves 8 / Serving size: 3 fish fingers + 2 tablespoons sauce

Marinade
- 8 tablespoons rice vinegar
- 2 tablespoons low-sodium soy sauce
- 1 tablespoon mirin
- 1 teaspoon unrefined sesame oil
- 2 teaspoons peeled and grated fresh ginger
- 1 small red chili pepper, seeded and chopped

Fish
- Four 4-ounce sea bass fillets
- 8 Swiss chard leaves, stems removed and cut in half, lengthwise
- 4 cups boiling water
- Pinch Atlantic sea salt
- Pinch ground black pepper

PREPARATION

1. Prepare marinade: In a non-reactive bowl, mix vinegar, soy sauce, mirin, and oil until combined. Mix in ginger and hot chili pepper.

2. Prepare fish: Slice fillets into 2-inch strips. Transfer strips to bowl with marinade and marinate in refrigerator for 30 minutes.

3. Pour boiling water into a heatproof bowl and soak a Swiss chard leaf for about 20 seconds,

Grilled Marinated Bass Fingers Wrapped in Swiss Chard

until softened. Remove leaf from bowl, shake off water, and lay on your work surface. Place another leaf to soak as you roll this one.

4. Place a strip of fish on the bottom edge of the leaf, and roll leaf into a cylinder around fish. Allow leaf to wrap fish no more than two times, then cut leaf with a sharp knife, and set aside rolled fish finger. Repeat process with remaining chard leaves and fish strips.

5. Heat a lined grill pan over medium heat. Grill several fish fingers at a time, roasting each for about 30 seconds per side, until opaque.

WHEN TO SAUTÉ

Sometimes, it's actually good to sauté foods lightly. Onions, for example, are best sautéed before being added to cooked dishes, because their aromatic elements are better released under high temperatures. The flavor of an onion that hasn't been sautéed simply isn't satisfying and could ultimately lead to the addition of more fat and salt afterwards, to compensate.

When sautéing onions, garlic, and other vegetables, oil is used in order to reach a high temperature, more than for flavor, so there is no need to use a lot of oil. For example, in the recipe on the facing page, a relatively small amount of oil is used to sauté a relatively large quantity of vegetables. Try to use just 1 to 3 tablespoons of oil whenever you sauté. If it helps, use a measuring spoon for precision. When you do sauté, heat oil until warm, make an effort not to heat the oil too much. Oil that smokes is burned, and it has reduced taste and nutritional quality.

An important criterion when selecting fat for sautéing is the temperature at which the fat burns or smokes. Burned oil is unpalatable and unhealthy, so if you need to reach a high temperature, select a fat that won't burn at that temperature. Olive oil and canola oil are two healthy oils commonly used in cooking. When frying foods at high temperatures for long periods of time, canola oil is more durable than olive oil. This means it's a better choice when searing meat, for example. If you are just lightly sautéing, both olive oil and canola oil are suitable, so select the oil you prefer according to taste. If you are sautéing onions for pasta sauce, olive oil may be just right; if you are making an Asian-style stir-fry, canola oil may be better.

THICKENING

Fat is often added at the end of the cooking process; for example, by adding cream to complete soups and other dishes. Many people like the texture of soup that has cream, but this texture can also be achieved with other ingredients, such as nuts that have been processed in a food processor (page 57). Soup can also be thickened by adding lentils at the beginning of the cooking process, as in the Fennel, Lentil, and Lemon Soup (page 33). Try adding a handful of split orange lentils the next time you prepare soup; it will thicken the texture, and make the soup more satisfying.

Soups can also be thickened without adding fat by using pureed vegetables (see facing page). To do this, just puree cooked vegetables with some of the cooking liquid. This technique can be used to make soups, sauces, or spreads; simply adjust the thickness by varying the amount of liquid you add.

Pumpkin and Sweet Potato Soup with a Touch of Orange

Thick soups are a traditional autumn favorite. This pureed soup is a bit tangy, thanks to the addition of fresh orange juice. You can also add freshly grated ginger just before serving. If you still long for the taste and texture of cream, try adding a bit of coconut milk just before serving. Although coconut milk does contain saturated fat, it has less fat and a much stronger flavor than cream, so less of it can be used for satisfying results.

INGREDIENTS

Serves 12 / Serving size: 1 cup

- 2 tablespoons extra-virgin olive oil
- 2 medium onions, diced
- 10½ ounces fresh pumpkin, peeled, seeded, and cut into chunks
- 4 medium sweet potatoes, peeled and cut into chunks
- 2 medium carrots, peeled and sliced into rounds
- 6 cups water
- 6 tablespoons vegetable stock (page 63), optional
- ¼ cup fresh orange juice
- ½ teaspoon Atlantic sea salt
- ½ teaspoon ground black pepper
- 4 tablespoons chopped fresh parsley, for garnish
- 2 tablespoons grated orange rind, for garnish

Calories	77
Total fat	2 g
Calories as fat	23%
Saturated fat	1 g
Cholesterol	0 mg
Carbohydrates	14 g
Dietary fiber	2 g
Sodium	116 mg
Protein	1 g
Carbohydrate choices	**1**

Exchanges:
½ starch, 1 vegetable, ½ fat

PREPARATION

1. In a pot, heat oil over medium-high heat and sauté onion for 3 minutes, until golden brown. Add pumpkin, sweet potatoes, and carrots, and sauté for 5 minutes, until lightly brown. Add water and stock and bring to a boil. Reduce heat to medium-low and cook, uncovered, for 40 minutes, until vegetables are soft.

2. Transfer soup to a food processor and process gradually until smooth. Return soup to pot and heat gently over low heat. Add water if necessary to reach desired consistency.

3. Add orange juice and cook for a few more seconds, then add salt and pepper to taste. Garnish with parsley and orange rind before serving.

USING LOW-FAT INGREDIENTS: PREPARING LEAN ROASTS

A significant quantity of the fat people consume doesn't come from fats that are added during the cooking process, but from the ingredients themselves. Many meat and dairy products are high in fat, some of which is saturated fat and cholesterol. However, if you select your ingredients carefully, high-fat products can be replaced with high-quality, low-fat products that won't diminish (and can even increase) the flavor of your food. For example, it is possible to reduce your consumption of fat and still eat beef by choosing lean cuts of meat that may even contain less fat than some poultry and fish. Furthermore, the taste of lean meat is often better than the taste of fatty meat. For example, beef tenderloin and beef sirloin are both high-quality lean meats that are prized in many kitchens.

Lean meats can be used to make delicious, gourmet foods—you just have to know how. Preparing lean meats using the same techniques you use for fatty meats can produce dishes that are dry and unpalatable. However, if you use the right techniques, the results are excellent. Lean meats are ideal for using in slow-cooked stews, for grinding and mixing with other ingredients, and for roasting. For examples of the first two methods, see the Persian Beef Stew with Quince and Pomegranate Seeds (page 167) and the Beef and Eggplant Hamburgers with Homemade Ketchup (page 194). In the following pages, you'll find tips on how to roast lean meats to perfection.

Start with a good cut of meat

For best results, choose fresh rather than frozen or pre-frozen and thawed meat. When choosing sirloin, opt for a cut that has been aged. The aging process makes meat tender, something that is critical when preparing leaner cuts of meats. Only fresh sirloin can be aged, so make sure the meat you buy has been properly aged. Once you find a store where the lean meat is aged properly, make an effort to shop there, since good cuts of meat are a valuable commodity.

Sear the meat properly

The first stage in preparing meat is to sear it. This prevents the meat from drying out while it is being roasted and keeps the flavor inside. To sear meat in a pan, heat 2 tablespoons of canola oil over high heat and sear for about 2 minutes on each side, or until brown all over (see Turkey Pastrami in Pistachio Pesto Sauce, page 56). An even better option is to sear meat in the oven. To do this, preheat the broiler, and sear the meat for about 5 minutes on each side. Once the meat is seared, adjust the oven to bake, reduce heat as instructed, and continue roasting (see Roast Sirloin with Thick Mushroom Sauce, page 54).

Roast meat with precision

To ensure that meat doesn't dry out during roasting, be precise about the temperature it reaches. Though some people use cooking timetables when roasting meat, these are based on factors such as oven heat, weight of meat, and level of readiness. However, since no two ovens are the same, and no two pieces of meat are the same shape, these timetables are not always precise enough for roasting lean meat to perfection. Lean meats are more susceptible to drying out if they are overcooked because they don't have extra fat to give them extra juiciness. The best way to cook them, therefore, isn't according to tables, but with the help of an instant-read meat thermometer that indicates the exact temperature.

To use a meat thermometer, just insert the pointed end into the middle of the meat. When roasting beef, and when the roast will sit for 15 minutes after it is removed from the oven before cutting and serving (see explanation next paragraph), the meat should reach a temperature of 142°F for rare, 158°F for medium, and 165°F for well-done. Turkey is always cooked until it is well-done and reaches a temperature of 165°F.

Finish with the correct cutting technique

When the meat reaches the desired temperature, take it out of the oven, cover it with aluminum foil, and let it rest for 15 minutes. During this time, the interior temperature of the meat will rise between 5°F and 10°F and complete the cooking process. Furthermore, during the cooking process, the liquids in the meat concentrate under high pressure in the center. If you slice the meat immediately after removing it from the oven, the liquids will still be concentrated in the center and will run out onto the cutting board. This means many of the meat slices will be dry. Letting the meat rest for a few minutes allows the juices to redistribute, improving the meat's texture and ensuring that every slice is flavorful and juicy.

Cut leftover roast into slices and freeze it

The roast you cooked in your oven is sure to be tastier than any cold cuts that are sold in supermarkets. It also has less fat, salt, and other additives than processed roast beef or pastrami. If you plan on keeping the leftovers for more than a couple of days, store them in the freezer. I recommend preparing two roasts at the same time. Serve one that day, and cut the other into thin slices, for freezing. Place pieces of parchment paper between each slice before freezing, so that the frozen slices can be separated with ease. The night before you want to take a roast beef sandwich to work, simply transfer a couple of slices to the refrigerator. In the morning, the meat will have defrosted, and it will be perfect for making a delicious and nutritious meat sandwich.

Roast Sirloin with Thick Mushroom Sauce

The mushroom sauce in this recipe is enriched with Porcini mushrooms, a tasty type often sold in a dried form. Shiitake mushrooms are also excellent for adding flavor to mushroom sauce, as in the Steamed Tilapia with Mushrooms (page 46). Generally speaking, try to include a few mushrooms with particularly dominant flavors when making any mushroom sauce. This upgrades the taste of the sauce, making it richer and more flavorful, without using mushroom soup powder, more salt, or artificial flavors.

INGREDIENTS

Serves 12 / Serving size: 2 slices roast + 2 tablespoons sauce

Roast

- One 3-pound aged lean sirloin roast
- ½ teaspoon Atlantic sea salt
- ½ teaspoon ground black pepper

Sauce

- ⅔ cups lukewarm water
- 1 tablespoon vegetable stock (page 63), optional
- ¾ ounce dried Porcini mushrooms
- 1 cup mixed sliced mushrooms (button, Portobello, oyster)
- 2 tablespoons extra-virgin olive oil
- 1 medium onion, chopped
- 2 cloves garlic, crushed
- ½ cup dry red wine
- 1 tablespoon unsweetened date honey
- ¼ cup chopped fresh parsley
- Pinch Atlantic sea salt
- Pinch ground black pepper

Calories	231
Total fat	11 g
Calories as fat	43%
Saturated fat	3 g
Cholesterol	66 mg
Carbohydrates	3 g
Dietary fiber	0 g
Sodium	166 mg
Protein	27 g
Carbohydrate choices	**None**

Exchanges: 4 lean meat

PREPARATION

1. Prepare roast: Preheat broiler and truss roast with kitchen twine. Season roast with salt and pepper, and place on an oven-safe wire rack. Place a baking dish directly underneath roast, for gathering fat, then roast for 5 minutes on each side, until seared all over.

2. Adjust oven to bake, and reduce temperature to 325°F. Leave oven door open to allow heat to escape until oven reaches desired temperature, then close door and continue roasting until an instant-read thermometer inserted in center of roast registers 140°F for rare or 165°F for medium. This will take about 60 minutes for rare (15 minutes for every 1 pound, + 15 minutes) and about 72 minutes for medium (18 minutes for every 1 pound, + 18 minutes). Remove meat from oven, lay a piece of aluminum foil over top, and let rest for 15 minutes before slicing.

Roast Sirloin with Thick Mushroom Sauce

3. In the meantime, prepare sauce: Transfer water and stock to a heatproof bowl. Add Porcini mushrooms and soak for about 10 minutes, until soft. Squeeze liquid from mushrooms, and reserve liquid. Combine mushrooms with mixed mushrooms in a medium bowl.

4. In a small saucepan, heat oil over medium-high heat. Add onion and garlic and sauté for 5 minutes, until onion is golden brown. Add mushrooms and sauté for 5 minutes, until brown. Add wine, date honey, parsley, and reserved liquid. Bring to a boil, then reduce heat to low and simmer until most of liquid evaporates and sauce thickens. Add salt and pepper to taste. To serve, slice roast into ¼-inch thick slices, and serve with sauce.

Turkey Pastrami in Pistachio Pesto Sauce

The delicate flavor of the turkey in this recipe is complemented by the aromatic sauce. If you plan to serve the turkey without sauce (sliced in sandwiches, for example), marinate it before roasting using one of the marinades in this book. You can also season the turkey with spices before searing it. To do this, mix together 6 tablespoons of olive oil with 1 tablespoon each of ground clove, ground cinnamon, ground black pepper, ground ginger, ground cardamom, and ground coriander. Rub the mixture on the turkey before searing.

Calories	255
Total fat	7 g
Calories as fat	25%
Saturated fat	1 g
Cholesterol	84 mg
Carbohydrates	1 g
Dietary fiber	0 g
Sodium	145 mg
Protein	34 g
Carbohydrate choices	**None**

Exchanges: 5 lean meat

INGREDIENTS

Serves 16 / Serving size: 2 slices roast + 2 tablespoons sauce

Turkey

- One 4-pound fresh lean turkey breast
- ½ teaspoon Atlantic sea salt
- ½ teaspoon ground black pepper
- 2 tablespoons unrefined canola oil

Sauce

- 3 ounces (2 bunches) fresh basil, leaves picked, rinsed, and patted dry
- 1½ ounces (1 bunch) fresh parsley, leaves picked, rinsed, and patted dry
- 2 cloves garlic, coarsely chopped
- 4 tablespoons extra-virgin olive oil
- 1 tablespoon fresh lemon juice
- Pinch Atlantic sea salt
- Pinch ground black pepper
- 1 ounce unsalted pistachios, toasted (page 57)

TIP *The pesto in this recipe uses pistachios rather than parmesan, primarily for the taste. For variety, substitute the pistachios for walnuts, almonds, hazelnuts, or another favorite nut. To maximize the taste and texture of the pesto, don't process the nuts too much.*

PREPARATION

1. Prepare turkey: Preheat oven to 275°F. Truss turkey breast with kitchen twine, and season with salt and pepper. Heat oil in a large frying pan over high heat and sear turkey on all sides for about 2 minutes, until seared all over.

2. Transfer turkey to a flat oven-safe wire rack. Place a baking dish directly underneath roast, for gathering fat, and roast until an instant-read thermometer inserted in center registers 165°F. This will take 2 to 2½ hours. Remove turkey from oven, lay a piece of aluminum foil on top, and let rest for 15 minutes before slicing.

3. In the meantime, prepare sauce: Place basil and parsley in a food processor and process until finely chopped. Add garlic, oil, and lemon juice, and process until well mixed. Season with salt and pepper, add pistachios and process for a few seconds. To serve, slice turkey into ¼-inch thick slices, and serve with sauce.

USING HEALTHIER FATS

Using nuts instead of other fats can improve the nutritional value of your food, and make the food tastier and more distinct. For example, just 1 ounce of pistachios in the Pistachio Pesto Sauce (page 56) makes a unique pesto that is just as delicious, if not more so, than ordinary pesto made with parmesan cheese. For other examples of dishes that are upgraded with nuts, see the Wild Rice and Beet Salad (page 26) and the Beef Stew with String Beans in Beer and Dried Fruit (page 87).

Choosing nuts

Every nut has its own flavor and nutritional benefits. Walnuts, for example, are rich in omega-3; Brazil nuts in selenium. The question isn't which nut is the most nutritious, but how to enjoy variety. With that approach, you'll gain both nutritional and culinary benefits from nuts. Another quality to consider is sweetness. Pistachios and cashews are sweeter nuts; using them in desserts can reduce the amount of sugar you add. Walnuts are more bitter, and suitable for other types of dishes. I recommend buying nuts that are raw and unsalted since you can always add salt, if you like. Store nuts in an airtight container in the pantry or refrigerator.

Raw or toasted?

Toasting nuts emphasizes their flavor, and means you need fewer nuts to obtain the same nutty taste. After all, even though nuts have healthy fats, they also have quite a few calories. However, the heat used to toast nuts partially damages their fatty acids, reducing their nutritional value. If the recipe uses relatively small quantity of nuts, and their purpose is just to give flavor, I recommend toasting them. To do this, simply place the nuts, such as the recipe on opposite page, in a small dry pan and heat them over medium-high heat until fragrant. If you are using a relatively large quantity of nuts, I recommend opting for raw nuts, since their flavor will be unmistakable, and you'll be taking full advantage of their nutritional qualities.

Use nuts to replace ingredients that are high in cholesterol and saturated fats

Nuts can be a practical substitute for cream, butter, and other thickeners. Ordinary cream, for example, is made up of low-fat milk, milk solids, and milk fats that have saturated fats and cholesterol. If you replace the milk solids with nut solids and the milk fats with nut fats, you'll have a healthier cream that has a unique flavor (see recipe on opposite page).

Nuts are also excellent for thickening salad dressing (see Baby Salad Greens with Nectarines and Walnut Vinaigrette, page 60). To do this, process nuts with a bit of oil, then add the mixture to the dressing ingredients. The result is a thick dressing with a texture similar to mayonnaise. To thicken soup using nuts, heat 1 tablespoon of olive oil in a frying pan over medium heat, then sauté 2 chopped shallots and 4 crushed garlic cloves until brown. Add a handful of nuts, such as walnuts, and sauté for 1 minute. Transfer the mixture to a food processor and process until smooth, then add to soup at the end of the cooking process, to thicken and add flavor.

Mango Cubes in Cashew Cream

Cashews mixed with walnut oil make the creamy, flavorful sauce in this recipe. Be sure to process the cashews thoroughly before adding the soy milk, and remember that the ratio between the cashews and milk determines the percentage of fat in the cream. The more milk you add, the lower the percentage of fat. Adding just a few tablespoons of milk will make nut butter. For variety, replace the cashews with almonds, hazelnuts, or any other type of nut you like. As for the walnut oil, it can be replaced with canola oil.

Calories	104
Total fat	7 g
Calories as fat	61%
Saturated fat	1 g
Cholesterol	0 mg
Carbohydrates	12 g
Dietary fiber	1 g
Sodium	4 mg
Protein	1 g
Carbohydrate choices	**1**

Exchanges: 1 fruit, 1 fat

INGREDIENTS

Serves 12 / Serving size: ⅓ cup mango cubes + 1 tablespoon cream

- **1¾ ounces raw cashews**
- **4 tablespoons unrefined walnut oil**
- **¼ cup unsweetened and unsalted soy milk**
- **1 tablespoon unsweetened date honey**
- **3 medium mangos, peeled, pitted, and cut into 1-inch cubes**
- **Fresh mint leaves, for garnish**

PREPARATION

1. In a food processor, process cashews and oil until smooth and creamy. Add milk gradually, while food processor is operating, until you achieve the desired consistency. Add date honey and process until combined.

2. Distribute mango cubes among serving dishes and pour cashew cream over top. Garnish with mint before serving.

Mango Cubes in Cashew Cream

Baby Salad Greens with Nectarines and Walnut Vinaigrette

The way ingredients are cut can reduce the amount of calories per serving. In this recipe, cut the nectarine into quarters, then cut each quarter into very thin slices. This results in a large number of pieces that can be evenly distributed throughout the salad, with a single nectarine adding flavor to every mouthful of salad. That probably wouldn't happen if you cut the nectarine into random chunks, since there would be far fewer nectarine pieces.

Calories	60
Total fat	6 g
Calories as fat	90%
Saturated fat	1 g
Cholesterol	0 mg
Carbohydrates	2 g
Dietary fiber	0.5 g
Sodium	118 mg
Protein	1 g
Carbohydrate choices	**None**
Exchanges: 1 fat	

INGREDIENTS

Serves 10 / Serving size: 1 cup

Dressing
- 4 tablespoons unrefined walnut oil
- 1 tablespoon coarsely chopped raw walnuts
- 4 tablespoons rice vinegar
- 1 tablespoon mirin
- ½ teaspoon peeled and grated fresh ginger
- ½ teaspoon wasabi
- ½ teaspoon Atlantic sea salt
- ½ teaspoon ground black pepper

Salad
- 1 red leaf lettuce, leaves torn into bite-size pieces
- 3 ounces (about 3 cups) baby arugula
- 5 ounces (about 5 cups) baby salad greens
- 1 nectarine, pitted, quartered, then thinly sliced

PREPARATION

1. Prepare dressing: In a food processor, process oil and walnuts until smooth. Add vinegar, mirin, ginger, and wasabi, and process until smooth. Add salt and pepper to taste.

2. Prepare salad: In a large serving bowl, mix together lettuce, baby arugula, baby salad greens, and nectarine. Pour dressing over salad, toss to coat, and serve.

Less Salt, More Flavor

Everybody knows that too much salt isn't healthy. Even people who love salt will agree that food seasoned with fresh herbs, diverse spices, delicious sauces, and salt is tastier than food seasoned only with salt. The main objective of this chapter, therefore, is to suggest ways in which you can reduce your salt consumption while increasing the flavor of your food.

Some people think cutting down on salt when they cook is the best way of reducing their sodium intake. This isn't completely true, since most of the sodium people consume comes from prepared food, such as canned broth, which is already sodium-heavy. Every time you eat homemade food rather than ready-made, frozen, or fast food, you are consuming less sodium. This is true even if you add a relatively large amount of salt to your food. One of the best ways of reducing the amount of sodium you consume and increasing the flavor of your food is to prepare the food yourself. Though preparing food takes longer than defrosting ready-made food or buying fast food, the food you make will have less sodium, provide more flavor, and be healthier. I hope the tips and techniques in this book help you manage your time in the kitchen more efficiently, and make it easier for you to cook more of the food you eat.

When it comes to cooking, use of salt has changed over time. In the past, salt was only used to emphasize the taste of food. Today, it is often the primary source of flavoring. There are many ways to increase the flavor of foods other than adding salt, and these methods don't have to take a lot of extra time. They include adding spices and fresh herbs, reducing excess water, soaking foods in marinades, and using diverse sauces. When using any of these methods, which are presented in the next chapter, taste the food after it is ready, and before you add salt. I'm sure you'll find that the amount of salt you add is significantly reduced.

People are exposed to large quantities of salt from a very young age these days, in the form of fast foods, frozen foods, and snacks. For this reason, many people are used to very salty flavors, and they don't notice the more delicate flavors found naturally in vegetables and fresh herbs. One method of combating this situation is to gradually adapt your palate to less salty foods. Don't eat bland food that doesn't taste good, but do try to gradually reduce the amount of salt you add. When you get used to a small reduction in salt, keep reducing the amount gradually over time. After a short while, you'll likely discover other flavors in the foods you eat, flavors that were previously masked by the salt. Not only will you develop a liking for foods that are less salty, but you'll also enjoy the other new flavors you encounter.

USING STOCK

A major source of sodium in many diets is found in prepared food such as canned broth and powdered soup. Even good quality canned broth that has lots of vegetables or meat often contains a large quantity of sodium. Furthermore, the taste of these products can't be compared to the flavor of the fresh stock they strive to replicate. Stock is a natural concentrate in various flavors such as vegetable, chicken, or beef. Stock can be made in a home kitchen (see recipe facing page), and is quite easy to prepare. I strongly recommend making the transition from canned broth to homemade stock. Use it to prepare aromatic liquids such as soups and sauces, as well as for upgrading other foods such as brown rice, stew, and baked dishes. Adding stock to a recipe will upgrade the taste and increase the flavor, and this means you won't feel the need to add on the salt. To make the transition easier, prepare a large batch of stock in advance, and freeze it in tablespoon servings using an ice cube tray. Transfer the frozen cubes to a freezer-safe storage bag, and store them for several months. Every time a recipe calls for canned broth, or whenever you want to upgrade a dish you're cooking, simply add one or two cubes of frozen stock. You'll increase the flavor and reduce the amount of salt needed, in one easy step.

How many tablespoons of stock to add?

It's hard to know, exactly. The more that stock is reduced as it cooks (and reducing foods in a home kitchen is not a precise process), the stronger it will be and the less you'll require. My recommendation is this: learn your stock, and after a few uses, you'll know how much is just right for adding flavor. Note that some cookbooks call for stock in tablespoons while others do so in cups. Recipes that list stock in tablespoons, such as in this book, are referring to concentrated stock; larger amounts indicate that the stock has been diluted with water so that it has the consistency of soup.

What is in the stock aside from taste?

Stock cooks for quite a long time, and you may wonder whether there are any vitamins or minerals left in it after it has been cooked. The answer to this question is complex, and discused it partially in the Lots of Vegetables chapter (pages 88–109). What's important to remember is that stock is added to food in order to increase taste, not nutrients. Its nutritional value lies in the fact that it helps you reduce your consumption of salt. When you prepare soup, most of the vitamins and minerals in the soup come from the vegetables and not the stock.

Stock can be made from a recipe, or from leftover vegetables

The recipe on the facing page is inspired by a French-style vegetable stock, but almost any vegetables—even the peels, ends, and stalks left over from other dishes you prepare can be used to make stock. Finished cooking? Collect the carrot peels, onion ends, parsley stalks, and celery leaves, and use them to prepare fresh stock by following the recipe's basic principles. If you don't have time to make stock on the same day you have lots of leftover vegetable pieces, simply store the vegetables in a freezer-safe storage bag and freeze them until you have time to cook. If you want to make chicken stock, add chicken bones to the pot and cook for 3 hours before straining; if you want to make beef stock, add meat bones, and cook for 6 hours before straining.

Vegetable Stock

When cooking vegetables to make stock, start with cold water for a flavorful result. If you use hot water, you'll actually blanch the vegetables, sealing the flavor inside rather than allowing it to enrich the liquid. Using tastier stock when you cook means you'll likely need to add less salt to achieve a flavorful result. Remember this technique the next time you make soup or sauce.

INGREDIENTS

Makes 2 cups stock /
Serving size: 1 tablespoon =
1 ice cube

- 3 tablespoons extra-virgin olive oil
- 1 leek, coarsely chopped
- 1 medium onion, coarsely chopped
- 4 celery stalks, sliced
- 2 medium carrots, peeled and sliced
- 1 parsley root, peeled and sliced
- 1 large tomato, cubed
- 8 button mushrooms, halved
- 10 cups water
- 1½ ounces (1 bunch) fresh thyme
- 1 bay leaf
- 5 black peppercorns
- 1 clove
- ¾ ounce (½ bunch) parsley

Calories	20
Total fat	1 g
Calories as fat	45%
Saturated fat	0 g
Cholesterol	0 mg
Carbohydrates	2 g
Dietary fiber	0 g
Sodium	8 mg
Protein	0 g
Carbohydrate choices	**None**
Exchanges: free food	

PREPARATION

1. In a large stockpot, heat oil over medium-high heat. Add leek, onion, and celery, and sauté for 5 minutes, until brown. Add carrots and parsley root and sauté for 1 minute, until brown. Add tomato and mushrooms and sauté for 1 minute, then add water. Bring to a boil, then add thyme, bay leaf, peppercorns, clove, and parsley. Reduce heat to low and simmer gently for 45 minutes.

2. Pour stock through a fine-mesh strainer into a large bowl. Discard vegetables, and return stock to pot. Simmer on low for 1 hour, until stock reduces by about three-quarters. Let stock cool, then transfer to ice cube trays by spooning 1 tablespoon stock into each cube. Freeze until solid, then transfer frozen stock cubes to freezer-safe storage bags, and freeze for up to 1 year.

SPICES

Spices are a simple, tasty replacement for salt. In fact, it's something of an insult to describe spices as salt replacements, since it should really be the other way around. Using spices doesn't make cooking more difficult or time consuming. Spices do upgrade the flavor of food, making it richer and more interesting. Make it a habit to use spices when you cook, and before you add salt to a dish, think about which spice could improve the taste. After adding that spice, you'll likely find you need to add less salt.

Several recipes in this book use spices you may be unfamiliar with, such as ground allspice berries, fennel seeds, and lavender blossoms. Get to know these spices, and add them to your spice collection. Pamper your spice rack by adding a new spice or two every now and then. When you've exhausted the selection at your supermarket, visit a spice shop, bulk food store, or health food store. You'll probably find a more diverse array of spices there, and the shopkeepers may offer you some tips for using them.

Choose high-quality spice mixtures
Spice mixtures such as curry and garam masala, both used in the recipe on the facing page, are quite common these days. These mixtures are excellent for upgrading the flavor of food, but they need to be of high quality. Many spice shops sell their own mixtures, which may contain salt or flour to increase their volume. Check the ingredients carefully before buying. If you find a spice shop that you like, go back for more.

Invest in a spice grinder or mortar and pestle
The flavor of freshly ground cardamom or cinnamon is incomparable to the flavor of these spices purchased already ground. If you equip your kitchen with a spice grinder or a mortar and pestle, you'll be able to buy whole spice seeds or beans and grind them up right before use. The result is excellent, and you'll barely feel the need for salt.

The recipe on page 66 calls for ground allspice, but if you have a spice grinder at home, you can purchase whole allspice and grind it. The recipe on page 69 uses fennel seeds and lavender blossoms. Grinding these spices gently before use increases their flavor immensely; in fact, their flavor is so strong you'll likely require very little additional salt. Try to create a similar situation when you cook other dishes, by combining strong, flavorful spices with less salt than usual.

Toasting some spices adds flavor
In the Indian kitchen, many spices are toasted before they are ground, to give them even more flavor. This technique can be used to enhance the taste of coriander seeds, for example, as demonstrated on facing page. To toast the seeds, place them in a small dry pan and toast them over medium heat, shaking the pan gently, until seeds are fragrant and start to brown. Remove the seeds from the pan and let them cool a bit before grinding.

Indian-Style Eggplant and Tomato Stew

Though many people think eggplant needs to be salted to remove bitterness, this simply isn't true. Eggplants that are smooth, shiny, and ripe don't need any salting at all. When selecting eggplants, look under the leaves at the narrower end. If the color there is the same as the rest, the eggplant is ripe, and ready to be cooked. When removing the peel from roasted eggplant, take care to remove only the thin purple peel, since the flesh just under it is the most flavorful.

INGREDIENTS

Serves 10 / Serving size: ⅔ cup

- 3 medium eggplants
- 2 medium tomatoes, cored and scored with an X at the bottom
- 3 tablespoons unrefined canola oil
- 3 medium onions, chopped
- 2 cups water
- 2 tablespoons vegetable stock (page 63), optional
- 1 teaspoon coriander seeds, toasted and ground (page 64)
- ½ teaspoon ground turmeric
- ½ teaspoon chili powder
- 1 teaspoon garam masala
- 1 teaspoon curry
- ½ teaspoon Atlantic sea salt
- ½ teaspoon ground black pepper

PREPARATION

1. Preheat oven to 400°F. Pierce eggplants with a fork several times, and place on a large baking sheet. Roast for 40 minutes, or until soft. When eggplants are cool enough to touch, remove peel and discard. Finely chop eggplant flesh, and transfer to a large bowl.

2. Bring a small pot of water to a boil over high heat. Place tomatoes in boiling water and blanch for 10 to 15 seconds, until skins loosen. Remove tomatoes with a slotted spoon and place them in an ice water bath. When tomatoes are cool enough to handle, remove skins with a paring knife and discard. Cut in halves, remove and discard seeds, and cut flesh into cubes.

3. In a medium pot, heat oil over medium-high heat. Add half the onions and sauté for 3 minutes, until golden brown. Add the tomatoes, ¼ cup water, and stock, reduce heat to medium-low, and cook for 5 minutes. Mix in chopped eggplant, remaining onions, remaining water, coriander, turmeric, chili powder, garam masala, and curry. Cook over medium-low heat for 20 minutes, until liquid evaporates. Season with salt and pepper, and serve.

Calories	66
Total fat	4 g
Calories as fat	55%
Saturated fat	1 g
Cholesterol	0 mg
Carbohydrates	7 g
Dietary fiber	3 g
Sodium	120 mg
Protein	1 g
Carbohydrate choices	½
Exchanges: 1 vegetable, ½ fat	

Aromatic Mixed Rice and Lentils

This popular dish traditionally combines rice and green lentils, but it is very adaptable. Replace the green lentils with black lentils or mung beans, or replace the brown rice with wheat seeds. For a quick version of the recipe, try using steamed seed sprouts instead of lentils, and whole-wheat couscous instead of brown rice. Adding vegetables to this recipe is an excellent way of enhancing the flavor. Sauté 1 chopped onion and 1 cup sliced button mushrooms in 2 tablespoons of unrefined canola oil, and spoon over rice and lentil mixture just before serving.

INGREDIENTS

Serves 10 / Serving size: ½ cup

- 1 tablespoon extra-virgin olive oil
- 1 large onion, chopped
- 1 clove garlic, crushed
- ½ teaspoon ground cardamom
- ½ teaspoon ground cinnamon
- ½ teaspoon ground allspice
- 1 cup brown rice, soaked overnight and drained
- Water
- 3 tablespoons vegetable stock (page 63), optional
- 1 cup green lentils, picked over and rinsed
- ½ teaspoon Atlantic sea salt
- ½ teaspoon ground black pepper
- ½ cup chopped fresh parsley, for garnish

Calories	156
Total fat	2 g
Calories as fat	12%
Saturated fat	0 g
Cholesterol	0 mg
Carbohydrates	28 g
Dietary fiber	7 g
Sodium	120 mg
Protein	7 g
Carbohydrate choices	**2**
Exchanges: 2 starch	

PREPARATION

1. In a large pot, heat oil over medium-high heat. Add onion and sauté until brown, about 5 minutes. Mix in garlic, cardamom, cinnamon, and allspice, and sauté for 1 minute. Add rice and mix to combine. Add enough water to reach ½ inch above the rice, then add stock and cover pot. Increase heat to high and bring to a boil; then reduce heat to low, and cook for about 30 minutes, until liquid is absorbed and rice is soft.

2. In the meantime, place lentils in a small pot, and add water with a pinch of salt to cover. Bring to a boil over high heat, then reduce heat and simmer, uncovered, for about 20 minutes, until lentils are soft. Periodically remove foam that forms on top.

3. Drain lentils and mix into rice. Add salt and pepper to taste, and garnish with parsley before serving.

Aromatic Mixed Rice and Lentils

Seared Tuna Steak with Lavender and Fennel Seeds in Mustard and Chive Sauce

Seared Tuna Steak with Lavender and Fennel Seeds in Mustard and Chive Sauce

Since the tuna is seared only to rare, using the right slicing technique is critical for its tenderness. In fact, it's the cutting that actually softens the fish in this recipe, not the heating. When fish or meat is cooked until rare, it should be sliced as thinly as possible, against the fibers of the fish or meat, to make it tender. If you don't have a mortar and pestle, use coarsely ground pepper, and crush the fennel seeds and lavender blossoms with the flat side of a wide knife blade.

INGREDIENTS

Serves 8 / Serving size: 5 slices

Sauce

- ½ teaspoon Dijon-style mustard
- ½ teaspoon honey
- 1 tablespoon extra-virgin olive oil
- 1 tablespoon fresh lemon juice
- 2 tablespoons chopped chives
- Pinch Atlantic sea salt
- Pinch coarsely ground black pepper

Tuna

- ¼ teaspoon Atlantic sea salt
- 1 teaspoon black peppercorns
- 1 tablespoon fennel seeds
- 1½ teaspoons dried lavender blossoms
- 1 tablespoon unrefined canola oil
- Two 3½-ounce ¾-inch thick red tuna steaks

TIP *For variation, replace the seasoning with mustard, cumin, and coriander seeds, and serve with a yogurt-based sauce such as the Fresh Herb and Yogurt Sauce (page 82). This dish can be served as a first course, antipasto, or can be mixed with baby leaves to make a salad.*

Calories	59
Total fat	4 g
Calories as fat	61%
Saturated fat	0 g
Cholesterol	11 mg
Carbohydrates	0 g
Dietary fiber	0 g
Sodium	82 mg
Protein	6 g
Carbohydrate choices	**None**
Exchanges: 1 lean meat	

PREPARATION

1. Prepare sauce: In a jar with a tight-fitting lid, combine mustard, honey, oil, lemon juice, chives, salt, and pepper. Close jar and shake vigorously.

2. Prepare tuna: Using a mortar and pestle, crush together salt, peppercorns, fennel seeds, and lavender blossoms. Spread mixture on a flat plate, and press tuna steaks into mixture to coat evenly on both sides.

3. In a medium frying pan, heat oil over medium-high heat. Add tuna and sear for 1 minute on each side. Be careful not to overcook. Transfer tuna to refrigerator to cool, then cut into very thin slices. Serve chilled, with sauce on the side.

HERBS

Another excellent way of enhancing flavor in food is to add fresh or dried herbs. Generally speaking, fresh herbs are best, since they are full of flavor and aroma, but dried herbs may be preferred in some cases, such as when making a crispy coating for baked chicken or fish (Sesame and Herb Chicken Fingers, page 215).

Since I grew up in the Mediterranean, the dishes of my childhood were rich in thyme, rosemary, fresh oregano, and sage. These herbs generally mix well with more common herbs such as basil, mint, cilantro and parsley. Other cuisines favor different types of herbs. Herbs of all types can be excellent additions to sauces, meat, chicken, and vegetable dishes. Start using them as often as you can and you'll soon find your dishes upgraded both in flavor and freshness. You'll also find you need to add much less salt to your food, since herbs bring with them enticingly rich flavors.

Adding herbs

Herbs may be added at the beginning of the cooking process, or at the very end. If you add the herb at the beginning, you'll get a delicate flavor that blends into the food you are preparing. If you add the herb at the end, like in Pea Soup with Fresh Mint (page 72), the flavor is much more dominant. Both options are fine, and you can alternate between them when you cook. Some herbs, such as basil, change color when they are cooked, so adding them at the end is important for aesthetic reasons.

Some herbs have stronger flavors than others. A successful herb mixture includes a primary herb with a delicate flavor, such as parsley, and smaller quantities of other herbs with slightly stronger flavors, such as thyme or oregano. A mixture that has too much of a dominant herb will likely be unappealing to many people's palates. See how these considerations guide the selection of fresh herbs in the mixtures used in the Whole-Wheat Couscous Salad with Roasted Vegetables (page 91) and the Tilapia and Swiss Chard with Green Tahini (page 74).

To see how herbs can reduce the amount of salt you need in a recipe, try the following experiment: prepare the Pea Soup with Fresh Mint (page 72) without the mint, and taste it. Then mix in the mint and taste it again. I'm sure you'll find you need to add much less salt after the mint has been added to achieve the flavor you want. Add fresh herbs to different foods you prepare, and discover how much less salt you need.

Storing fresh herbs

Storing herbs properly is critical for preserving their flavor and freshness. Since many people go shopping only once a week, proper storage techniques are really important. Fresh herbs should always be refrigerated, and may be stored in one of two ways. You can wrap them in absorbent paper or place them in a plastic bag that has been punctured in a few places, to allow moisture to escape. Either one of these methods should keep your herbs fresh and full of flavor for up to one week.

Another method of preserving the flavor of herbs, particularly those that are only in season for a short time, is to make Herb-Infused Olive Oil (page 75). Such oils are excellent for adding flavor to salads or lightly fried dishes. Any fresh herb is suitable for this technique. You can also try using a combination of herbs, although this can limit the possibilities for using the oil. In fact, if you want to use different herbs to make herb-infused oils, I recommend preparing separate bottles, each with its own herb. If you want to combine the flavors, simply combine the oils.

Pesto sauce

Pesto is a delicious Mediterranean sauce made with olive oil and fresh herbs that is suitable for adding to meats, starches, and vegetables. Classic pesto is made with basil, but you can also use other seasonal fresh herbs, such as fresh oregano or thyme, with a bit of parsley to soften the flavor. Pesto can be frozen for several months and is excellent for preserving the taste of fresh herbs long after they are out of season.

Pea Soup with Fresh Mint

For variety in this recipe, alter the vegetable, the herb, or both. My preferred variations are zucchini with mint and pumpkin with sage. Notice that if you replace the peas with a non-starchy vegetable, you'll be reducing the carbohydrate choices in this dish. Consider the strength of the herb's flavor when substituting fresh herbs. For example, oregano and sage have relatively strong flavors, so I recommend using small quantities; if you use parsley, increase the amount since its flavor is quite mild.

INGREDIENTS

Serves 10 / Serving size: 1 cup

- 3 tablespoons extra-virgin olive oil
- 1 small onion, chopped
- 2 cloves garlic, chopped
- ½ leek, sliced
- 2 celery stalks, sliced
- 4 cups water
- 4 tablespoons vegetable stock (page 63), optional
- 1 pound peas, fresh or frozen
- 1 cup fresh mint leaves, plus more for garnish
- ¼ teaspoon Atlantic sea salt
- ¼ teaspoon ground black pepper

Calories	81
Total fat	4 g
Calories as fat	44%
Saturated fat	1 g
Cholesterol	0 mg
Carbohydrates	9 g
Dietary fiber	3 g
Sodium	101 mg
Protein	3 g
Carbohydrate choices	½
Exchanges: ½ starch, 1 fat	

PREPARATION

1. In a large pot, heat oil over medium-high heat. Add onion, garlic, leek, and celery, and sauté for 5 minutes, until brown. Add water and stock, increase heat to high, and bring to a boil. Reduce heat to low and simmer for 10 minutes. Add peas, increase heat to high and bring to a boil, then reduce heat to low and simmer for 20 minutes.

2. Mix in mint, then transfer to a food processor, or use an immersion blender, and puree until smooth. Return soup to pot, and heat gently. Add salt and pepper to taste. Transfer to serving plate and garnish with mint leaves before serving.

Pea Soup with Fresh Mint

Tilapia and Swiss Chard with Green Tahini Cream

Tahini is a fat that comes from sesame seeds. When mixing tahini with water, gradually mix small amounts at a time, so that the tahini absorbs the water. I recommend making the tahini cream relatively thin, so that it has a delicate flavor that mixes well with the flavor of the fish. For variety, replace the sautéed Swiss chard with tomato cubes, sautéed zucchini, slices of fennel, or with cubes of your favorite root vegetables. The fish can be replaced with any other type of white fish, or with lean ground beef. If using ground beef, arrange it in a ¾-inch thick layer on top of the vegetables and pour the tahini over top.

INGREDIENTS

Serves 8 / Serving size: 1 fillet +
4 tablespoons vegetables

Tahini

- 4 tablespoons pure tahini
- 2 tablespoons pure unsweetened pomegranate juice concentrate
- 4 tablespoons fresh lemon juice
- ½ cup water
- 2 cloves garlic, crushed
- 2 tablespoons chopped fresh thyme
- 4 tablespoons chopped fresh parsley
- 4 tablespoons chopped scallions
- 2 tablespoons chopped fresh oregano
- Pinch teaspoon Atlantic sea salt
- Pinch teaspoon ground black pepper

Fish

- 1 tablespoon extra-virgin olive oil
- 1 medium onion, chopped
- 2¼ pounds Swiss chard, sliced
- ¼ teaspoon Atlantic sea salt
- ¼ teaspoon ground black pepper

- Eight 4-ounce tilapia fillets, with or without skin
- 1 tomato, halved
- 4 tablespoons pomegranate seeds, for garnish
- 4 tablespoons fresh chopped parsley, for garnish

Calories	202
Total fat	8 g
Calories as fat	36%
Saturated fat	2 g
Cholesterol	48 mg
Carbohydrates	9 g
Dietary fiber	3 g
Sodium	468 mg
Protein	26 g
Carbohydrate choices	½

Exchanges: 4 lean meat, 2 vegetable

PREPARATION

1. Prepare tahini: In a medium bowl, mix together tahini, pomegranate juice concentrate, lemon juice, and water. Mix in garlic, thyme, parsley, scallions, and oregano. Add salt and pepper to taste, and set aside.

2. Prepare fish: Preheat oven to 350°F. Place wok over medium-high heat, and add oil, swirling to coat. When oil is hot, add onion and sauté for 3 minutes until golden brown. Add Swiss chard and cook for 5 minutes. Add salt and pepper to taste.

3. Transfer Swiss chard mixture to a 14 x 10-inch baking dish. Arrange fillets on top, skin-side down. Season with salt and pepper. Gently squeeze tomatoes over top.

4. Pour tahini mixture evenly over fish. Bake for 10 minutes, until fish are soft, then set oven to broil and cook for 1 minute, until top is brown. Sprinkle fish with pomegranate seeds and parsley before serving.

Herb-Infused Olive Oil

Olive oil is likely to become oxygenated and damaged if it is stored in direct light, so pour it into a dark bottle and keep it in a dark place. In the following recipe, the addition of fresh herbs may accelerate the oxidation process. To stop this from happening, I recommend adding a bit of wheat germ oil. Wheat germ oil lacks flavor, but is very rich in vitamin E and helps reduce damage from oxygen. Wheat germ oil is sold in a variety of forms and used for various purposes. Make sure you purchase cold-pressed wheat germ oil intended for consumption.

The best way of releasing the aromatic elements in fresh herbs is to gently heat the mixture over steam from a pot, a technique known as a bain-marie or water bath (see instructions below). This technique helps transfer the flavor from the herbs to the olive oil without damaging the taste or quality of the oil. Because steam heat is gentler than direct heat from the stove, it's easier to ensure that the oil doesn't reach a too high temperature.

After you are skilled at making flavored olive oil, try infusing nut oils with mint, sage, vanilla sticks, or cloves. These oils are excellent for preparing desserts. Try spreading flavored nut oil between pieces of phyllo pastry in the Apple-filled Phyllo Pastry in Pomegranate and Red Wine Sauce (page 143), or when preparing pastry dough that will be filled with a sweet filling (see page 134).

Calories	46
Total fat	5 g
Calories as fat	100%
Saturated fat	1 g
Cholesterol	0 mg
Carbohydrates	0 g
Dietary fiber	0 g
Sodium	0 mg
Protein	0 g
Carbohydrate choices	**None**
Exchanges: 1 fat	

INGREDIENTS

Makes 32 ounces / Serving size: 1 teaspoon

- **28 ounces extra-virgin olive oil**
- **3½ ounces wheat germ oil**
- **1½ ounces (1 bunch) fresh herbs (such as tarragon, oregano or thyme)**

PREPARATION

1. Mix together olive oil, wheat germ oil, and herbs in a large stainless steel bowl. Place a pot of water over medium heat, and place bowl on pot. Make sure the bottom of the bowl does not come in contact with the water in the pot. Bring to a boil over medium-high heat, reduce heat to low, and heat gently for 3 minutes, allowing flavors to blend.

2. Pour oil and herbs into a dark bottle, and store in a dark place for 10 days, shaking gently every day. May be then stored for up to 4 months.

REDUCE THE QUANTITY OF WATER YOU USE WHILE COOKING

People are seldom aware of the amount of water they add when cooking. Using too much water dilutes the flavor of the food. This makes the flavor less satisfying, often resulting in the addition of extra salt. In the recipe on the facing page, the beef is roasted in a pot without any water. It is still a wet roasting technique, since the meat and vegetables have enough water already; adding any more water would simply dilute the taste. If you do need to add a bit of liquid while preparing a dish to keep it moist, I suggest using liquids that will increase rather than diminish flavor. Try using dry red wine or stock instead of water.

When cooking some starches, adding the right amount of water is very important. When cooking most other foods, however, try to reduce the amount of water you normally add. If you cook with a covered pot, the steam in the pot will produce enough moisture to eliminate the need for anything more than a small amount of additional liquid. When cooking in an uncovered pot, add just enough water to cover the food in the pot. Cook with less water and your food will be more flavorful and require less salt.

Cook with an uncovered pot when possible

One method of reducing the amount of liquid is to cook with an open pot. This takes a bit longer than cooking with a covered pot, but the result is richer, tastier, and will require less salt for flavoring. I highly recommend it, when possible. See the recipes in this chapter for demonstrations of this technique.

The next time you find that the flavor of a sauce or soup you are cooking isn't quite strong enough, allow the dish to simmer uncovered for another 5 or 10 minutes before adding salt. After the liquid has been reduced, taste it again. You'll likely find that the flavor is much richer than before and may not even require additional salt. Try this technique with the Indian-Style Eggplant and Tomato Stew (page 65). At the beginning of the cooking process, immediately after you add the spices, you'll probably find that the taste isn't satisfying, and you'll want to add salt. Wait until the end of the cooking process and then try it again. Still needs salt? Wait a few more minutes and check again. Excess water will have evaporated by then, and that is the right time to add a bit of salt, if necessary.

Beef Shoulder in Fresh Oregano and Root Vegetable Sauce

Two groups of ingredients I highly recommend are onions and root vegetables. Though higher in carbohydrates than other vegetables, they are very aromatic, and even a small quantity can add a lot of flavor to your food, while maintaining a suitable amount of carbohydrate. Many people add garlic, onions, leeks, and celery for flavor; try adding parsley and celery root as well. The following recipe shows how these vegetables, cut into cubes, can be combined and added to a cooked dish. They can also be grated and added raw to foods, as demonstrated in the Cucumber and Parsley Root Salad (page 159).

INGREDIENTS

Serves 12 / Serving size:
2 slices + 4 tablespoons sauce

- One 3½-pound lean beef shoulder roast
- ½ teaspoon Atlantic sea salt
- ½ teaspoon ground black pepper
- 1 tablespoon unrefined canola oil
- 2 medium onions, coarsely chopped
- 1 head garlic, cloves separated and peeled
- 1 medium kohlrabi, peeled and cut into ½-inch cubes
- 2 medium carrots, peeled and cut into ½-inch cubes
- 1 medium parsley root, peeled and cut into ½-inch cubes
- 1 medium celery root, peeled and cut into ½-inch cubes
- ½ cup fresh oregano leaves

TIP *To vary this recipe, replace the onions with leeks or shallots, or add splashes of color with pumpkin or beet cubes. Fennel can be used instead of kohlrabi, and thyme or sage can be used instead of oregano.*

Calories	170
Total fat	7 g
Calories as fat	37%
Saturated fat	2 g
Cholesterol	53 mg
Carbohydrates	4 g
Dietary fiber	1 g
Sodium	179 mg
Protein	22 g
Carbohydrate choices	**None**
Exchanges: 3 lean meat, 1 vegetable	

PREPARATION

1. Truss beef with kitchen twine, and season with salt and pepper. In a wide-based pot, heat oil over high heat. Add beef and sear for about 2 minutes on each side. Remove beef from pot and set aside.

2. Reduce heat to medium-high, add onions and garlic to pot, and sauté for about 3 minutes, until onions are golden brown. Add kohlrabi, carrots, parsley root, and celery root. Season with salt and pepper, and sauté for 5 minutes. Add oregano, and mix.

3. Return beef to pot, placing it on vegetable mixture, and cover. Reduce heat to low and cook for 2 hours, turning the beef over every 30 minutes until soft.

4. Remove beef, season vegetable mixture with salt and pepper before serving. Slice beef into ¼-inch thick slices, and serve with vegetable mixture.

MARINADES

Another way to enrich the flavor of almost any ingredient, including vegetables and starches, is to marinate. Foods don't always need to be marinated in advance, and cooked foods can actually be added to marinades so that they soak up flavor before being served (see Grilled Zucchini in Mint Vinaigrette, page 230).

Marinating in advance doesn't need to take a long time, either. Even a short period of marinating can lead to excellent results if the food you are marinating is small or cut into thin slices. That's how the shrimp in the Baby Salad Greens with Stir-Fried Shrimp and Avocado (page 149) get their flavor. In that dish, the shrimp marinate while the vegetables are being stir-fried, so the process doesn't actually require any additional time at all. Use marinades as often as you can to upgrade the flavor of raw ingredients. Even a simple marinade such as plain yogurt or wine mixed with olive oil and mustard are delicious marinades. Remember, when food is marinating, it doesn't actually require any attention; it just marinates in the refrigerator or on the counter while you do other things.

Make a successful marinade with the ingredients you have at home

All types of aromatic ingredients are suitable for making marinades. Spices, fresh herbs, root vegetables, onions, fruit juices, and alcoholic beverages are all excellent marinade ingredients. Don't hesitate to try new combinations with various ingredients that you have at home, since that's often the best way of succeeding. As a general guideline, I suggest choosing an aromatic liquid for the marinade base, then adding a variety of herbs and spices. If the liquid you choose is bitter, such as beer, or sour, such as lemon juice, add a small amount of sweetening agent, such as honey or mirin (Japanese cooking wine), to balance the flavors.

To practice making your own marinades, use the recipe on the facing page as your base, and replace one ingredient at a time. For example, first replace one of the herbs in the recipe with a different fresh or dry herb you have in your refrigerator or pantry. Next, try replacing all of the herbs with spices. For example, if you are in the mood for an Indian-style dish, replace the herbs with coriander, mustard, and cumin seeds. Once you have succeeded with making small changes, try making larger ones by replacing several ingredients. For example, alter the color of the marinade by substituting the white wine, honey, and herbs with red wine, unsweetened date honey, and a mixture of mushrooms. Remember, a good marinade will upgrade the taste of your food, and this ultimately helps you reduce the amount of salt you consume.

Sea Bass with Beet and Fennel in Yogurt and Pomegranate Sauce

Lemon cubes can add wonderful color and flavor to any dish. Try adding them to fish dishes such as the Baked Trout with Fresh Herbs and White Wine (page 156), to poultry dishes such as the Chicken Drumsticks with Peppers and Cherry Tomatoes (page 201), and to vegetable dishes such as the Wild Rice and Beet Salad (page 26). Select a lemon that is yellow and juicy, scrub peel well, then cut lemon into small chunks. As for the fish, you can replace the sea bass with another type of low-fat white fish such as tilapia.

INGREDIENTS

Serves 8 / Serving size: 1 fillet + 4 tablespoons sauce

Calories	188
Total fat	5 g
Calories as fat	24%
Saturated fat	1 g
Cholesterol	39 mg
Carbohydrates	16 g
Dietary fiber	4 g
Sodium	222 mg
Protein	19 g
Carbohydrate choices	**1**
Exchanges: 2 lean meat, 3 vegetable	

Marinade

- 1 cup plain low-fat goat yogurt
- ½ cup dry white wine
- 2 tablespoons pure unsweetened pomegranate juice concentrate
- 1 tablespoon honey
- 3 tablespoons chopped scallions
- 3 tablespoons chopped fresh mint
- 3 tablespoons chopped fresh basil
- 4 tablespoons fresh lemon juice

- 1 tablespoon chopped parsley, for garnish
- ½ lemon, cut into ¼-inch cubes, for garnish

Fish

- Eight 4-ounce sea bass fillets, with or without skin
- 4 medium fennel bulbs, thinly sliced
- 1 small beet, cut into ½-inch cubes
- 4 cloves garlic, peeled
- Pinch Atlantic sea salt, or more to taste
- Pinch ground black pepper, or more to taste
- 2 tablespoons extra-virgin olive oil

PREPARATION

1. Prepare marinade: In a medium bowl, mix together yogurt, wine, pomegranate juice concentrate, and honey. Add scallions, mint, basil, and lemon juice, and mix until combined.

2. Prepare fish: Place fillets in a shallow non-reactive dish, and pour marinade over top. Cover with plastic wrap and marinate in refrigerator for 1 hour, mixing every 20 minutes.

3. Preheat oven to 400°F. In a 14 x 10-inch baking dish, combine fennel, beet, garlic, salt, and pepper. Add oil, and mix to coat. Bake for 10 minutes, stirring occasionally, until golden brown.

4. Remove fennel mixture from oven and reduce temperature to 350°F. Place fish on fennel mixture, skin-side down, and season with salt and pepper. Pour marinade over top, and bake for 15 minutes, or until fish flakes easily with a fork. Garnish with parsley and lemon cubes before serving.

SAUCES

A classic method of adding flavor to food is to add sauce. Foods that are served with rich sauce will be of a higher quality and won't require a lot of salt. Here are a few tips that will help you make sauces quickly and without too much effort. I hope this encourage you to use sauces more often.

Use yogurt

A single tablespoon of yogurt can sometimes be just what a dish needs to make its flavor complete. Yogurt is excellent for upgrading soups, such as the Fennel, Lentil, and Lemon Soup (page 33), enhancing starches, such as the Aromatic Mixed Rice and Lentils (page 66), or adding a touch of creaminess to vegetable dishes, such as the Indian-Style Eggplant and Tomato Stew (page 65). I recommend keeping some plain low-fat yogurt in your refrigerator at all times.

Many quick and delicious sauces can be made without cooking at all and are excellent flavor enhancers. In the following pages, you'll see the Fresh Herb and Yogurt Sauce (page 82), an example from the Turkish kitchen, and salsa the famous sauce from Spanish cooking traditions. Though it can be purchased ready-made, making it at home means you can ensure that it is low in salt. For a distinct salsa made with fruit, see the Baked Salmon with Nectarine and Chili Salsa (page 84).

Sauces can be served with meats, poultry, fish, starches, or vegetables. Try to create sauces by adding your favorite vegetables, and use them to upgrade foods as often as you can. Not only will these sauces enhance the flavor of your food, but they'll also increase the quantity of vegetables you consume. For a vegetable-rich salsa fusion using Asian ingredients, see the Broccoli, Tofu, and Leek Dim Sum with Asian Salsa (page 43).

Cooking sauces can be fast

Making a sauce with pureed roasted vegetables is easy and quick. The next time your oven is on, put in a few red peppers to roast (page 39). After the peppers are roasted and peeled, put them in a food processor with a bit of garlic, water, vegetable stock, salt, and pepper. Puree until thick. You'll have a colorful, tasty sauce that can be frozen and defrosted whenever you like. Replace the peppers with any other vegetables you like, roast them in the oven or boil them on the stove, and you have the basis for a delicious and easy sauce. When you have some time, try upgrading this basic technique, as explained in Red Pepper and Basil Sauce (page 83).

Make a double batch and freeze

If you are already preparing a sauce, make a large batch and freeze part of it. Frozen sauce can be stored for several months. Imagine coming home from work and finding small containers of sauce in your freezer that you made in advance. Having these sauces on hand will not only help you reduce the amount of salt you consume. They will also make you very happy when you realize that you can add a homemade sauce to your dinner with very little effort!

Fresh Herb and Yogurt Sauce

This cold sauce does not require any cooking and can be stored in the refrigerator for several days. Just mix well before serving. It is excellent for serving with a starch or meat dishes, such as the Stuffed Peppers with Brown Rice in Tomato Sauce (page 30) or the Roast Sirloin with Thick Mushroom Sauce (page 54). It can also be used as a dressing for a cold salad, such as the Wild Rice and Beet Salad (page 26), or alongside the Pumpkin Carpaccio with Nigella (page 232). Use it as a dip for the Beet and Sesame Crackers (page 217), or as a marinade when cooking chicken or fish.

Calories	17
Total fat	1 g
Calories as fat	53%
Saturated fat	0 g
Cholesterol	1 mg
Carbohydrates	1 g
Dietary fiber	0 g
Sodium	29 mg
Protein	1 g
Carbohydrate choices	**None**
Exchanges: free food	

INGREDIENTS

Makes 2½ cups / Serving size: 2 tablespoons

- 2 cups plain low-fat yogurt
- 2 tablespoons extra-virgin olive oil
- 2 tablespoons fresh lemon juice
- 2 cloves garlic, crushed
- 4 tablespoons chopped fresh parsley
- 2 tablespoons chopped fresh mint
- 1 tablespoon sumac
- Pinch Atlantic sea salt
- Pinch ground black pepper

PREPARATION

1. In a small bowl, mix together yogurt, oil, and lemon juice. Add garlic, parsley, mint, and sumac, and mix well. Let sauce sit for at least 30 minutes, for flavors to blend.
2. Mix well before serving, and add salt and pepper to taste. May be refrigerated for up to 10 days.

Red Pepper and Basil Sauce

With a few portions of this sauce stored in your freezer, a world of culinary possibilities is open to you. You can serve it warm over oven-baked or steamed fish, or alongside whole-grain pasta, bulgur, or another quick-cooking starch. Another use of the frozen sauce can be to place it in a saucepan with a bit of stock and water and heat until warm. Then you can use it to cook meatballs, drumsticks, or cubes of chicken breast. Refrigerate leftover sauce, and use it to prepare lunch the next day by spreading it on bread to upgrade a lunchtime sandwich or dressing up cold whole-grain pasta salad.

Calories	13
Total fat	1 g
Calories as fat	70%
Saturated fat	0 g
Cholesterol	0 mg
Carbohydrates	1 g
Dietary fiber	0 g
Sodium	21 mg
Protein	0 g
Carbohydrate choices	**None**

Exchanges: free food

INGREDIENTS

Makes 2 cups / Serving size:
2 tablespoons

- 2 tablespoons extra-virgin olive oil
- 1 medium onion, quartered
- ½ leek, coarsely chopped
- 2 cloves garlic, peeled and halved
- 1 stalk celery, coarsely chopped
- 1 medium carrot, cut into slices
- 3 medium red bell peppers, roasted, peeled, seeded (page 39), and sliced
- 2 medium tomatoes, quartered
- 2 cups water, plus more as necessary
- 2 tablespoons vegetable stock (page 63), optional
- ¼ teaspoon Atlantic sea salt
- ¼ teaspoon ground black pepper
- 2 tablespoons fresh chopped basil

PREPARATION

1. Place wok over medium-high heat, and add oil, swirling to coat. When oil is hot, add onion, leek, garlic, and celery, and sauté for 2 minutes. Add carrot and sauté for 2 minutes. Add peppers and tomatoes, and cook for another 3 minutes. Add water and stock, increase heat to high, and bring to a boil. Reduce heat to low and cook for 25 minutes until soft.

2. Transfer sauce to a food processor and puree until smooth. Return mixture to wok, and add more water if necessary to reach desired consistency. Add salt, pepper, and basil to taste.

Baked Salmon with Nectarine and Chili Salsa

Fruits usually contain more carbohydrates and calories than vegetables, but if one uses a small quantity of fruit to make a large amount of sauce, their use is legitimate and even recommended. Salsa can be made from many types of fruit, just consider whether the fruit is sour or sweet. Sour fruit such as Granny Smith apples should be balanced with a small amount of sweet ingredients such as honey; sweeter fruit such as mangoes should be balanced with sour ingredients such as lemon juice. Fruit salsas are excellent alongside meat, poultry, seafood, and fish dishes.

Calories	227
Total fat	14 g
Calories as fat	55%
Saturated fat	3 g
Cholesterol	72 mg
Carbohydrates	3 g
Dietary fiber	1 g
Sodium	148 mg
Protein	22 g
Carbohydrate choices	**None**

Exchanges: 3 lean meat, 1 fat

INGREDIENTS

Serves 12 / Serving size: 1 slice + 2 tablespoons salsa

Fish

- One 3½-pound salmon fillet, without skin, cut into 12 pieces
- ½ teaspoon Atlantic sea salt
- ½ teaspoon ground black pepper
- 2 tablespoons walnut oil

Salsa

- 2 nectarines, pitted and cut into ¼-inch cubes
- 1 tablespoon seeded and finely chopped red hot chili pepper
- 1 tablespoon finely chopped fresh cilantro
- 1 clove garlic, crushed
- 1 teaspoon mirin
- Pinch Atlantic sea salt
- Pinch ground black pepper

PREPARATION

1. Prepare fish: Preheat oven to 350°F and line a baking sheet with parchment paper. Season salmon with salt and pepper, and brush with oil. Place on baking sheet and bake for 8 minutes, or until salmon is cooked through. Do not overcook.

2. In the meantime, prepare salsa: In a medium bowl, mix together nectarines, pepper, cilantro, garlic, mirin, salt, and pepper. Serve each salmon slice with 2 tablespoons of salsa.

Baked Salmon with Nectarine and Chili Salsa

HOW TO USE SALT

The best way to end this chapter on salt is with a few words on how to use it. An important factor to consider when adding salt is how to use it for best effect, without obscuring other flavors. Once you know how to do this, you'll be able to use the least amount of salt and obtain its maximum flavor. The longer a dish cooks, the more liquids evaporate, and the stronger the flavor. One may think this means salt should be added at the end of the cooking process, since that's when the full flavor of the dish is realized, making it easy to judge how much salt should be added. Although this strategy has its merits, it is only partly valid. When vegetables are sautéed and meat seared, the heating process seals them and prevents the salt from penetrating. If you add salt afterward, its effect will be minimized, and you'll probably end up adding more salt to achieve a satisfactory result.

In such cases, therefore, salt should actually be added before the food is cooked, so that it achieves its maximum effect. This ensures that the salt penetrates into the food and brings out its flavor. I suggest adding a moderate amount of salt before searing the raw ingredients, and correcting the flavor, if necessary, at the end of the cooking process.

If you're already adding salt, should you choose fine or coarse grain salt?
Generally speaking, choosing a type of salt is a matter of personal taste. When fine salt is added to foods, the taste of the salt is quite evenly distributed; when coarse salt is added, some portions are saltier than others. Some people prefer fine salt because they like the even flavor; others prefer coarse salt because they like flavor that is varied and surprising. You can try both types of salt and choose the variety that ultimately helps you cut down on your salt consumption. These distinctions are eliminated by cooking since the salt distributes itself evenly when it melts. In baking, fine salt is generally recommended over coarse salt, since it mixes more evenly into the batter or dough.

What about Atlantic sea salt and Fleur de Sel?
There are many salts on the market today. The real difference between them lies in taste, not the sodium. It's hard to compare the taste of Fleur de Sel with regular table salt, and therefore it's hard to compare the amounts you will add to your dishes. Generally speaking, the higher the quality of the salt, the richer its taste. This means people may add less of it to their food. Atlantic sea salt is an excellent compromise that takes into account both good taste and price.

Beef Stew with String Beans in Beer and Dried Fruit

Stews are easy to prepare and can be made with ingredients you have at home. Stews are also rich in flavor, meaning they require little additional salt. In this recipe, most of the alcohol in the beer evaporates during the cooking process. Use a lighter beer for a less bitter flavor, or replace the beer with ¾ cup red wine and ¾ cup water. When cooking for children, or for people who can afford a larger intake of carbohydrates, replace the beer with apple juice. The beef can be replaced with turkey or chicken drumsticks.

INGREDIENTS

Serves 8 / Serving size: 1 cup

- 1 tablespoon unrefined canola oil
- 1 large onion, chopped
- 3 cloves garlic, chopped
- 1¾ pounds lean beef round, cut into 1-inch cubes
- ½ teaspoon Atlantic sea salt
- ½ teaspoon ground black pepper
- 2 cups fresh green beans, trimmed and cut into 2-inch pieces
- 2 cups fresh yellow beans, trimmed and cut into 2-inch pieces
- 1 ounce prunes, pitted
- ⅔ ounce raw Brazil nuts
- 1 heaping tablespoon
- Dijon-style mustard
- 12 ounces dark beer
- 1 tablespoon unsweetened date honey
- 1 cup water
- 1 tablespoon vegetable stock (page 63), optional

Calories	207
Total fat	9 g
Calories as fat	39%
Saturated fat	2 g
Cholesterol	63 mg
Carbohydrates	9 g
Dietary fiber	2 g
Sodium	210 mg
Protein	23 g
Carbohydrate choices	½

Exchanges: 2 lean meat, 2 vegetable

PREPARATION

1. In a large pot, heat oil over medium-high heat. Add onion and garlic and sauté for 3 minutes, until onion is golden brown.

2. Season beef cubes with salt and pepper, then add to pot. Sear over high heat until beef whitens, about 3 minutes. Add beans, prunes, and Brazil nuts, and sauté gently over medium heat for about 5 minutes. Stir in mustard, beer, date honey, water, and stock. Add water, if necessary, to cover all ingredients. Increase heat to medium-high and bring mixture to a boil. Reduce heat to low and cook until beef softens, about 90 minutes.

3. Continue cooking until liquid reduces and stew is the desired flavor and consistency. Add salt and pepper to taste.

Lots of Vegetables

Cooking with vegetables is great fun since there is no need to reduce or change anything. In fact, healthy cooking actually means consuming more vegetables and eating a wide variety of them. Vegetables don't just add vitamins, minerals, and fiber to food; they also enrich it with color and flavor. Every vegetable has its own flavor and nutritional benefit. The best way to make the most of these qualities is to eat a wide variety. If your grocery cart contains at least five different colors of vegetables, you are heading in the right direction.

Many vegetables can be eaten either raw or cooked. Although raw vegetables are considered healthier to eat, in some cases cooking vegetables makes their vitamins more accessible to the body. The bottom line: don't worry about how you eat your vegetables, they can even be frozen and thawed. This chapter contains many tips and techniques for incorporating vegetables into your daily cooking. To begin, I discuss a number of vegetable cooking techniques; most of these don't require even a drop of oil.

Blanching

Bringing vegetables to a boil in water that is cold from the start can cause many of the vitamins and minerals, along with the flavor, to seep out of the vegetable and into the water. Though this may be fine when cooking soups or sauces, it is unfortunate when cooking vegetables for other purposes. Blanching is a technique that prevents some of this loss. It involves plunging the vegetables into boiling water, thereby sealing more of the flavor, vitamins, and minerals inside. Blanching is perfect for cooking hard vegetables such as cauliflower, broccoli, Brussels sprouts, beans, and asparagus. After the vegetables have been blanched, place them in a bowl of ice water to stop the cooking process and keep the color bright.

Steaming

Vegetables that can be blanched can also be steamed using a bamboo steamer. Like blanching, steaming uses water, but none of the vegetables' benefits are lost to the water. Steaming can be done relatively quickly, since there is no need to boil water in advance, and you can steam large quantities of vegetables at one time using more than one steamer. See page 42 for more information on steaming.

Oven roasting

Many types of vegetables can be roasted in the oven, in large quantities and without any oil. Just heat the oven to 350°F or 400°F, and keep your eye on the vegetables as they roast, to make sure they don't dry out. I recommend roasting vegetables with their peels, and cutting or peeling them after they have finished baking, in order to keep liquids inside. If the vegetables you choose don't have peels, or if you prefer a crunchy surface, brush a thin layer of oil on the vegetable before roasting.

Grilling

Grilling on a lined grill pan is an elegant and oil-free way of preparing vegetables. Make sure you slice the vegetables quite thin before roasting, and don't flip the vegetables more than once, since this will damage the appearance. Grilling is perfect for vegetables that require relatively short cooking times, such as zucchini or pumpkin slices, or vegetables that don't need to be completely cooked before eating, such as carrots and beet. See page 47 for more information on grilling.

INCORPORATING VEGETABLES INTO YOUR DISHES

Buying vegetables

Try to buy vegetables in season whenever possible, since their nutritional value and taste are highest. For example, I recommend making the Sea Bass with Beet and Fennel in Yogurt and Pomegranate Sauce (page 79) when fennel is in season, for best flavor. Fennel that is fresh will add aroma and flavor to the dish, while fennel that is out of season will have little flavor, and will actually negate the flavor of the dish. When selecting fennel, look for a bulb that is closed and has straight stalks rather than one that has split stalks or looks shriveled and dried out.

In fact, you should consider which vegetables are in season before you choose the recipes you want to prepare. If you're not sure, ask someone in the produce section of your supermarket. Foods made with vegetables that are in season will have more natural flavor, and require less salt, oil, and other flavorings to make them tasty. You may also want to try organic vegetables when you cook. Although studies have yet to prove any nutritional advantage to organic vegetables, some are simply tastier, and increased flavor means healthier food.

Dried vegetables

Some supermarkets sell dried vegetables such as mushrooms, tomatoes, and peppers. Make sure you select vegetables that have been dried without salt, since salt is actually unnecessary in the drying process. Try the Dried Tomato and Thyme Spread (page 109) and you'll see that the flavor is so concentrated that only a tiny quantity of salt is necessary for emphasis. Be sure to soak dried vegetables in lukewarm rather than hot water before using, since hot water can damage the flavor. If you'd like to prepare dried tomatoes yourself, I recommend using plum tomatoes. Cut them in half lengthwise, arrange them on a baking sheet, cut-side up, and bake at 300°F for 6 hours. For best results, leave the oven door ajar while the tomatoes bake, to allow moisture to dissipate. Dried tomatoes mixed with a bit of extra-virgin olive oil can be stored in an airtight jar for several weeks in a dark place.

How to integrate different vegetables

After you have purchased high-quality fresh or dried vegetables, it's time to integrate them into the right foods. In addition to combining harmonious colors and flavors, consider the importance of texture. People's palates generally like contrasting textures. Just think about the Mediterranean classic salad combination of cucumber and tomatoes; the cucumber is crunchy and the tomatoes are soft, making for an attractive and interesting combination. This same contrast is found in the Quinoa with Sautéed Cherry Tomatoes and Asparagus (page 19). Keep this type of combination in mind when choosing vegetables for any type of dish.

UPGRADING DISHES

One of the challenges of healthy eating is to feel satisfied after eating foods that contain the appropriate amount of carbohydrates and calories. Vegetables help to overcome that challenge. By adding vegetables to a dish, you can reduce the amount of calories and starches in every serving, without eliminating ingredients that are high in calories and carbohydrates. The technical term for this is reducing the "energy density" of a food, and it is an excellent way for making food healthier and, in many cases, tastier. Imagine a serving of pasta that has more of a healthy tomato-based sauce, or a rice dish that has more mushrooms. A single serving has a lower amount of calories than a regular serving of the same dish, and it is also much tastier. It may sound hard to believe, but by consuming foods that are richer and tastier, you'll actually be eating foods have fewer calories!

How to do it

The easiest way to reduce energy density is to simply add more vegetables. In the recipe on the opposite page, for example, the taste of whole-wheat couscous is enhanced with a variety of vegetables—asparagus, roasted red peppers, and zucchini. A satisfying serving of salad that is enriched with diverse vegetables like that has fewer calories than one that contains only tomatoes. The enriched salad is tastier too. If you want to upgrade the salad even more, add another vegetable or two. Try adding roasted yellow pepper or a handful of baby arugula, since these add both color and taste.

Adding vegetables can also reduce the amount of carbohydrates and calories in a serving of baked goods. For a full description on how to do this, turn to Baked Goods (pages 129–145), or take a look at the Beet and Sesame Crackers (page 217) or the Pumpkin Dinner Rolls with Flakes of Thyme (page 132). In baking, as in cooking, the tastier way is also healthier. The second recipe in this chapter shows how you can even upgrade desserts by adding vegetables. Add vegetables whenever you can; they'll upgrade the dish you are preparing and help you feel satisfied with far fewer calories.

Whole-Wheat Couscous Salad with Roasted Vegetables

As with most wheat products, couscous is available in a whole-wheat version. It requires a relatively short preparation time; combine the same amounts of couscous and boiling water for a few minutes, season, and serve. I recommend adding whole-wheat couscous to your pantry. It can be served cold, as in the following recipe, or warm alongside chicken, meat, or a vegetable dish. A word about the hot pepper: when using hot chili pepper, you can get a strong hot flavor by including the seeds or a rich delicate hot flavor by removing them. In this dish, I recommend removing the seeds.

INGREDIENTS

Serves 10 / Serving size: ¾ cup

- 6 ounces whole-wheat couscous
- ½ teaspoon Atlantic sea salt, or to taste
- 1 cup water, boiling
- 1 tablespoon vegetable stock (page 63), optional
- 4 tablespoons chopped scallions
- 2 tablespoons chopped fresh thyme
- 2 tablespoons chopped fresh mint
- 4 tablespoons chopped fresh parsley
- 1 tablespoon chopped fresh cilantro
- 2 tablespoons chopped fresh basil
- 1 red hot chili pepper, seeded and chopped
- 6 tablespoons fresh lemon juice
- 5 tablespoons extra-virgin olive oil
- ½ teaspoon ground black pepper, or to taste
- 3 firm medium zucchini, sliced lengthwise and grilled (page 89)
- 10 asparagus spears, trimmed, cut into 2-inch pieces, and blanched (page 88)
- 2 medium red bell peppers, roasted (page 39) and sliced

Calories	130
Total fat	6 g
Calories as fat	42%
Saturated fat	1 g
Cholesterol	0 mg
Carbohydrates	19 g
Dietary fiber	2 g
Sodium	115 mg
Protein	0 g
Carbohydrate choices	**1**

Exchanges:
1 starch, 1 vegetable, 1 fat

PREPARATION

1. Place couscous, salt, water, and stock in a bowl. Cover and let sit 7 minutes, until liquid is absorbed.

2. In a large bowl, mix together scallions, thyme, mint, parsley, cilantro, basil, hot pepper, lemon juice, oil, and pepper. Add couscous, zucchini, asparagus, and peppers mix until combined.

3. Cover and refrigerate for 2 to 3 hours to allow flavors to blend. Add salt and pepper to taste before serving.

Fruit and Vegetable Salad with Hot Coconut Sauce

Although coconut milk comes from a plant, it contains saturated fats. Many supermarkets sell three types of coconut liquid products: coconut water, coconut milk, and coconut cream. The most diluted version is coconut water, and its taste is quite weak. Coconut cream is the richest version, but it contains a large amount of fat. I recommend using small amounts of coconut milk, and only every now and again: a little goes a long way because its flavor is distinct and dominant.

Calories	61
Total fat	1 g
Calories as fat	15%
Saturated fat	1 g
Cholesterol	0 mg
Carbohydrates	14 g
Dietary fiber	2 g
Sodium	90 mg
Protein	1 g
Carbohydrate choices	**1**

Exchanges: 1 vegetable, ½ fruit

INGREDIENTS

Serves 8 / Serving size: ¾ cup

Salad

- 1½ ounces green beans, trimmed, cut into 2-inch pieces, and blanched (page 88)
- 2 medium mangos, ripe but firm, peeled, pitted, and cut into ½-inch cubes
- ½ medium Granny Smith apple, cored and sliced
- 8 fresh lychees, peeled and pitted
- ½ medium Bermuda onion, halved and sliced into thin rings
- ½ medium Lebanese cucumber, sliced into strips
- 1½ ounces bean sprouts
- 1 scallions, chopped
- ½ tomato, peeled, seeded, and sliced into strips

Dressing

- 2 tablespoons coconut milk
- 1 teaspoon mirin
- ½ red chili pepper, seeded and chopped
- ½ tablespoon fish sauce
- 2 tablespoons fresh lemon juice

PREPARATION

1. Prepare salad: In a medium bowl, mix together mangos, apple, lychees, onion, cucumber, bean sprouts, scallions, and tomato.

2. Prepare dressing: In a jar with a tight-fitting lid, combine coconut milk, mirin, hot pepper, fish sauce, and lemon juice. Close jar and shake vigorously. Pour dressing over salad and toss to coat. Let sit for 2 to 3 minutes before serving, for flavors to blend.

Fruit and Vegetable Salad with Hot Coconut Sauce

UPGRADING MEALS

Vegetables can help reduce the energy density of both individual dishes and entire meals. Adding more vegetable dishes to a meal is particularly useful if you are having trouble changing your eating habits, because it means you don't have to eliminate foods you like, or change them. You can still enjoy your favorite foods. You'll just end up eating less of them with the added vegetables. Young people may also be tempted to try new foods once they see the interesting new variety, especially if they see others setting an example. Here are some types of food that can do the trick.

Vegetable-based salads

Salads can reduce the energy density of a meal, but only if they have the right amount of dressing. Salads that have healthy ingredients but are drowned in dressing can actually increase the energy density of your food. A dressing is supposed to add flavor to a salad by wrapping all of the salad's elements in an aromatic sauce. As long as the dressing is just on the salad, it adds flavor. Once the dressing pools at the bottom of the salad bowl, there is too much. The next time you add dressing to a salad, add it gradually, and toss intermittently. If the dressing starts accumulating at the bottom of the salad bowl, you'll know you have added enough.

Vegetable dishes

Cooked vegetable dishes such as the Grilled Eggplant with Tomato Sauce (page 96) and Mediterranean Ratatouille with Millet (page 177) are excellent for upgrading meals and reducing their energy density. One advantage of cooked dishes over salads is the fact that cooked dishes can usually be refrigerated for up to 5 days. This means you can prepare them in advance and serve them at several meals. Once the dish is in the refrigerator, it is readily available for upgrading meals or for serving as a base for a quick meal. For example, the Grilled Eggplant with Tomato Sauce can be nibbled on when you feel like having a snack, or it can be used to enrich a cheese or meat sandwich. It can also be heated up and served warm alongside whole-grain pasta or brown rice, or used as a sauce for baked fish or roast chicken. Make an effort to keep at least one vegetable dish in your refrigerator. It can serve as the base for many other dishes.

Vegetable-based soups

Soups are excellent for reducing the energy density of a meal. They can also be eaten on their own as a quick meal or a snack. Soups can also include interesting and varied ingredients; see for yourself in the recipe on page 100. Soups are excellent for freezing; just store them in single-serving plastic containers in your freezer.

Gather recipes for vegetable dishes from various sources and make use of all them. This will keep your food choices interested and varied, upgrading your meals and reducing their energy density.

Grilled Eggplant with Tomato Sauce

When making homemade tomato sauce, eliminate bitterness by removing the tomato seeds at the beginning of the process. If you do this, you won't need to compensate for the bitterness by adding sugar or another sweetener to the sauce. In fact, by using just the flesh of the tomato, you'll be making a much tastier, less watery sauce right from the beginning. To remove the seeds, simply cut the tomato in half and scoop out the seeds with a spoon. The eggplant in this recipe can be deliciously replaced with zucchini or pumpkin.

INGREDIENTS

Serves 8 / Serving size: 1 cup

- **2 medium eggplants, cut into ¼-inch thick rounds**
- **¼ teaspoon Atlantic sea salt, or to taste**
- **¼ teaspoon ground black pepper, or to taste**
- **5 large tomatoes, cored and scored with an X at the bottom**
- **1 tablespoon extra-virgin olive oil**
- **2 cloves garlic, crushed**
- **2 teaspoons sweet paprika**
- **½ cup water**
- **1 tablespoon vegetable stock (page 63), optional**
- **2 tablespoons chopped fresh thyme**

PREPARATION

1. Season eggplant slices with salt and pepper. Heat a lined grill pan over medium heat, and grill eggplant slices for 4 minutes on each side, until brown lines appear.

2. Bring a small pot of water to a boil over high heat. Place tomatoes in boiling water and blanch for 10 to 15 seconds, until skins loosen. Remove tomatoes with a slotted spoon and place them in an ice water bath. When tomatoes are cool enough to handle, remove skins with a paring knife and cut in half. Remove and discard seeds, and cut flesh into cubes.

3. In a medium pot, heat oil over medium heat. Add garlic and sauté for 3 minutes, until brown. Add tomatoes and paprika and cook for 5 minutes. Add water and stock, increase heat to high, and bring to a boil. Reduce heat to low and simmer for 5 minutes.

4. Add eggplant and thyme and bring to a boil. Reduce heat to low and simmer for 15 minutes, until almost all the liquid evaporates. Adjust seasoning with salt and pepper before serving. Serve warm or cold.

Calories	63
Total fat	2 g
Calories as fat	29%
Saturated fat	0 g
Cholesterol	0 mg
Carbohydrates	11 g
Dietary fiber	3 g
Sodium	82 mg
Protein	2 g
Carbohydrate choices	**1**
Exchanges: 2 vegetable, ½ fat	

Grilled Eggplant with Tomato Sauce

Baby Salad Greens and Plum Salad with Dill Dressing

Baby Salad Greens and Plum Salad with Dill Dressing

This recipe includes whole-herb leaves, which I really like to use when making green leafy salads. Unlike other salads, in which fresh herbs are chopped, whole leaves mix nicely into green leafy salads, enhancing both their appearance and taste. This salad is particularly suited to mint, but whole basil or parsley leaves can also be added. Cilantro leaves are excellent for adding to salads that have an Asian flavor. Try adding whole-herb leaves to other salads that you make.

Calories	81
Total fat	7 g
Calories as fat	78%
Saturated fat	1 g
Cholesterol	0 mg
Carbohydrates	3 g
Dietary fiber	1 g
Sodium	123 mg
Protein	1 g
Carbohydrate choices	**None**
Exchanges: 1 vegetable, 1 fat	

INGREDIENTS

Serves 10 / Serving size: ¾ cup

Salad
- 5 ounces (about 5 cups) baby salad greens
- 3 ounces (about 3 cups) baby arugula
- 3 medium Lebanese cucumbers, sliced into thin rounds
- 1 ounce raw walnuts, coarsely chopped
- ½ cup fresh mint leaves
- 1 medium plum, pitted, quartered and thinly sliced

Dressing
- 4 tablespoons extra-virgin olive oil
- 2 tablespoons fresh lemon juice
- 1 tablespoon balsamic vinegar
- 2 tablespoons chopped fresh dill
- 1 teaspoon honey
- ½ tablespoon Atlantic sea salt
- ½ tablespoon ground black pepper

PREPARATION

1. Prepare salad: In a medium bowl, mix together baby salad greens, baby arugula, cucumbers, walnuts, mint leaves, and plum.

2. Prepare dressing: In a jar with a tight-fitting lid, combine oil, lemon juice, vinegar, dill, honey, salt, and pepper. Close jar and shake vigorously. Pour dressing over salad and toss to coat. Let sit for 2 to 3 minutes before serving, for flavors to blend.

Roasted Eggplant Soup with Fresh Herbs

The technique used for this soup can be used to make many different types of soups. Simply replace the eggplant with tomato or zucchini, and use a variety of fresh herbs. Roasting the vegetables first gives the soup an unforgettable flavor. For a really attractive serving option, prepare two pureed soups that have contrasting colors. Serve both soups in the same bowl, pouring in each at the same time from a different side of the bowl.

INGREDIENTS

Serves 10 / Serving size: 1 cup

- 3 medium tomatoes, cored and scored with an X at the bottom
- 2 medium eggplants, cut into 1-inch cubes
- 1 medium onion, quartered
- 2 medium zucchini, cut into ½-inch cubes
- 1 head garlic, cloves separated and peeled
- 10 ounces button mushrooms
- ½ teaspoon Atlantic sea salt, or to taste
- ½ teaspoon ground black pepper, or to taste
- 4 tablespoons extra-virgin olive oil
- 2½ cups water
- 3 tablespoons vegetable stock (page 63), optional
- ½ cup dry red wine
- 4 tablespoons fresh chopped thyme
- 4 tablespoons fresh lemon juice

PREPARATION

1. Preheat oven to 350°F and line a baking sheet with parchment paper. Bring a small pot of water to a boil over high heat. Place tomatoes in boiling water and blanch for 10 to 15 seconds, until skins loosen. Remove tomatoes with a slotted spoon and place them in an ice water bath. When tomatoes are cool enough to handle, remove skins with a paring knife and cut in half. Remove and discard seeds, and cut flesh into cubes.

2. In a medium bowl, mix together eggplants, onion, zucchini, tomatoes, garlic, and mushrooms. Season with salt and pepper, then add oil and mix until coated.

3. Arrange vegetables on baking sheet in a single layer and bake for 45 minutes, mixing once or twice, until lightly browned. Remove vegetables from oven, and set some aside for garnish. Transfer the rest to a food processor and process until smooth.

4. Transfer pureed vegetables to a large pot, and add water, stock, and wine. Bring to a boil over medium-high heat. Reduce heat to low, add thyme and lemon juice, and simmer for 3 minutes. Season with salt and pepper and serve with reserved roasted vegetables on top of each serving.

Calories	106
Total fat	6 g
Calories as fat	51%
Saturated fat	1 g
Cholesterol	0 mg
Carbohydrates	11 g
Dietary fiber	5 g
Sodium	129 mg
Protein	3 g
Carbohydrate choices	**1**
Exchanges: 2 vegetables, 1 fat	

Roasted Eggplant Soup with Fresh Herbs

REPLACING STARCHES WITH VEGETABLES

Vegetables aren't just excellent additions to starches. They can also be used to replace them, and to upgrade dishes by making them more colorful, more attractive, and tastier. Of course, this doesn't mean replacing or avoiding all starches. It does mean that if you are trying to reduce the amount of starch you eat in order to eat only your recommended amount, increasing your consumption of vegetables can help you feel satisfied. At the same time, you'll also be increasing your consumption of vegetables, which is an important goal in itself.

For example, Swiss chard can be stuffed with filling instead of rice paper wrapping (see recipe on page 104) or lettuce can replace tortillas. Vegetables can even be used instead of pasta. Consider the following recipe for a deliciously unique eggplant ravioli. Take slices of grilled eggplant, then sandwich a spoon of mixed cheese filling between two eggplant slices. Press down all around the eggplant edges with a fork to secure the filling inside, and serve with tomato sauce.

In the recipe on the facing page, vegetables are used to make a dough that doesn't contain any flour. Dough made with vegetables and eggs does not have any gluten, making it an excellent option for people who are sensitive to gluten.

The more you use these techniques and recipes in your kitchen, the more variety you'll add to your meals. You'll also find it easier to succeed in balancing your blood glucose levels and watching your weight.

Spinach Pastry with Goat Cheese and Smoked Salmon

When blanching spinach for this recipe, do so for just a few seconds, since overcooking will cause it too shrivel and make it unsuitable for preparing dough. The filling made with cheese and salmon features a combination of colors that look lovely with the delicate green of the pastry. If you'd like to try a different filling, choose a spread with complementary colors, such as the Red Tahini Spread (page 108), the Dried Tomato and Thyme Spread (page 109), or the Pumpkin and Caraway Seed Spread (page 107). As for the salmon, it can be replaced with roasted chopped mushrooms.

Calories	81
Total fat	5 g
Calories as fat	56%
Saturated fat	3 g
Cholesterol	88 mg
Carbohydrates	2 g
Dietary fiber	1 g
Sodium	426 mg
Protein	8 g
Carbohydrate choices	**None**

Exchanges: 1 medium-fat meat

INGREDIENTS

Serves 8 / Serving size: Two
¾-inch slices

- **¾ pound fresh spinach, blanched (page 88) and drained**
- **3 large eggs, separated**
- **¼ teaspoon Atlantic sea salt**
- **¼ teaspoon ground black pepper**
- **Pinch nutmeg**
- **3½ ounces low-fat, soft (spreadable) goat cheese**
- **3½ ounces smoked salmon, sliced**
- **Unrefined canola oil, for greasing**

PREPARATION

1. Preheat oven to 400°F. Line a 10 x 12-inch baking sheet with parchment paper and grease lightly.

2. In a food processor, combine spinach, egg yolks, salt, pepper, and nutmeg. Process until smooth.

3. Separately, beat egg whites with a pinch of salt until stiff peaks form, then fold in the spinach mixture.

4. Spread mixture on baking pan, and bake for 10 minutes. Cover work surface with a clean kitchen towel and lay a piece of parchment paper on top. Turn out hot pastry onto parchment paper, then roll into a cylinder. Let sit on work surface, seam side down, to cool.

5. Carefully unroll pastry and spread inside with cheese. Lay strips of salmon on cheese, then roll pastry back into a cylinder. Cut into slices and serve.

Swiss Chard Dim Sum with Sea Bass and Water Chestnuts

Swiss chard leaves are large, flexible, and excellent for wrapping fillings. They have a hard white stem down the middle that can be removed, leaving separate leaf halves for making smaller dim sum. To make larger dim sum, or if the Swiss chard leaves aren't big enough for halving, simply shave down the stem using a sharp knife or vegetable peeler and soak it in the boiling water longer, so that the leaf is flexible enough to be rolled. Always roll Swiss chard leaves with their natural curve, and don't worry too much if the leaf doesn't stay tightly rolled before it is steamed, since the steaming process will help the leaf stick.

INGREDIENTS

Makes 30 dim sum / Serving size: 2 dim sum

- **2 pounds skinless sea bass fillet, ground**
- **6 tablespoons soda water**
- **4 tablespoons dry white wine**
- **3 tablespoons peeled and grated fresh ginger**
- **1 cup chopped scallions**
- **8 water chestnuts, peeled and sliced**
- **4 cloves garlic, crushed**
- **½ teaspoon Atlantic sea salt**
- **½ teaspoon ground black pepper**
- **4 cups boiling water**
- **10 large Swiss chard leaves, halved lengthwise and stems removed**
- **2 cups water**
- **2 jasmine teabags**

PREPARATION

1. In a medium bowl, mix together sea bass, soda water, wine, ginger, scallions, chestnuts, garlic, salt, and pepper.

2. Separately, pour boiling water into a heatproof bowl. Soak 1 chard leaf for 20 seconds, until it softens. Remove leaf, gently shake off excess water, and lay on work surface. Place another leaf to soak.

3. Trim top and bottom of soaked leaf, if these areas are too narrow for rolling. Arrange ⅟₃₀ of fish mixture in a horizontal mound near bottom of leaf. Leave space at left and right sides. Fold in sides and roll up leaf, using your fingers to press filling firmly inside, to form a cylinder. Roll leaf 2 or 3 times, then cut dim sum from leaf and place in steamer basket. Repeat process with remaining leaves and fish mixture. Depending on the size of the leaves, you should be able to roll 1 or 2 dim sum from every half leaf.

4. In a pot, the size of the steamer basket, bring water and teabags to a boil. Place steamer basket with dim sum on top, cover, and reduce heat to low. Steam dim sum over low heat for 10 minutes. Serve hot.

Calories	58
Total fat	2 g
Calories as fat	31%
Saturated fat	0 g
Cholesterol	18 mg
Carbohydrates	2 g
Dietary fiber	0 g
Sodium	100 mg
Protein	8 g
Carbohydrate choices	**None**
Exchanges: 1 lean meat	

Swiss Chard Dim Sum with Sea Bass and Water Chestnuts

TIP *An interesting way of using fresh herbs is to steep them. In this recipe, I use a jasmine teabag rather than fresh herbs, but the jasmine can be replaced with a variety of other herbs. You can also create a fusion of flavors by combining Chinese steaming techniques with Mediterranean herbs. For example, fill the Swiss chard leaves with a mixture of cheeses and dried tomatoes, and steam them over steeping oregano. This dish can be served with any of the Mediterranean-style sauces in this book.*

SPREADS

Sandwiches, those quick meals placed between two pieces of bread, are one of the most popular foods in the Western world. At home, people don't always feel like cooking a meal, and many make do with a quick sandwich for lunch or supper. Outside the house, sandwiches are the most common brown-bag meal for school or work. If you've already decided to eat a sandwich, then I recommend a vegetable-rich spread for the bread. Not only will this enrich the color and flavor of your sandwich, but it will also increase your consumption of vegetables.

The spreads described on the following pages can be stored in the refrigerator for several days. In addition to upgrading sandwiches, they can also be used to enhance cooked dishes. For example, the Dried Tomato and Thyme Spread (page 109) can enrich starch dishes such as the Quinoa with Sautéed Cherry Tomatoes and Asparagus (page 19), chicken dishes such as the Chicken Drumsticks with Peppers and Cherry Tomatoes (page 202), and even a cold salad such as the Avocado and Pearl Barley Salad (page 160). Mix ½ cup water and stock with 2 tablespoons of Dried Tomato Spread to create an excellent base for cooking quick meals. Use it to marinate chicken, seafood, or fish, or as a sauce for starches.

Many spreads are really quite easy to make, requiring relatively little time and attention. They are perfect for making on days when you are already cooking, and they can be stored for several days in the refrigerator. I recommend making one spread from fresh vegetables that can be refrigerated for several days, and one spread from dried vegetables that can be stored for more than a week.

Pumpkin and Caraway Seed Spread

This spread is excellent for adding to meat or cheese sandwiches. In other recipes in this book, I recommend roasting vegetables in the oven to retain maximum taste. However, a puree made of roasted vegetables has a grainy texture, one that isn't ideal for making a smooth spread. That's why I recommend boiling the vegetables in this recipe. Because the vegetables will absorb extra water while boiling, heat the boiled vegetables in an empty pot over low heat for a few minutes to allow excess water to evaporate. This makes for a more flavorful spread and reduces, or even eliminates, the need to add seasoning such as salt.

INGREDIENTS

Makes 2 cups / Serving size:
1 tablespoon

- 1 pound fresh pumpkin, peeled and cubed
- 1 teaspoon Atlantic sea salt
- 6 cups water
- ½ medium sweet potato, peeled and cubed
- 2 medium carrots, unpeeled and sliced
- 4 cloves garlic, crushed
- ½ teaspoon hot paprika
- ½ teaspoon sweet paprika
- 1 heaping teaspoon ground caraway
- 2 tablespoons fresh lemon juice
- 2 tablespoons extra-virgin olive oil
- ½ teaspoon ground black pepper

Calories	15
Total fat	1 g
Calories as fat	60%
Saturated fat	0 g
Cholesterol	0 mg
Carbohydrates	2 g
Dietary fiber	0 g
Sodium	81 mg
Protein	0 g
Carbohydrate choices	**None**
Exchanges: free food	

PREPARATION

1. In a large pot, bring water with a pinch of salt to a boil over high heat. Add pumpkin, sweet potato and carrots, reduce heat to medium, and cook until soft, about 40 minutes. Drain vegetables and return to dry pot. Heat over low heat for 3 minutes, while stirring, to allow liquid in vegetables to evaporate.

2. Transfer vegetables to a food processor. Add garlic, paprikas, caraway, lemon juice, and oil, and puree until smooth. Add salt and pepper to taste.

Red Tahini Spread

This bright spread is excellent for enriching meat, poultry, or vegetable sandwiches. Tahini contains healthier fat, and is an excellent alternative to butter or margarine. Pomegranate juice complements the lemon juice here, creating a tangy flavor that is much more interesting than lemon juice alone. Try integrating pomegranate juice concentrate into other recipes that call for lemon juice, and enjoy the difference. When buying pomegranate juice concentrate, be sure to select one that has no added sugar. Of course, if pomegranates are in season, use freshly squeezed juice.

Calories	56
Total fat	5 g
Calories as fat	80%
Saturated fat	1 g
Cholesterol	0 mg
Carbohydrates	2 g
Dietary fiber	1 g
Sodium	62 mg
Protein	2 g
Carbohydrate choices	**None**
Exchanges: 1 fat	

INGREDIENTS

Makes 1¼ cups / Serving size:
1 tablespoon

- **12 tablespoons pure tahini**
- **2 tablespoons fresh lemon juice**
- **2 tablespoons pure unsweetened pomegranate juice concentrate**
- **4 cloves garlic, chopped**
- **1 medium red bell pepper, roasted (page 39), peeled, seeded, and cut into strips**
- **½ cup water**
- **½ teaspoon Atlantic sea salt**
- **½ teaspoon ground black pepper**

PREPARATION

1. In a food processor, process tahini, lemon juice, pomegranate juice concentrate, and garlic until smooth.

2. Add pepper and puree until smooth. Slowly add water until mixture is desired consistency. Add salt and pepper, to taste.

Dried Tomato and Thyme Spread

This spread is excellent for upgrading any sandwich, especially one that contains pastrami, chicken, or cheese. Rinse the dried tomatoes before soaking them, then save the soaking water for other uses. For example, add a bit of the reserved liquid to the spread to thin it and make a delicious sauce (page 106). You can also use the liquid to cook brown rice, make vegetable stock, or prepare any other food that would be complemented by a light tomato flavoring.

Calories	21
Total fat	2 g
Calories as fat	86%
Saturated fat	0 g
Cholesterol	0 mg
Carbohydrates	1 g
Dietary fiber	0 g
Sodium	57%
Protein	0 g
Carbohydrate choices	**None**
Exchanges: ½ fat	

INGREDIENTS

Makes ¾ cup / Serving size:
1 tablespoon

- **2 cups warm water, for soaking**
- **1 cup salt-free, naturally dried tomatoes, rinsed**
- **4 tablespoons extra-virgin olive oil**
- **1 tablespoon chopped fresh thyme**
- **Pinch Atlantic sea salt**
- **¼ teaspoon ground black pepper**

PREPARATION

1. In a small bowl, place dried tomatoes to soak in warm water for several hours. Drain tomatoes and reserve soaking liquid for another use. Transfer tomatoes to a food processor, add oil and thyme, and process until smooth.

2. Add salt and pepper to taste, then transfer to a glass jar and refrigerate. May be stored for several weeks.

Sweetening Without Sugar

Dessert, of course, is the ultimate challenge. How can you consume less sugar and still enjoy life? One way of doing this is to replace sugar with sugar substitutes, but we'll try taking on the task without them. Rich, enjoyable, and satisfying desserts can be made using a variety of techniques and ingredients, as well as small quantities of regular sweeteners to enhance flavors. But if you want to replace the small amount of sweeteners that I use with sugar substitutes, that's fine.

Notice that most of the desserts in this chapter contain regular sweeteners, but no more than one carbohydrate choice. To achieve the sweet flavors in these recipes, I used several cooking techniques and a variety of ingredients.

Sweeten with spices
Basic sweet flavors can be achieved using sugar, honey, or other sweeteners, but more varied flavors are possible using spices such as cinnamon, cloves, cardamom, and allspice. These spices emphasize sweetness and enhance it. They are excellent for making sweetness richer, in contrast to sugar, which makes sweetness stronger. They also add variety to sweetness, which can ultimately result in the use of less sweetener. Try adding them to your recipe every time you make dessert.

Using aromatic liquids
Cooking or baking with aromatic liquids such as alcoholic beverages, flavored teas, and flavored extracts (vanilla or rose, for example), enhances the taste of desserts and reduces the amount of sweetener necessary to achieve a satisfying taste. Try using these ingredients instead of water, or in addition to it, whenever possible.

Using herbs
Herbs are often added to savory dishes before adding salt. Herbs such as mint, sage, and lemon verbena, as well as basil and thyme, can also be used to enhance the flavor of desserts. Adding these herbs before you add sweetener can help you make tastier food and reduce the amount of sweetener you use.

Keep the texture coarse
Though it may seem hard to believe, the texture of a food can affect our perception of sweetness. Take two apples, and grate one of them finely and the other coarsely. Taste both apples, and you'll likely find that the coarsely grated apple has a sweeter taste. This may be because it stays on your tongue longer and activates your flavor glands more. Make sauces with a coarse texture and you'll see that you need to add less sweetener to reach a satisfying flavor.

Cook raw ingredients

Sometimes, cooking can change the structure of the food you are using, and make it much sweeter. For example, compare the taste of a raw onion to one that is sautéed. Sautéed onions are often sweet enough to balance a cooked dish. For an even sweeter example, consider onion jam, in which onions play a central role. Use this technique to get a rich sweet flavor without adding any sweetener at all.

Heating to sweeten

The temperature of a dessert when it is served has a big effect on how it tastes. Sweetened tea that has just the right amount of sweetness when it is warm will not taste as sweet when it is cold. Cold desserts require a larger amount of sweetener than warm desserts to provide the same sweet flavor. Serve warm desserts, so you'll require less sweetener to get high-quality results.

Sauces and toppings

A dessert does not need to be extremely sweet to be enjoyed. Sometimes, a sweet sauce or topping is all you need to emphasize a sweet flavor. Furthermore, the contrast between a delicately flavored cookie with a sweet topping, or an unsweetened fruit cake topped with honey, can be tastier than heavily sweetened alternatives.

The principles for using sweetener are quite similar to those for using salt. Just as the flavor of a dish can be enriched with herbs and spices before salt is added, the flavor of desserts can be enhanced before adding sweetener. The recipes in this chapter demonstrate how to use these techniques simply and quickly, so that they are practical in your own kitchen. Most of the recipes use two or more techniques in order to create an especially fine result. Adopt these techniques when preparing other sweet foods at home. I hope they help you cook better and reduce your consumption of sugar and sugar substitutes.

Another similarity between salt and sugar is the habit: have you ever wondered why children don't seem to like fruit as much today as they did in the past? Some people say fruit has less flavor today, since it has been genetically enhanced to extend its shelf life, and that in the past, fruit was simply tastier. This could be right, but another reason could also be possible: perhaps it is harder for people to detect the delicate natural flavors of fruit because they are so used to the high level of sweetness found in sweetened and artificially-sweetened foods and drinks. Try to get used to adding less sweeteners. Start by reducing the amount of sweetener a bit, so that the beverage or dessert is still tasty. After you get used to this change, reduce the amount of sugar a bit more. In a shorter amount of time than you might expect (just a few weeks!) you'll find that you need to add a smaller amount of sweetener to enjoy your food and drink, and that foods you once liked are now too sweet for you. You'll also discover new flavors in your foods—flavors that were masked by sugar or sugar substitutes in the past.

CHOOSING FRUIT FOR DESSERT

Note the proportion of fruit-based desserts and pastries in this chapter and in this entire book. I suggest adopting a similar proportion in your kitchen, too. In order to succeed when preparing attractive and sweet fruit-based desserts, it's important to choose the right fruit. There are sweet fruits such as pears and melons and sour fruits such as kiwis and Granny Smith apples. Remember that sour fruits don't necessarily contain fewer carbohydrates than sweet ones, but using them may require the addition of larger quantities of sweetener in order to achieve satisfyingly sweet results. When selecting fruits for dessert, for example, in the Mango Sorbet and Fruit Salad with Maple Tahini (page 126), I recommend choosing fruit that are naturally sweet and require only a small amount of sweetener in order to obtain a satisfying taste. See how the use of pears in the recipe on page 114 and of other naturally sweet fruits in the fruit salad on page 126 allows us to make a rich and tasty dessert while adding very little sweetener. Also, remember that fruit in season is sweeter and has more flavor than fruit that is out of season. Consider this the next time you choose fruit for your dessert.

Get to know the different varieties of your favorite fruits – it can cut down your sweetener consumption

Many supermarkets sell a variety of apples, and each one has its own flavor. Granny Smith apples, for example, are sour; Gala and Red Delicious apples are generally sweet. There isn't a significant difference in the amount in the carbohydrate content of various types of apples, so if you are looking for a sweet flavor for your dessert (for example, when making filling for the Apple-filled Phyllo Pastry in Pomegranate and Red Wine Sauce, page 143), choose apples that are naturally sweet. If you are cooking apples with fish, you may prefer an apple that is more sour. Use this principle when selecting plums, pomegranates, or other fruit that comes in sweet and sour varieties. If you aren't familiar with a fruit's different varieties, ask the manager of the fruit section in your supermarket.

Dried fruit

In most cases, I recommend using fresh fruit rather than dried fruit for one simple reason: even dried fruit with no added sugar contains the same amount of sugar as fresh fruit, but in a serving that is much smaller in size. Since the size of a dessert is important to many people, they will tend to consume a larger amount of fruit in a dessert made with dried fruit, and therefore they'll consume more carbohydrate than if they were to eat a dessert made with fresh fruit. However, if you are using dried fruit to upgrade the taste of a dessert and not to increase its portion, dried fruit can be beneficial due to its more concentrated flavor. For example, note how dried apricots are an excellent base for the sauce in the Almond Cookies in Apricot Sauce (page 184); and how a thin layer of fruit leather provides a satisfying contrast with the cheese in the Rolled Apricot Fruit Leather with Goat Cheese and Basil (page 118).

Fruit leather is fruit that has been pureed, cooked, spread, and dried into a thin and dry sheet. The most common type of fruit leather is made from apricots, but you can also find papaya and pineapple fruit leathers. Whenever you buy fruit leather, or any type of dried fruit, make sure it doesn't have any added sugar. Many manufacturers add sugar in order to facilitate the drying process and emphasize the fruit's flavor, but this is completely unnecessary.

If you want to make fruit leather at home, try making it with apricots to start. Remove the pits and puree the fruit in a food processor. Transfer the pureed fruit to a saucepan and cook over low heat while stirring until the liquid evaporates. This may take as long as 1 hour. Line a baking pan with plastic wrap and spread the apricot mixture in a ⅛-inch layer. Let the mixture dry in the sun for a couple of days, or bake it at 200°F for about 6 hours, turn off the oven, and leave it to dry overnight in the oven with a closed door. When the fruit leather is stiff but still pliable, peel it from the plastic wrap, and you'll have delicious, unsweetened fruit leather.

Pears in Spiced White Wine Sauce

Make sure you don't overcook the pears in this recipe, so that they maintain their shape. Also, take care not to add too much cornstarch to the warm sauce, since it will thicken naturally as it cools. Chill the pears and sauce separately, so that the pears don't become soft in the refrigerator. For variety, replace the pears with apples, quince, or any other hard fruit. For a lovely upgrade, try filling the pears with coarsely chopped nuts of any type you like, or process ¾-ounce ground toasted walnuts or pecans with every 1 cup sauce. You can also cook the pears in red wine, rather than white.

INGREDIENTS

Serves 8 / Serving size: 1 pear + 2 tablespoons

- **One 25-ounce bottle dry white wine**
- **1 vanilla stick**
- **1 cinnamon stick**
- **4 whole allspice berries**
- **4 cardamom pods**
- **4 cloves**
- **1 tablespoon honey**
- **8 medium Anjou pears, peeled and cored from the bottom, with stems intact**
- **Cornstarch, for thickening**

Calories	89
Total fat	0 g
Calories as fat	0 %
Saturated fat	0 g
Cholesterol	0 mg
Carbohydrates	23 g
Dietary fiber	5 g
Sodium	2 mg
Protein	0 g
Carbohydrate choices	**1½**
Exchanges: 1½ fruit	

PREPARATION

1. In a pot over medium-high heat, mix together wine, vanilla, cinnamon, peppercorns, cardamom, cloves, and honey, and bring to a boil. Add pears and bring to a boil, then reduce heat to low and simmer for about 20 minutes, or until pears are soft but still hold their shape.

2. Remove pears from pot using a slotted spoon, and chill. Pour sauce through a fine mesh strainer, then return to pot and heat over low heat until sauce reduces to about one-third. If sauce is too thin, mix in a bit of cornstarch to thicken. Transfer to refrigerator and chill. To serve, pour 2 tablespoons chilled sauce over pear.

Pears in Spiced White Wine Sauce

SWEETENING WITH AROMATIC MATERIALS

Using spices and aromatic liquids

The previous recipe shows how to use sauce, spices, and an aromatic liquid to enrich flavor. The aromatic liquid in which the pears are cooked is wine. The alcohol in the wine, as in other alcoholic beverages, evaporates almost completely during cooking, so the only sugar that remains is the wine sugar. Dry wines such as Sauvignon Blanc and Viognier have especially low sugar content and are therefore suitable for this recipe. I highly recommend using dry wine when preparing sweets and for cooking and baking in general. Many recipes can be upgraded by replacing half the quantity of water with dry white or red wine. Try it yourself, and savor the difference.

The previous recipe also uses cardamom, cloves, allspice, and cinnamon for flavor, but you can use other spices as well, such as star anise. Another possible flavor enhancer is brandy-soaked chopped dried fruit, such as prune, which can be added to upgrade any dessert recipe in this book, or any other favorite dessert.

Using herbs in desserts

Herbs are used in most of the recipes in this chapter to enrich the flavor. Mint is often used in desserts, but herbs such as thyme and basil, ones that are usually used in savory dishes, can also enrich desserts. For example, note how thyme and lemon verbena are used to upgrade the flavor of the strawberries in the Strawberries in Lemon Verbena and Thyme Marinade, with Ricotta (page 122), and how the basil enriches the Rolled Apricot Fruit Leather with Goat Cheese and Basil recipe on page 118. In fact, the basil and fruit leather enrich the flavor in this dessert so much, you don't need to add any sweetener at all. Try using diverse herbs to upgrade your own desserts, and enjoy the results.

Soak fruit in fresh herbs to enrich their flavor

Soaking fruit in a marinade of fresh herbs, as in the Strawberries in Lemon Verbena and Thyme, with Ricotta (page 122) is an excellent way of enriching flavor. If you do this, I recommend cutting the fruit first so that it absorbs more flavors. Don't soak fruit for more than 2 or 3 hours, or it will become soggy. When making the Melon and Cherry Minestrone (page 123), try soaking the melon cubes in lemon verbena before grinding them; when making the Pears in Spiced White Wine Sauce (page 114), try soaking the pears in mint leaves before cooking. Try other combinations of fruit and fresh herbs; for example, I like to marinate strawberries in lemongrass before serving.

Rolled Apricot Fruit Leather with Goat Cheese and Basil

Rolled Apricot Fruit Leather with Goat Cheese and Basil

The apricot fruit leather in this recipe can be replaced with other types of fruit leather. If you can't buy fruit leather in the store, try making it yourself by following the instructions on page 113. You can replace the fruit leather in this recipe with whole dried apricots or fresh fruit such as figs. Just slit the fruit down the middle and fill with the cheese mixture. To vary the filling, replace the basil with mint, sage, or coarsely chopped nuts such as pistachios. If you'd like to make the dessert a bit sweeter, serve the stuffed fruit with one of the sweet sauces described in this book.

INGREDIENTS

Serves 8 / Serving size: 2 slices

- Two 8 x 8-inch sheets unsweetened apricot fruit leather
- 6 tablespoons low-fat soft (spreadable) goat cheese
- 6 tablespoons chopped fresh basil

Calories	34
Total fat	2 g
Calories as fat	53%
Saturated fat	1 g
Cholesterol	1 mg
Carbohydrates	4 g
Dietary fiber	0 g
Sodium	28 mg
Protein	0 g
Carbohydrate choices	**None**
Exchanges: ½ fat	

PREPARATION

1. Lay one fruit leather flat on your work surface, and spread ½ the cheese on top in a thin, even layer. Sprinkle evenly with ½ the basil. Repeat with second fruit leather.

2. Roll up fruit leathers into a tight roll, and chill for at least 15 minutes, until cheese hardens. Cut into ½-inch slices, then let sit at room temperature for about 10 minutes before serving.

TIP *Using low-fat cheese when making desserts can be a bit challenging, since it tends to lose its form when you work with it. The higher the percentage of fat, the more it stays solid. If the low-fat cheese you are working with becomes too soft to handle, return it to the refrigerator for 5 to 10 minutes. Chilling the cheese will cause it to solidify again, and make it easier to handle. Try this technique in the following recipe: after you have spread the cheese mixture on the fruit leather, roll the fruit leather and refrigerate it for at least 15 minutes before cutting it. Once the roll has been cut, let the pieces sit at room temperature for a few minutes. Allowing the temperature of the dish to increase will make it tastier.* **Note how refrigeration can help you significantly reduce the amount of fat and sugar in a dish.**

SWEETENING BY CHANGING THE CHARACTERISTICS OF INGREDIENTS

Sweetening through a change in temperature

The recipe on the next page is one of the most surprising I have come across recently. It takes excellent advantage of a simple technique: heating. The next time you barbecue, bring with you some aluminum foil and fruit. Make a roasting bag with the aluminum foil and put the fruit inside, along with some aromatic ingredients such as orange juice or red wine. Add a teaspoon of honey and close the roasting bag. If you really want a surprise, throw in a bit of red hot chili pepper as well. When you sit down to eat and there is still space on the barbecue, place the bag of fruit on top and let it roast for a few minutes, turning it over every now and then. By the time the meal is over, a delicious dessert will be waiting.

To make a roasting bag, cut off a 3-foot piece of heavy-duty aluminum foil, and fold it in half widthwise. Make double folds along the right and left edges to close the sides securely. Place the fruit and aromatic ingredients inside the bag, then make a double fold along the top edge to seal it. You can also use this technique to roast fruit in your oven. Simply put the oven on broil; I'm sure it will be happy to host a roasting bag like this.

Sweetening by cooking

The introduction to this chapter describes how an onion becomes sweeter through heating. Reduced balsamic vinegar is another example of how cooking can cause a change in flavor. In its natural state, balsamic vinegar is made up of little carbohydrates and a lot of acid. Therefore, it's the taste of the acid that dominates the flavor of the vinegar. Gentle heating causes the acid to evaporate and emphasizes the sweet flavor. The reduced liquid is rich, sweet, and excellent for serving with desserts, such as the recipe on page 122. When reducing balsamic vinegar, take care not to reduce it to too much. Remember that the sauce is served cool, and it will thicken as it cools; if you reduce balsamic vinegar too much, it will likely be too thick.

Reduced balsamic vinegar can be stored in the refrigerator for several days, and served with fruit desserts or pastries. Try pouring some on the Mango Cubes in Cashew Cream (page 58), the Rolled Apricot Fruit Leather with Goat Cheese and Basil (page 118), on frozen desserts such as the Mango Sorbet (page 126), or on baked goods such as the Apple-filled Phyllo Fingers (page 143).

Sweetening through texture

The fruit soup on page 123 demonstrates how a dessert with a coarse texture can be sweet enough to the palate without adding sweeteners. Instead of simply pureeing all of the fruit to the same coarse texture, I puree some of it to a fine texture and add whole cherries to make a combination that is reminiscent of minestrone soup. These types of textures can also be achieved by adding various types of nuts.

Nectarines Roasted in Orange Juice and Date Honey

The next time you attend a barbecue, use the technique described below to create a delicious appetizer of barbecued vegetables that can be eaten while the meat is being cooked. Simply make a roasting bag with aluminum foil (page 119) and fill it with zucchini, cauliflower, fennel, mushrooms, and any other type of vegetable you like. Add a bit of olive oil and put the bag on the grill. You can also add hot pepper to upgrade the flavor even more. If you want to avoid direct contact between food and aluminum foil, place a piece of parchment paper on the aluminum foil before folding it into the bag.

Calories	71
Total fat	0 g
Calories as fat	0%
Saturated fat	0 g
Cholesterol	0 mg
Carbohydrates	17 g
Dietary fiber	3 g
Sodium	0 mg
Protein	2 g
Carbohydrate choices	**1**
Exchanges: 1 fruit	

INGREDIENTS

Serves 4 / Serving size: 2 nectarine halves + 1 tablespoon sauce

- **4 nectarines, halved**
- **2 tablespoons fresh orange juice**
- **1 teaspoon unsweetened date honey**

PREPARATION

1. Preheat barbecue or oven to 350°F, and prepare a roasting bag with aluminum foil (page 119).

2. Place nectarines, orange juice, and date honey inside, and close bag securely. Place bag on barbecue or oven and roast for about 30 minutes, turning occasionally.

Nectarines Roasted in Orange Juice and Date Honey

Strawberries in Lemon Verbena and Thyme, with Ricotta

Low-fat ricotta is an excellent cheese for upgrading desserts thanks to its texture, flavor, and low percentage of fat. Just make sure you are using natural-flavor, unsalted ricotta. Ricotta is best used when combined with fruit, such as a base for strawberries in this recipe. In Pears in Spiced White Wine Sauce (page 114) you can mix the ricotta with the wine sauce to make the sauce even richer. Ricotta is delicious when combined in baked dishes, as well. For more on that, see Ricotta and Pear Dim Sum in Pistachio and Apple Sauce (page 144).

Calories	47
Total fat	0 g
Calories as fat	19%
Saturated fat	1 g
Cholesterol	3 mg
Carbohydrates	8 g
Dietary fiber	2 g
Sodium	14 mg
Protein	1 g
Carbohydrate choices	**½**
Exchanges: ½ fruit	

INGREDIENTS

Serves 4 / Serving size:
1 tablespoon ricotta + ½ cup
strawberries + 1 tablespoon sauce

- **10 ounces strawberries, stemmed and halved**
- **½ cup fresh lemon verbena leaves**
- **1 tablespoon fresh thyme leaves**
- **½ cup balsamic vinegar**
- **4 tablespoons low-fat unsalted ricotta cheese**

PREPARATION

1. In a medium bowl, mix together strawberries, lemon verbena, and thyme. Cover and refrigerate for 2 hours.

2. In a small saucepan, heat vinegar over low heat, stirring occasionally, until vinegar reduces to about a third of its original volume. Transfer to refrigerator and chill.

3. To serve, spread 1 tablespoon cheese on each serving dish. Top with ¼ of the strawberries, and pour sauce on top.

Melon and Cherry Minestrone with Apple-filled Phyllo Fingers

The simple technique used in the following recipe can be used to make a variety of desserts with fruit and herbs. Upgrade it in the summer by processing the soup with ice cubes or by adding frozen fruit (see page 161). Try kiwi and mint, watermelon and ginger, or mixed berries with more exotic flavors. You can also decorate the soup with a spoonful of sliced toasted almonds.

INGREDIENTS

Serves 16 / Serving size: ¾ cup minestrone + 1 phyllo finger

Fruit soup
- **1 medium cantaloupe, peeled, seeded, and cubed**
- **½ cup mint leaves, separated**
- **1 tablespoon vanilla vodka**
- **1 pound cherries**
- **4 passion fruits, halved, for garnish**

Phyllo fingers
- **1 Royal Gala apple, cored and cut into ½-inch cubes**
- **5 tablespoons water**
- **Four 12½ x 14-inch sheets phyllo pastry**
- **2 tablespoons walnut oil**

PREPARATION

1. Prepare fruit soup: Place melon, mint, and vodka into a food processor and process until blended. Transfer to a large bowl, and mix in cherries. Cover and chill for at least 1 hour.

2. Prepare phyllo fingers: In a small non-stick frying pan, cook apple with water for about 5 minutes, until apple softens. Drain liquid and transfer apple to a small bowl. Cover and let cool to room temperature.

3. Preheat oven to 425°F and line a baking sheet with parchment paper. Lay 1 phyllo sheet on your work surface and brush with 1 tablespoon oil. Top with a second sheet of phyllo, and cut into 8 even rectangles. Place a thin row of apple filling along a long edge of each rectangle, fold sides over filling, and roll up into a cylinder. Repeat process with remaining phyllo sheets, oil, and filling to make 16 cylinders. Arrange cylinders on baking sheet and bake for 4 minutes, until golden brown.

4. To serve, distribute fruit soup evenly among martini glasses. Scoop seeds from passion fruit with a small spoon, and sprinkle on each serving. Insert a phyllo finger and serve immediately.

Calories	69
Total fat	2 g
Calories as fat	26%
Saturated fat	0 g
Cholesterol	0 mg
Carbohydrates	10 g
Dietary fiber	2 g
Sodium	10 mg
Protein	1 g
Carbohydrate choices	**½**
Exchanges: ½ fruit, ½ fat	

USING SUGAR SUBSTITUTES

If the desserts described in this chapter aren't sweet enough for you, you can add your preferred sugar substitute to make them sweeter, at least until your palate becomes accustomed to enjoying foods that are less sweet. Notice that these desserts depend on a variety of natural sweetening techniques, so if you do decide to add some sugar substitute, you'll probably need less than you normally would when making dessert. In this manner, the taste of the sugar substitute mixes well with the flavors in the dessert, and the aftertaste that often accompanies sugar substitutes will be minimized. If you choose to replace sugar with sugar substitute in ordinary recipes, here are several suggestions to keep in mind:

Choose recipes that require small quantities of sweeteners and combine a variety of natural flavors

Try to find recipes that have a variety of flavors, and a relatively small quantity of sweetener. In those cases, replace a third to two-thirds of that sugar with a sugar substitute. Take into account that if the dominant flavor of the recipe is sugar, the sugar substitute flavor will be highly noticeable.

Vary the types of sugar substitutes that you use

That way you'll be consuming relatively smaller quantities of the various substitutes. If you plan on cooking or heating the dish you are preparing, read the fine print on the sugar substitutes in your pantry. Make sure you choose one that will retain its sweetening power when heated.

Sugars do more than just sweeten

It's important to know that sugar does more than just sweeten when used in preparing foods. For example, sugar doesn't freeze in a household freezer. When it's included in sorbet it prevents the sorbet from freezing completely, and helps retain its texture. If you replace the sugar with sugar substitute in an ordinary sorbet recipe, the sorbet will be sweet enough, but the texture will be brittle rather than creamy and smooth. In order to make sorbet without adding sugar you can do one of two things. One technique is to heat the fruit puree and reduce it before freezing the sorbet. This eliminates unnecessary liquids that could cause the sorbet to become too frozen. Another strategy, and the one used in the recipe on the next page, is to use fruit (like mango) that has a fibrous texture but relatively little liquid. The role of sugar in baking is complex, and replacing it with sugar substitutes can cause significant changes to the baked product. If you are planning to make substitutions, consider the following tips:

- The rich brown color of many baked products is due to the caramelization of sugar. Dough or batter in which sugar has been replaced with a sugar substitute will be paler than usual in color. This can be partially overcome by brushing a thin layer of oil on the dough before baking it.

- Baked items made with sugar substitutes are usually ready 5 to 10 minutes before baked items made with sugar.

- Sugar acts as a preservative in baked goods. A baked item that contains a sugar substitute will have a shorter shelf life. I recommend freezing such items to preserve freshness (see page 130).

- In yeast dough, yeast feeds on sugar, and this helps the dough to rise. Yeast dough in which sugar has been replaced with sugar substitutes will not rise as expected. It is possible to add more yeast to the dough, or to leaven the dough for a longer period of time.

If you decide to use sugar substitutes when baking, choose the right baked goods (ones that contain a lot of fruit, and not too much sugar, such as in the recipe on page 127) and the results can be relatively good. However, I am sure that if you accustom yourself to eating desserts that are less sweet, you'll reduce the amount of sugar substitute you use. As a result, the desserts will be tastier and you'll enjoy them more.

THE QUANTITY

In French cuisine, portions of food are often known for being high in taste and relatively small in size. I recommend adopting this approach to all foods, especially desserts, since their purpose is to imbue flavor and not satisfy hunger. Portions can be small but flavorful. The reason is simple: if you are satisfied with a smaller quantity of dessert, you can use a larger quantity of sweetener without increasing your consumption of sugars.

Confused? Notice that in the recipe on page 127, a serving comprises of four biscotti. If you are satisfied with just two biscotti instead of four, then you can double the amount of regular sweetener you use, and you'll still be consuming the same amount of sugar. You can relate in the same manner to all of the recipes in this chapter: the more you can be satisfied with a smaller serving, the more regular sweetener you'll be able to add, while staying within the recommended limits.

Strive for servings that are small and of high quality when making desserts. When eating them, take small bites. Move the morsel to the center of your tongue, close your mouth, and shut your eyes. Let the taste spread through your mouth. Only after the flavor has spread, chew the dessert again. Continue eating your dessert, very slowly, in this manner. I'm sure you'll enjoy the taste more than usual. Practice eating this way as often as possible. You'll get more pleasure from your food for a longer time, and the amount of sugars you consume will be reduced.

Mango Sorbet and Fruit Salad with Maple Tahini

Make an ordinary fruit salad extraordinary by adding a few nuts as well as exotic fruits such as pineapple, mango, persimmon, or avocado. (Although combining avocado with sweet foods may be unusual in Western cuisines, it is common in Asian cuisine, where salting avocado is considered unusual.) The sauce in your fruit salad can also make it special. This recipe mixes fruit juice with tahini, but you can replace the tahini with natural peanut butter or cashew butter. If the fruit you choose is sweet enough, try adding ginger, hot pepper, or cumin to spice it up a bit.

INGREDIENTS

Serves 15 / Serving size: ⅓ cup salad + 1 scoop sorbet + 1 tablespoon sauce

Calories	82
Total fat	2 g
Calories as fat	22%
Saturated fat	0 g
Cholesterol	0 mg
Carbohydrates	15 g
Dietary fiber	3 g
Sodium	3 mg
Protein	0 g
Carbohydrate choices	**1**
Exchanges: 1 fruit	

Sorbet

- 3 ripe medium mangos, peeled, halved, and pitted
- 1 teaspoon fresh lemon juice
- 2 tablespoons vanilla vodka
- Sugar substitute equivalent to 1 teaspoon sugar, optional
- Boiling water, if necessary

Sauce

- 1 teaspoon pure tahini
- 1 tablespoon unsweetened 100% maple syrup
- ¼ cup orange juice

Fruit salad

- 1 passion fruit, halved
- 1 medium Anjou pear, cored and cut into ½-inch cubes
- 1 medium persimmon, cut into ½-inch cubes
- 1 medium Red Delicious apple, cored and cut into ½-inch cubes
- 1 medium banana, cut into ½-inch cubes
- 1 medium avocado, ripe but firm, peeled, cored, and cut into
- ½-inch cubes

PREPARATION

1. Prepare sorbet: Grate mango and transfer to a medium bowl. Mix in lemon juice, vanilla vodka, and sugar substitute until well combined. Cover with plastic wrap, and transfer to freezer until frozen, at least 3 hours.

2. Transfer frozen mango mixture to a food processor and puree. If mango is too cold to process, add a tablespoon of boiling water. Return to bowl, cover, and refreeze.

3. Prepare fruit salad: Using a spoon, scoop seeds out of passion fruit halves and transfer to a medium bowl. Mix in pear, persimmon, apple, banana, and avocado.

4. Prepare sauce: In a small bowl, mix together tahini, maple syrup, and orange juice.

5. Just before serving, remove mango mixture from freezer, transfer to a food processor, and puree. Distribute fruit salad evenly among serving dishes. Top each serving with a scoop of mango sorbet and sauce.

Dried Fruit and Nut Biscotti

The ratio between the dried fruit and nuts in this recipe and the flours is almost 1:1, making it rich in flavor, attractive, and naturally sweet. Feel free to make variations in this recipe by using your favorite dried fruit and nuts. Because of its large quantity of dried fruit and nuts, the dough has a delicate texture that requires a different method of handling from other cookie recipes. After the dough is partially baked as a log, it is transferred to the freezer, frozen and then sliced into very thin slices. These slices are then baked again to make crispy biscotti that are just right for serving with coffee.

INGREDIENTS

Makes 300 biscotti /
Serving size: 4 biscotti

- 21 ounces (about 5 cups) whole-wheat flour
- 14 ounces (about 3 cups) all-purpose white flour
- 1 teaspoon baking powder
- 4 tablespoons brown sugar
- Powdered sugar substitute equal to 4 tablespoons sugar
- Pinch Atlantic sea salt
- 5½ ounces raw almonds, coarsely chopped
- 5½ ounces raw hazelnuts, coarsely chopped
- 11 ounces unsweetened dried figs, coarsely chopped
- 11 ounces unsweetened dried apricots, coarsely chopped
- 3 ounces unsweetened raisins, coarsely chopped
- 8 large eggs
- 4 large egg yolks
- Rind from 1 orange

PREPARATION

1. In the bowl of an electric mixer, combine whole-wheat flour, all-purpose flour, baking powder, brown sugar, sugar substitute, and salt. Add almonds, hazelnuts, figs, apricots, and raisins, and mix until combined. Add eggs, egg yolks, and orange rind, and mix until combined. Shape batter into six logs, flatten slightly, then chill for about 30 minutes.

2. Preheat oven to 350°F and line 2 baking sheets with parchment paper. Lay logs on baking sheets and bake for 25 minutes. Remove logs from oven and let cool, then wrap each log in plastic wrap, transfer them to the freezer, and freeze for 2 to 3 hours, until frozen. At this stage, logs may be stored for several weeks.

3. Preheat oven to 350°F and line baking sheets with parchment paper. Remove logs from freezer and slice into very thin slices. Arrange slices on baking sheets, and bake for 10 minutes. Cool on a wire rack before serving. May be stored in an airtight container for up to 3 to 4 weeks.

Calories	98
Total fat	3 g
Calories as fat	28%
Saturated fat	1 g
Cholesterol	34 mg
Carbohydrates	15 g
Dietary fiber	2 g
Sodium	37 mg
Protein	3 g
Carbohydrate choices	**1**

Exchanges:
½ starch, ½ fruit, ½ fat

Dried Fruit and Nut Biscotti

Baked Goods

Even people who excel at healthy cooking may run into trouble when it comes to healthy baking. The unfamiliar texture of whole-grain flour, along with efforts to reduce fat and sugars, can make the task a bit challenging. The recipes in this chapter demonstrate the secrets of healthy baking.

My first suggestion is to start with healthy recipes. It may be tempting to use your regular recipes and simply replace white flour with whole-wheat flour or part of the butter with canola oil, but the results of such substitutions can be mediocre, even disappointing. Dough is a complex mixture, and since making successful substitutions is difficult, I recommend using healthy recipes from the start.

If you do decide to make your own healthier baked dishes, I suggest you try a culinary trend that involves incorporating vegetable puree into the dough. One of the most noticeable qualities of dough made from whole-wheat flour is its dense texture. Though some people like this texture, others prefer the light, airy texture of dough made with white flour. A common solution is to add more fat to the dough, but clearly that's not something you want to do. In my opinion, one of the best solutions is to incorporate vegetable puree into the dough. Dough made with vegetables has a rich color, a lower calorie and carbohydrate count, and an airy texture that allows for the use of less fat too. A large portion of the recipes in this chapter are influenced by this trend, which I hope becomes permanent.

I'll conclude with some advice: working with dough made from whole-wheat flour is different than working with dough made from white flour. The texture of the resulting baked good is also different. Getting used to these two differences may take a bit of time, just as it takes time to adjust to a change in the quantity of salt and sugar you consume. To make the transition to whole-wheat flour easier, start with a mixture of white flour and whole-wheat flour. Rather than using 100% whole-wheat flour, try using 75% or even 50% whole-wheat flour. In this chapter, you'll find recipes that use various mixtures of flours, from 50% whole-wheat flour and 50% white flour to 100% whole-wheat flour. If you find that you aren't accustomed to whole-wheat flour, replace part of it with white flour. As you gain confidence with whole-wheat flour, increase its percentage of the total flour. As long as you are using at least 50% whole-wheat flour when you bake, you are heading in the right direction. **Remember: it's better to make baked goods with 50% whole-wheat flour that will be eaten with pleasure, than with 100% whole-wheat flour that isn't eaten at all, or that requires high calorie pastry as a compensation.**

Yeast Dough

The main challenge in making healthier yeast dough is how to incorporate whole-wheat flour. One of the qualities of whole-wheat flour is that it contains less gluten than white flour. (Gluten is found in the wheat seed, and because whole-wheat flour includes the wheat kernel coating, there is relatively less gluten in whole-wheat flour than in white flour.) In order for yeast dough to rise properly it needs a high quantity of gluten. Here are a few techniques that can be used to help yeast dough made with whole-wheat flour rise properly:

Add 1 tablespoon of gluten powder for every 2 pounds (7½ cups) whole-wheat flour. Maintain the same ratio for mixed flours as well; for example, add ½ tablespoon gluten if you use 2 pounds of flour comprised of 50% whole-wheat flour and 50% white flour. Gluten powder is found in many health food stores and can be stored in the freezer for several months.

Knead yeast dough made with whole-wheat flour more thoroughly than usual. Kneading helps the gluten particles connect with each other, and this helps the dough rise.

Add liquids that are lukewarm in temperature. This helps dough reach the ideal temperature for rising.

Achieving an airy texture

To reduce the density of dough made with whole-wheat flour, try aerating it by adding pureed vegetables. The Pumpkin Dinner Rolls with Flakes of Thyme (page 132) demonstrates how to make high-quality dough with 100% whole-wheat flour and without any added oil. For variety, replace the pumpkin with kohlrabi, parsley root, or any other root vegetable. Baked goods made with vegetable puree have a shorter shelf life than store-bought baked goods. This is always true of homemade baked goods since they don't contain the large quantity of additives, salts, and sugars that are added to mass-produced baked goods to extend their shelf life. Therefore, in order to make things easier for yourself and to preserve the freshness of your baked foods, try to prepare a large quantity of baked items whenever you bake, and then freeze most of them. This means you'll have healthy, homemade baked goods on hand whenever you want them. The Beer and Almond Bread recipe on the opposite page is an example how to make bread without pureed vegetables or gluten. In fact, with this recipe, you don't even need to wait for the dough to rise. In the time it takes to chop a salad and set the table, you'll have bread—made from whole-wheat flour and a bottle of beer—baking in the oven.

How to prepare baked goods for freezing

Reduce the baking time for items you know you'll be freezing. Make sure the baked items are completely cooled before freezing. Wrap them well with plastic wrap or place them in freezer-safe storage bags. Packaging baked goods properly before freezing protects them from moisture that can build up and damage their texture. When you want to eat the baked goods, take them out of the freezer and place them directly in a preheated oven to defrost them and complete the baking process.

Beer and Almond Bread

I suggest using light beer in this recipe, for a delicate flavor. The almonds can be substituted with another type of nut, such as walnuts, or with fresh herbs, such as thyme. The texture of the mixture before baking is a batter, so you'll need a pan with high sides for baking this bread. If you want to make rolls, use a muffin pan. Don't fill the pan or muffin cups more than halfway with batter to allow room for the bread to rise. After you have mastered the basic recipe, trying adding 3½ ounces grated, low-fat, semi-soft, white cheese and 1½ ounces dried tomatoes to the batter.

Calories	83
Total fat	1 g
Calories as fat	11%
Saturated fat	0 g
Cholesterol	0 mg
Carbohydrates	15 g
Dietary fiber	2 g
Sodium	167 mg
Protein	3 g
Carbohydrate choices	**1**
Exchanges: 1 starch	

INGREDIENTS

Makes one 1 loaf (20 slices) /
Serving size: One ½-inch thick slice

- **Unrefined canola oil, for greasing**
- **9 ounces (about 2 cups) whole-wheat flour**
- **4½ ounces (about 1 cup) all-purpose white flour**
- **2 teaspoons baking powder**
- **1 tablespoon brown sugar**
- **1 teaspoon Atlantic sea salt**
- **One 16-ounce bottle light beer**
- **1½ ounces raw almonds**

PREPARATION

1. Preheat oven to 350°F. Grease a 10 x 5 x 3-inch loaf pan with oil. In a large bowl, mix together flours, baking powder, sugar, and salt until combined. Whisk in beer and mix until batter is smooth and there are no lumps. Mix in almonds until evenly distributed.

2. Transfer batter to loaf pan and bake for 40 minutes, until a toothpick inserted into center comes out dry. Cool before slicing.

Pumpkin Dinner Rolls with Flakes of Thyme

The amount of liquid in every vegetable is different, so when you add water to the pureed vegetables in this recipe, do so slowly, and just until the desired consistency is reached. Be patient when you mix the dry and wet ingredients together to form dough since whole-wheat flour takes a bit of time to absorb liquids. Add the remaining liquid, if necessary, at this stage. In addition to thyme leaves and pumpkin seeds, you can also sprinkle nigella seeds and sesame seeds on the rolls. To make the tops crispy, place a small bowl with water in the oven while the rolls are baking.

INGREDIENTS

Makes 45 rolls / Serving size: 1 roll

- 1½ pounds fresh pumpkin, peeled, seeded, and cut into chunks
- 6 cups water
- 2⅗ pounds (about 8 cups) whole-wheat flour, plus more for dusting
- 1¼ ounces (2 tablespoons) fine Atlantic sea salt
- 1 tablespoon gluten, optional
- 1⅖ ounces (4 tablespoons) brown sugar
- ½ ounce (2 packages) dry active yeast
- ¾ cup lukewarm water
- ½ egg, beaten
- 4 tablespoons thyme leaves
- 2 tablespoons raw pumpkin seeds

PREPARATION

1. In a large pot over high heat, bring water with a pinch of salt to a boil. Add pumpkin, reduce heat to low, and cook for about 30 minutes, until pumpkin is soft. Drain, mash pumpkin with a fork, and let cool.

2. Separately, in a large bowl, mix together flour, salt, gluten, and sugar until combined. Add yeast and mix well.

3. Place pumpkin and ½ cup water in a food processor, and process until smooth. Add pumpkin puree to dry ingredients and knead until thoroughly combined. Add remaining water, if necessary, and knead well.

4. Cover bowl with a clean kitchen towel and let rise in a warm place for about 45 minutes, until dough doubles in size. Line 2 baking sheets with parchment paper.

5. Turn out dough on a lightly floured surface, and gently knead to reduce its size. Divide dough into 45 even pieces and shape each piece into a roll. Arrange rolls on baking sheets, and let rise in a warm place for 1 hour.

6. Preheat oven to 400°F. Brush rolls with egg, sprinkle with thyme and pumpkin seeds, and score tops with a sharp knife. Bake for 13 minutes, until tops are golden brown.

Calories	83
Total fat	1 g
Calories as fat	11%
Saturated fat	0 g
Cholesterol	1 mg
Carbohydrates	18 g
Dietary fiber	3 g
Sodium	183 mg
Protein	3 g
Carbohydrate choices	**1**
Exchanges: 1 starch	

Pumpkin Dinner Rolls with Flakes of Thyme

PASTRY DOUGH

Pastry dough is an art unto itself and entire books are dedicated to making it to perfection. Many elements affect the flakiness, softness, color, and taste of pastry dough. Unlike yeast dough, pastry dough should not be too dense, so the use of whole-wheat flour that contains less gluten is actually an advantage. The challenge that remains, however, is the quantity and type of fat you use. How can you obtain a desirable texture while using a reasonable quantity of healthier fat? Here, too, vegetables come to the rescue, by upgrading the taste, texture, and flakiness of the pastry.

There are a few important differences in the preparation of yeast dough and pastry dough. First of all, the ingredients are added in a different order. When making pastry dough, all the dry ingredients are mixed together first, and then the oil is added. The liquid is added at the end. Another difference is the amount of kneading. Pastry dough should be kneaded as little as possible. **Precise measurements and techniques are always important when making dough, but they are especially important when using healthier ingredients. The more you adhere to the right technique, the higher the quality of your pastry.**

The pastry dough described on the facing page can be used in any baked goods recipe calling for pastry dough. I use canola oil and olive oil for savory baked goods. If you want to make a sweet pastry, replace the olive oil with walnut oil, since the taste of olive oil doesn't generally suit sweet flavors, and replace the eggplant with banana, which has a dominant flavor, or with pumpkin, which has a more delicate flavor. For a sweet alternative filling, mix together 7 ounces of unsalted ricotta cheese with 6 cored and cubed plums or apples and 6 sliced fresh figs (which have been cooked in ½ cup of dry red wine and chilled).

Buckwheat and yogurt dough

This dough is surprisingly simple to make and has a high-quality texture that doesn't include any fruits or vegetables. Its taste is suitable for either savory or sweet dishes. The ratio between flour and yogurt depends on the liquidity of the yogurt. To make this dough, place buckwheat flour in a bowl, add a pinch of salt, and slowly add yogurt while mixing. When the mixture has the texture of dough, transfer it to the refrigerator for 30 minutes, then roll it out, as thin as you can, and fill as desired. Bake at medium heat until ready.

Eggplant Pastry Filled with Cheese and Swiss Chard

The pastry dough in this recipe can be paired with a wide variety of fillings. To make a savory filling with a velvety texture, heat 1 tablespoon olive oil, and sauté 2 leeks, 5 ounces sliced mushrooms, and a bit of fresh thyme. For a more substantial dish, fill the dough with a mixture of 1 pound lean ground beef, 1 cup chopped parsley, 1 chopped onion, and 2 tablespoons tahini. Remember, it is essential to strain and chill the filling.

INGREDIENTS

Serves 24 / Serving size: 1 slice

Filling

- 1 tablespoon extra-virgin olive oil
- 4 pounds Swiss chard, thinly sliced
- ¼ teaspoon Atlantic sea salt
- ¼ teaspoon ground black pepper
- 9 ounces low-fat, semi-soft white cheese, such as feta, cut into ½-inch cubes

Pastry dough

- 9 ounces whole-wheat flour
- 9 ounces all-purpose white flour, plus more for dusting
- 2 teaspoons baking powder
- 1 teaspoon fine Atlantic sea salt
- 3 tablespoons extra-virgin olive oil
- 3 tablespoons unrefined canola oil
- 10 tablespoons finely chopped roasted eggplant (page 89)
- 6 tablespoons fresh orange juice
- ¼ egg, beaten
- 1 teaspoon nigella seeds
- 1 teaspoon sesame seeds

PREPARATION

1. Prepare filling: In a medium frying pan, heat oil over medium-high heat. Add Swiss chard, and sauté for about 15 minutes, until liquid evaporates. Add salt and pepper to taste, then transfer to a colander and drain. Mix in cheese, and transfer to a medium bowl. Cover and chill until ready to use.

2. Prepare pastry dough: Preheat oven to 400°F and line a baking sheet with parchment paper. In a large bowl, mix together flours, baking powder, and salt. Add olive oil and canola oil, and mix until texture is sandy. Mix in eggplant and orange juice, and knead until dough is uniform. Take care not to knead too much.

3. Divide dough in half. On a lightly floured surface, roll one half into a rectangle that is about ¼-inch thick. Place half of filling in a row along a long end of the rectangle, then roll up into cylinder and fold sides. Repeat process with remaining dough and filling. Brush the tops of both rolls with beaten egg, and sprinkle nigella and sesame seeds over top. Place rolls on baking sheet, and bake for 15 minutes, until golden brown. Let cool slightly before slicing into 1-inch thick slices.

Calories	128
Total fat	6 g
Calories as fat	42%
Saturated fat	2 g
Cholesterol	7 mg
Carbohydrates	14 g
Dietary fiber	1 g
Sodium	199 mg
Protein	5 g
Carbohydrate choices	**1**
Exchanges: 1 starch, 1 fat	

Eggplant Pastry Filled with Cheese and Swiss Chard

VEGETABLE BAKES

These versatile dishes use mainly simple ingredients and require relatively little preparation time. A single vegetable bake, which usually provides several servings, can be kept in the refrigerator for four or five days, or frozen for several weeks. If you plan on freezing a vegetable bake, I recommend cutting it into serving-size pieces before freezing. When you want a light and easy meal, simply take a serving out of the freezer and defrost. Serve with a side salad for a lovely light lunch, or with some fish or chicken as a quick and satisfying dinner.

Vegetable bakes are excellent recipes for improvisation. They can be made with a diverse list of healthy ingredients and are very easy to alter. Simply chop up vegetables you have in the refrigerator, mix them with eggs, whole-wheat flour, and a liquid, and bake in the oven at 350°F. About 40 minutes later, you'll have a warm, filling dish, ready to be savored. If you aren't sure about quantities, use the recipe on the page 138 as a template, and substitute with the vegetables you have at home. Because every vegetable has a different quantity of liquid, I recommend draining vegetables with lots of liquid first, then adding liquid separately until the desired consistency is reached. If you do this, the recipe will always work. A bit of low-fat, semi-soft cheese or low-fat yogurt and fresh herbs are excellent additions that will always upgrade the final dish.

Replace eggs with tofu to reduce fat

Another ingredient I recommend integrating into baked goods in general, and vegetable bakes in particular, is tofu. Tofu can even help you reduce the amount of fat you use to make dough. To do this, puree 3 ounces of soft silken tofu and 1 tablespoon of oil in a food processor until you have a smooth cream. Use this mixture to replace 1 egg. This combination can replace half the quantity of eggs in most recipes. Give it a try with the Dried Fruit and Nut Biscotti (page 127).

BAKING WITH WHOLE AND CRUSHED STARCHES

Another way of making whole-grain baked goods that have an airy texture is by using coarsely ground whole-grain flour, crushed whole grain such as bulgur, whole grain such as oats, or even pre-cooked whole grains. These items can be used to bake excellent breads, vegetable bakes, even cakes that have a unique, sometimes, very delicate texture.

If you want variety, try replacing whole-wheat flour in Zucchini and Cherry Tomato Bake (page 140) with bulgur, cooked brown rice, or quinoa. If you choose bulgur, add just half the usual amount of liquid; if you prefer using a cooked whole grains, leave out the liquid altogether. Polenta is used in the Carrot Cake with Pears in Honey and Almonds Glaze (see page 139). Made from coarsely ground corn, polenta is a staple in traditional Italian cooking. When combined with liquid, polenta absorbs it and takes on a porridge-like texture. When integrated into a relatively dry mixture, it can make a delicious airy and grainy cake.

Carrot Cake with Pears and Honey Almond Glaze

Nut butters made from almonds, walnuts, cashews, and pistachios are available in many health food stores these days. You can use any of these butters in this cake. If you can't find the nut butter you want, try making it yourself by processing the nuts in a food processor, gradually adding walnut oil until you achieve the desired texture (see page 58). Note that all of the sweetness in this cake comes from the pears, carrots, almond butter, and a sweet glazing of honey at the end that completes the dessert.

INGREDIENTS

Serves 18 / Serving size:
one ½-inch slice

- 3 medium Anjou pears, peeled, cored, and cut into eighths
- 6½ cups water
- 2¾ pounds carrots, peeled and cut into large chunks
- Pinch Atlantic sea salt
- 6 tablespoons almond butter
- 5 drops pure almond extract, optional
- 6 ounces polenta
- 1 tablespoon honey
- 1 tablespoon boiling water
- Canola oil, for greasing
- 1 ounce unsalted sliced almonds, toasted (page 57)

PREPARATION

1. Arrange pear slices in a large frying pan. Add ½ cup water and steam over high heat for about 5 minutes, until pears are a little soft. Set aside.

2. In a large pot over high heat, bring 6 cups water with a pinch of salt to a boil. Add carrots, reduce heat to medium, and cook for about 40 minutes, until carrots are very soft. Drain, let carrots cool, then transfer to a food processor and puree until smooth.

3. Transfer pureed carrots to a large bowl, and mix in almond butter and almond extract until combined. Gradually add polenta while mixing constantly with a wooden spoon to prevent lumps from forming.

4. Preheat oven to 350°F. Brush the sides of a 10-inch round baking pan with oil. Pour batter into baking pan, and flatten top with a rubber spatula. Arrange pear slices in a tight ring on top, and press in gently. Bake for about 30 minutes, until cake pulls away from sides of pan. Place on a wire rack to cool.

5. In a small bowl, mix together honey and boiling water. Brush on cooled cake, then sprinkle with almonds.

Calories	127
Total fat	4 g
Calories as fat	28%
Saturated fat	1 g
Cholesterol	0 mg
Carbohydrates	19 g
Dietary fiber	5 g
Sodium	81 mg
Protein	3 g
Carbohydrate choices	**1**

Exchanges: 1 starch, 1 fat

Carrot Cake with Pears and Honey Almond Glaze

Zucchini and Cherry Tomato Bake

Vegetable bakes may turn out too liquidy when you start using unfamiliar flours, or when you use vegetables that have unexpectedly large quantities of liquid. An excellent way of preventing this is by sprinkling dry grains such as bulgur, whole-wheat couscous, or quinoa on the bottom of the pan to absorb excess liquid. Make sure you choose a grain that has the same cooking time as the vegetable bake, or even a bit shorter.

INGREDIENTS

Serves 20 / Serving size:

One 2 x 3-inch piece

- 4 tablespoons extra-virgin olive oil, plus more for greasing
- 1 cup whole-wheat flour
- ½ cup all-purpose white flour
- 1 teaspoon baking powder
- 5 medium zucchini, finely grated and drained
- ¾ cup water
- 1 tablespoon vegetable stock (page 63), optional
- 4 large eggs
- 3½ ounces low-fat, semi-soft white cheese, such as feta
- ¼ teaspoon Atlantic sea salt
- ¼ teaspoon ground black pepper
- 2 tablespoons quinoa
- 3½ ounces cherry tomato

Calories	94
Total fat	5 g
Calories as fat	48%
Saturated fat	1 g
Cholesterol	45 mg
Carbohydrates	9 g
Dietary fiber	1 g
Sodium	103 mg
Protein	4 g
Carbohydrate choices	½
Exchanges: ½ starch, 1 fat	

PREPARATION

1. Preheat oven to 320°F. Grease a 10 x 12-inch baking dish with olive oil. In a medium bowl, mix together flours and baking powder. Add zucchini, water, stock, oil, eggs, cheese, salt, and pepper, mixing until combined.

2. Sprinkle quinoa into baking dish, then add zucchini mixture. Arrange cherry tomatoes on top, in any design you like, and press in gently.

3. Bake for 40 to 50 minutes, or until a toothpick inserted into the center comes out clean. Cool for a few minutes before cutting.

BAKING WITH READY-MADE DOUGH

The first recipes in this chapter demonstrated how to make various types of dough. The two final recipes demonstrate how you can use two types of ready-made dough to make high-quality dishes.

The first one is a Mediterranean dough known as phyllo, made from wheat flour and water. Note that ready-made foods made with phyllo might contain large quantities of added fats, sugars, and salt, but if you are preparing with phyllo, you can achieve results that are tasty and nutritious. Although phyllo is made with white flour, it is very thin and contains no fat. Take a look at the recipe on page 143, and you'll see that a single serving of dessert made with phyllo, fruit filling, and sauce contains less than one carbohydrate choice.

Phyllo can be used to prepare both savory and sweet dishes. Ideas for fillings are described in the recipes on the following pages, but once you are comfortable working with phyllo, I recommend creating your own fillings with your favorite ingredients. When you do this, just remember a few simple tips. Phyllo can be baked for a relatively short time; the recipe on page 143 is baked for just 5 minutes at high heat. A suitable filling when preparing phyllo in this manner will require a relatively short baking time, or will be one that can be eaten without being completely cooked. If you want to use a filling that requires a longer cooking time, cook the filling on its own in advance. Because phyllo pastry is fat-free, a few principles should be followed to ensure a high-quality result.

Do not refreeze raw phyllo dough. If you decide to use phyllo dough, defrost the whole package, prepare it and bake it, then freeze the baked item. Working with phyllo that has been defrosted and refrozen is problematic. Phyllo dough defrosts quickly, so when you buy it at the supermarket, add it to your shopping cart right before going to the checkout. When you get home, make sure it's the first thing you put in your freezer.

Cover phyllo with a damp cloth when working with it. Exposure to the air is likely to dry out defrosted phyllo. After phyllo has been defrosted and is on your work surface, cover it with a damp cloth until you are ready to use it. Every time you remove a sheet of phyllo from the stack, replace the damp cloth to prevent the rest of the sheets from drying out.

Always bake with two layers of phyllo. For best results, use two layers of phyllo, and brush a thin layer of oil between them. The benefit of phyllo is that other ready-made dough already has oil in it; with phyllo, you add the oil yourself. This means you can control both the quantity and quality of oil you use. I recommend using olive oil for savory dishes and walnut oil for sweet dishes. For a more neutral flavor, or if you don't have these oils, canola oil can be used.

Use a dry filling. Because phyllo is quite delicate, excess liquid in the filling can damage the dough. Make sure that the filling you choose is completely dry. If you cook the filling in advance and it contains excess liquid, drain it before filling the phyllo dough.

The second type of ready-made dough I recommend can be stored in the pantry. Rice paper wrappers, of the kind used to make savory dishes such as the Broccoli, Tofu, and Leek Dim Sum with Asian Salsa (page 43) and Cheese and Vegetable Spring Rolls with Mediterranean Vinaigrette (page 198), can also be used for desserts. These wrappers are an excellent fat-free dough that can be filled with surprising sweet fillings, whenever you want. Easy, simple, and elegant, the rolled pastries you make with these wrappers can be baked in the oven, or served at room temperature without any baking at all. The sweet filling on page 144 doesn't require any cooking; this is a great advantage when you want to make a quick dessert. If you want an uncooked savory filling, try combining vegetables and savory cheeses as in the recipe on page 198. Upgrade any of these options by serving sauce on the side—warm sauce is ideal if the pastry is cold.

Apple-filled Phyllo Pastry in Pomegranate and Red Wine Sauce

The apples in this recipe are not peeled, adding both nutritional and culinary value to the filling. The peels upgrade the quality of the pastry by providing a crispy contrast to the delicate texture of the apple flesh. Try leaving on peels with other ingredients that you use, too. For variety, replace the apples with pears, nectarines, or any other fruit, or with a mixture of fruit. You can also add ricotta cheese, nuts, or your favorite spice. To make a savory dish, fill the phyllo with cheeses, vegetables, poultry, meat, or fish.

INGREDIENTS

Serves 12 / Serving size: 1 pastry +
1 tablespoon sauce

- 1 cup dry red wine
- 3 tablespoons pure unsweetened pomegranate juice concentrate
- 1 tablespoon unsweetened date honey
- Cornstarch, for thickening
- 1½ medium Red Delicious apples, cored and cut into cubes
- 2 tablespoons water
- 1 ounce raw walnuts, coarsely chopped
- Four 12½ x 14-inch sheets frozen phyllo dough, thawed
- 2 tablespoons unrefined walnut oil

PREPARATION

1. In a small pot, heat wine, pomegranate juice concentrate, and date honey over medium-high heat. Bring to a boil, reduce heat to low, and continue to heat, stirring occasionally, until mixture reduces to a third, about 15 minutes. Thicken with cornstarch if necessary. Set aside.

2. Preheat oven to 425°F and line a baking sheet with parchment paper. Place wok over medium heat, cook apples with water for 3 minutes, until slightly soft. Mix in walnuts, heat for a few more seconds, then transfer to a colander, and drain. Set aside.

3. Lay a sheet of phyllo on your work surface and brush with 1 tablespoon oil. Lay another sheet of phyllo on top, and cut into 6 equal rectangles. Arrange an equal amount of apple mixture in a strip down the center of each rectangle, and bring the ends of phyllo together, pinching them gently. Repeat with remaining phyllo and apple mixture, then arrange on baking sheet. Bake for 5 minutes, until tops are golden brown. Reheat wine sauce before serving, and pour over pastries.

Calories	81
Total fat	4 g
Calories as fat	44%
Saturated fat	1 g
Cholesterol	0 mg
Carbohydrates	8 g
Dietary fiber	1 g
Sodium	31 mg
Protein	1 g
Carbohydrate choices	½
Exchanges: ½ starch, 1 fat	

Ricotta and Pear Dim Sum in Pistachio and Apple Sauce

I highly recommend adding low-fat, unsalted ricotta to the list of ingredients you use to make sweet fillings. Rich in calcium, ricotta mixes well, both in taste and in texture, with fruits such as pears, plums, or apples, as well as nuts, to create fillings that are sweet and attractive. Try it as a filling with phyllo dough, or with the pastry dough (see page 134). Ricotta can also be delicious in more complex desserts. Try combining 7 ounces unsalted ricotta, 6 sliced fresh figs, 2 ounces unsalted pistachios, 1 tablespoon chopped fresh basil, and 1 tablespoon licorice-flavored liquor.

Calories	126
Total fat	2 g
Calories as fat	14%
Saturated fat	0 g
Cholesterol	1 mg
Carbohydrates	24 g
Dietary fiber	3 g
Sodium	50 mg
Protein	2 g
Carbohydrate choices	**1½**

Exchanges: 1 starch, ½ fruit

INGREDIENTS

Serves 6 / Serving size: 1 dim sum +
1 tablespoon sauce

Dim sum

- 2 medium Anjou pears, cored and cut into ¼-inch cubes
- 2 tablespoons low-fat, unsalted ricotta
- Six 8½-inch rice paper wrappers

Sauce

- ¾ cup pure apple juice
- ½ cup dry red wine
- Cornstarch, for thickening
- ⅔ ounce unsalted pistachios, toasted (page 57) and coarsely chopped

PREPARATION

1. Prepare dim sum: In a small bowl, mix together pears and ricotta. Set aside.

2. Partially fill a large heatproof bowl with warm water by mixing together boiling water and tap water. Soak 1 wrapper for 10 to 20 seconds, until it softens. Remove wrapper, gently shake off excess water, and lay on work surface. Place another wrapper to soak.

3. Arrange ⅙ of pear mixture in a horizontal mound below center of wrapper, leaving left and right sides of wrapper bare. Fold sides over filling and roll up wrapper, using your fingers to press filling

Ricotta and Pear Dim Sum in Pistachio and Apple Sauce

firmly inside, to form a tight cylinder (see page 44 for photos). Repeat process with remaining wrappers and pear mixture.

4. Prepare sauce: In a small pot, bring apple juice and wine to a boil over medium-high heat. Reduce heat to medium and cook, stirring occasionally, until mixture reduces to about one-third. Thicken with cornstarch, if necessary. Mix in nuts. Serve dim sum cool, with warm sauce on the side.

Part 2

Making Healthy Eating
a Habit

Quick Meals

Most of us don't have a lot of free time these days. We want everything as quickly as possible, including food. Whether it's at home in the morning or after work, or at work during a lunch break, the range of possibilities and the amount of time we have to prepare food is quite limited. When you're in a hurry, it's easy to eat ready-made frozen foods, fast foods, or sandwiches. However, these foods may be high in calories, salt, and fats, or insufficient to satisfy your hunger. As for quality, these foods are often mediocre at best. I recommend that you reduce your consumption of standard fast food options and try to prepare quicker and healthier meals both for eating at home and at work.

Though these techniques won't objectively add time to your busy day, and though it may still be easier and quicker to stop at a fast food outlet, try to make a small change in your priorities, and devote a little bit more time and attention to cooking. Sometimes, this may mean dedicating a few minutes in the morning or before you go to bed. However, like other changes, this will become easier as time goes on, and many goals that took a lot of energy and attention in the beginning will become increasingly easier to achieve over time.

Remember: if you succeed, you'll have more control over your blood glucose level and weight, and will enjoy food that tastes better. You'll also have another bonus to look forward to: many studies show people who eat healthy food are more alert than people who don't eat properly. Of course, there is also extensive information about the importance of eating breakfast every morning. Try to spend a bit more time preparing healthy foods. You'll likely find that the small amount of time you invest in eating properly returns to you, with interest, through increased effectiveness in your daily life, increased satisfaction from the food you eat, and from all that you invest in yourself.

ne. We get home after a busy day at work and have

ve want to do so as quickly and easily as possible.

volve very little cooking, and stir-frying certainly fits

nd cooking time. Cut an assortment of colorful, quick-

ips. Heat a few tablespoons of canola oil in a wok over

medium heat, and sau...   t and pepper. When the vegetables are cooked but still

crunchy, add a bit of soy sauce, and serve. To upgrade .   add freshly grated ginger, rice vinegar, chopped scallions,

sliced fruit, mirin, or a handful of nuts.

Add a protein-rich ingredient for a more satisfying stir-fry

Poultry, fish, or seafood are excellent stir-fry additions, since as they can be cooked in a relatively short time. Shrimp or thin strips of fish or chicken breast work very well. Cook this ingredient in the wok first, then remove it and put in some vegetables. When the vegetables are ready, add the pre-cooked seafood or fish along with soy sauce. Stir-fry everything for a few seconds before serving so that the flavors are integrated and absorbed.

Stir-fry can be served alongside a starch that was prepared in advance, or one that was made while the stir-fry cooked. You can also add a quick-cooking starch such as brown rice noodles to the stir-fry as it cooks. Add cooked noodles (see instructions on page 153) to the wok only after the vegetables are ready, along with the stir-fried protein-rich ingredient and soy sauce. You can also add leftover cooked starches such as brown rice or whole-wheat pasta at this stage.

Dishes similar to stir-fry can be found in cuisines around the world. For example, to give your stir-fry an Indian flavor, use curry and garam masala instead of ginger and soy sauce, and cut the vegetables into cubes rather than strips. This dish is delightful served with brown rice and lentils. If you use olive oil and whole-wheat pasta and include vegetables such as kohlrabi and leek, you'll create a Mediterranean-style dish. Cut the vegetables any way you like, mix them with your favorite selection of herbs and spices, and you'll create a variety of dishes that are quick and delicious.

Baby Salad Greens with Stir-Fried Shrimp and Avocado

The radishes and avocado in this stir-fry make it quite distinct. If you're tempted to try some substitutions, go right ahead; just be sure to choose ingredients that are suitable for quick cooking or can be eaten when only partially cooked, such as carrots, pepper, onions, cherry tomatoes, and a small portion of fruit. Don't use vegetables such as potatoes and sweet potatoes that require quite a long cooking time. Add ingredients in a descending order, from hardest to softest, so that none of them is over or undercooked.

INGREDIENTS

Serves 8 / Serving size: 1 cup

Marinade

- 1 tablespoon fresh lemon juice
- 3 tablespoons rice vinegar
- 1 tablespoon mirin
- 1 tablespoon low-sodium soy sauce
- ½ teaspoon unrefined sesame oil
- 1 teaspoon grated lime rind

Stir-fry

- 1 pound medium shrimp, peeled and deveined
- Pinch ground black pepper, or to taste
- Pinch Atlantic sea salt, or to taste
- 2 tablespoons unrefined canola oil
- 2 cloves garlic, peeled and sliced
- 1 teaspoon peeled and grated fresh ginger
- 4 small radishes, thinly sliced
- 2 medium carrots, peeled and cut into matchsticks
- 1 medium avocado, ripe but firm, peeled, pitted, and cut into ½-inch cubes

- 5 ounces (about 5 cups) baby salad greens
- 2 teaspoons sesame seeds, toasted (page 64), for garnish

Calories	142
Total fat	8 g
Calories as fat	51%
Saturated fat	1 g
Cholesterol	110 mg
Carbohydrates	4 g
Dietary fiber	2 g
Sodium	284 mg
Protein	13 g
Carbohydrate choices	**None**
Exchanges: 2 lean meat, ½ fat	

PREPARATION

1. Prepare marinade: In a medium bowl, combine lemon juice, vinegar, mirin, soy sauce, and sesame oil, until combined. Mix in lime rind and set aside.

2. Prepare stir-fry: Season shrimp with salt and pepper, tossing gently to coat. Place wok over medium heat, and add 2 tablespoons oil, swirling to coat. When oil is hot, add shrimp and stir-fry for 1 to 2 minutes, until shrimp are a pinkish color. Transfer shrimp to bowl with marinade, and stir to coat.

3. Return wok to heat, and add remaining 2 tablespoons oil, swirling to coat. When oil is hot, add garlic and ginger, and stir-fry for 30 seconds, until onion is golden brown. Add radishes and carrots, season with salt and pepper, and stir-fry for about 30 seconds.

4. Add avocado and shrimp with marinade, and stir-fry for a few seconds, just until mixed. To serve, place baby salad greens on a large serving dish and spoon stir-fry over top. Garnish with sesame seeds.

Whole-Wheat Pasta with Broccoli and Cherry Tomatoes, in Yogurt and Basil Sauce

Whole-Wheat Pasta with Broccoli and Cherry Tomatoes, in Yogurt and Basil Sauce

This stir-fry uses yogurt for flavor and has a distinct Mediterranean taste. The leftovers are great for serving at lunch the next day, so make a double batch from the start and set aside the extra before adding the yogurt. Bring the dish to work in a plastic container, and add yogurt and a bit of olive oil for flavor just before you sit down for lunch. To vary the recipe, replace the basil with thyme or the broccoli with asparagus or zucchini.

INGREDIENTS

Serves 8 / Serving size: 1 cup

- **7 ounces whole-wheat durum penne pasta**
- **2 tablespoons extra-virgin olive oil**
- **2 cloves garlic, chopped**
- **9 ounces broccoli florets, blanched (page 88)**
- **½ pound cherry tomatoes**
- **¼ teaspoon Atlantic sea salt, or to taste**
- **¼ teaspoon ground black pepper, or to taste**
- **½ cup plain, low-fat goat yogurt**
- **4 tablespoons coarsely chopped fresh basil**
- **¼ lemon, cut into small cubes**

Calories	142
Total fat	5 g
Calories as fat	32%
Saturated fat	1 g
Cholesterol	1 mg
Carbohydrates	23 g
Dietary fiber	2 g
Sodium	97 mg
Protein	5 g
Carbohydrate choices	**1½**

Exchanges:
1 starch, 1 vegetable, 1 fat

PREPARATION

1. Prepare pasta according to instructions on bag, and drain.

2. Place wok over medium-high heat, and add oil, swirling to coat. When oil is hot, add garlic and stir-fry for 30 seconds. Add broccoli, cherry tomatoes, salt, and pepper, and stir-fry for 3 minutes, until cherry tomato skins begin to crack.

3. Mix in pasta and yogurt, and stir-fry for 20 seconds. Remove from heat, and mix in basil and lemon cubes. Season with salt and pepper and serve.

LEFTOVERS

An excellent way of making fast meals is to use leftovers, and the best way to make sure you have leftovers is by making more of the recipe right from the start. Try to plan in advance when shopping for ingredients. This will make your cooking more cost effective, and save you time in the kitchen. If you prepare a dish with chicken breasts for dinner, prepare a few extra pieces to use in a stir-fry, salad, or sandwich the next day. If you're not the type to plan in advance, just make a bit more in the first place. I'm sure that over the next couple of days, you'll find something to do with the leftovers.

Leftover meat, poultry, seafood, or fish

As leftovers, these foods can be integrated into a fresh meal on another day. For example, chicken breast leftovers from an evening meal can be served with vegetables and Red Tahini Spread (page 108) in a sandwich the next day. You can also cut the leftover chicken breasts into cubes to add to a lunchtime salad, or slice them into strips to wrap with vegetables in a rice paper wrapper (see page 210). Diced chicken breast can be used to make hot meals, too. Add it to a stir-fry just before serving, mix it into the Grilled Eggplant with Tomato Sauce (page 96), or use it to replace the cheese in the Whole-Wheat Pasta with Zucchini, Basil, and Cheese (page 16). If these ideas haven't already convinced you to prepare a few extra chicken breasts, then the recipe on the facing page certainly will.

Leftover starches

Day-old cooked starches such as whole-wheat pasta or brown rice can be used to make a variety of meals. Leftover pasta can be added to a stir-fry (see previous page), mixed with vegetables to make a chilled salad, or topped with warm pasta sauce to make a hot meal. To reheat pasta that has been refrigerated overnight, place it in a colander and pour boiling water over it. Leftover rice that is two or three days old is perfect for making fried rice. Don't be turned off by the name of this dish. When prepared properly (see recipe on page 154) fried rice can be colorful, flavorful, and nutritious. You can make it with almost any type of vegetable you have in the refrigerator, as well as leftover cooked chicken or ground beef.

Leftover vegetables

Leftover cooked vegetables can be integrated into a new dish the next day or even several days later. If you are preparing vegetables for a specific recipe, for example, sautéed zucchini for the Whole-Wheat Pasta with Zucchini, Basil, and Cheese (page 16), prepare a bit more zucchini than you need for the recipe, and store the extra in the refrigerator. These vegetables can be used in cold salads, baked dishes, stir-fries, or antipasti. For example, the sautéed zucchini can replace the cucumber in the Avocado and Pearl Barley Salad (page 160), or the broccoli in the stir-fry on the previous page.

Schezuan Chicken and Brown Rice Noodle Salad

Rice noodles come in various widths and require very little preparation time. In this salad, I recommend using ¼-inch wide noodles, but if you are making a stir-fry, thinner ones are better. Brown rice noodles, available in an increasing number of health food stores and supermarkets, are an excellent type of whole-grain to add to your pantry. Cook them for just 2 minutes in boiling water, then serve with sauce. Although this recipe can be made with leftover chicken, I have included simple instructions for cooking fresh chicken with Schezuan pepper.

INGREDIENTS

Serves 10 / Serving size: ¾ cup

Chicken

- ½ cup dry white wine
- 1-inch piece fresh ginger, cut into slices
- 1 tablespoon chopped scallions
- 1 teaspoon Schezuan pepper
- 4 cups water
- 4 tablespoons vegetable stock (page 63), optional
- Pinch Atlantic sea salt
- Pinch ground black pepper
- Two 4-ounce chicken breasts

Sauce

- 1½ tablespoons unrefined sesame oil
- 1½ tablespoons unrefined canola oil
- 4 tablespoons low-sodium soy sauce
- 1 tablespoon black rice vinegar
- 1 tablespoon mirin
- 1 small red chili pepper, seeded and chopped
- 1 clove garlic, crushed
- 1½ tablespoons chopped scallions

Salad

- 1 cup cooked wide brown rice noodles
- 6 medium Lebanese cucumbers, cut into matchsticks
- 2 tablespoons chopped scallions, for garnish

Calories	103
Total fat	5 g
Calories as fat	44%
Saturated fat	1 g
Cholesterol	13 mg
Carbohydrates	7 g
Dietary fiber	1 g
Sodium	289 mg
Protein	6 g
Carbohydrate choices	½

Exchanges:
1 lean meat, ½ starch, ½ fat

PREPARATION

1. Prepare chicken: In a small pot over medium-high heat, combine wine, ginger, scallions, Schezuan pepper, water, stock, salt, and pepper. Bring to a boil. Add chicken breasts and cook for 7 minutes, until completely cooked. Remove chicken, refrigerate until cool, then slice.

2. Prepare sauce: In a jar with a tight-fitting lid, combine sesame oil, canola oil, soy sauce, rice vinegar, and mirin. Add chili pepper, garlic, and scallions, and shake until combined.

3. Prepare salad: In a large bowl, mix together rice noodles, cucumbers, and chicken. Pour in sauce and toss until evenly coated.

Fried Rice with Cashews and Scallions

This delicious dish makes the most of rice that has been in the refrigerator for a few days. For best results, keep a few general principles in mind. First, make sure the rice is dry, preferably a couple of days old. Second, when adding the rice to the sautéed onion and garlic, mix it well, making an effort to separate any chunks of rice into individual grains. Do this patiently and thoroughly before you add the egg. Third, when you add the beaten egg, mix it quickly into the rice, since your goal is to coat every grain before the egg solidifies.

INGREDIENTS

Serves 8 / Serving size: ¾ cup

- 2 tablespoons unrefined canola oil
- ½ medium onion, finely chopped
- 4 garlic cloves, crushed
- ½ medium carrot, cut into ¼-inch cubes
- ½ medium red bell pepper, cut into ¼-inch cubes
- Pinch Atlantic sea salt, or to taste
- Pinch ground black pepper, or to taste
- 4 cups cooked brown rice (2 or 3-days old, if possible)
- 1 large egg, beaten
- 1 tablespoon low-sodium soy sauce
- ½ tablespoon fish sauce
- ½ tablespoon clam sauce
- 4 tablespoons thinly chopped scallions
- 2 tablespoons coarsely chopped raw cashews

Calories	173
Total fat	6 g
Calories as fat	31%
Saturated fat	1 g
Cholesterol	27 mg
Carbohydrates	26 g
Dietary fiber	2 g
Sodium	473 mg
Protein	4 g
Carbohydrate choices	**1½**
Exchanges: 1½ starch, 1 fat	

PREPARATION

1. In a large frying pan, heat oil over medium-high heat. Add onion and garlic and sauté for about 3 minutes, until onion is golden brown. Add carrot, red pepper, salt, and pepper, and sauté while stirring for another 3 minutes.

2. Add rice and continue to cook, stirring constantly, to separate all of the grains. Add egg to mixture, stirring constantly and quickly so that the egg coats every grain. Add soy sauce, fish sauce, and clam sauce. Sauté until dry, then mix in scallions and cashews. Add salt and pepper to taste. Serve with soy sauce on the side.

FISH: MAKE THE MOST OF IT

When preparing quick meals, cutting up vegetables and serving them with a starch is relatively easy. Finding a quick-cooking, protein-rich ingredient can be a bit more challenging. Many people solve this problem by eating quick meals that don't include protein, or by adding processed foods that contain protein but don't contribute to good health, such as cold cuts, burgers, or hot dogs.

Fish, both whole and fillet, is an ideal ingredient that provides high-quality protein without much time and effort on your part. Buy fresh fish when possible; cook some of it right away, and store the rest in your freezer for up to several weeks.

For an easy, flavorful, and nutritious meal, place fresh or frozen and thawed fish in a pan, and top with a marinade made from fresh herbs, lemon juice, and white wine, such as in the recipe on the next page. Bake the fish at 350°F for about 8 minutes, and you'll have a dinner. You'll know the fish is ready to eat when it flakes easily with a fork. Fish cooks quickly, so take care not to overcook.

If you don't have any fresh herbs or lemon juice on hand, simply wrap the fish in parchment paper and aluminum foil, and bake as instructed above. A good quality fish will be delicious without any marinade, and can be seasoned with a bit of salt and pepper before serving. By the way, the best way of defrosting fish for an evening meal is by transferring it from the freezer to the refrigerator in the morning, so that it is defrosted and ready to cook by evening.

Want to be even more efficient? Cook a double quantity of fish. Eat the leftovers within one or two days, or freeze them for another time. If you plan on freezing the fish, remove it from the oven about 3 minutes before it is fully cooked. To defrost the cooked fish, place it directly in a preheated oven to complete the baking process. If you bake the fish completely the first time, it could dry out when reheated after freezing.

Baked Trout with Fresh Herbs and White Wine

Most of us eat with our eyes as much as our stomachs. This means we enjoy seeing a serving that really fills our plate. Here is a technique you can use to fill your plate with a seemingly large portion of fish: rather than buying fish fillets with tails and heads removed, buy a whole fish that has been halved lengthwise. Prepare the fish as if it were a fillet, and when you serve it, place an entire fish half on each plate. The serving will look larger than otherwise and much more impressive.

Calories	155
Total fat	6 g
Calories as fat	35%
Saturated fat	1 g
Cholesterol	49 mg
Carbohydrates	3 g
Dietary fiber	0 g
Sodium	125 mg
Protein	18 g
Carbohydrate choices	**None**

Exchanges: 2 lean meat

INGREDIENTS

Serves 8 / Serving size: ½ fish

- **8 tablespoons fresh lemon juice**
- **1 cup dry white wine**
- **1 cup chopped mixed fresh herbs (basil, parsley, chives, sage, dill, thyme)**
- **1 leek, thinly sliced**
- **4 fresh whole 13-ounce trouts, halved lengthwise**
- **¼ teaspoon Atlantic sea salt**
- **¼ teaspoon ground black pepper**
- **2 whole lemons, cut into wedges**

PREPARATION

1. Preheat oven to 350°F. In a small bowl, mix together lemon juice and wine. Stir in mixed herbs and leek.

2. Place fish, skin-side down, in a baking dish. Sprinkle with salt and pepper, then pour wine mixture on top. Bake for 10 minutes, or until fish flakes easily with a fork. Serve with lemon wedges.

TIP *If you have the time, enhance this dish by letting the fish marinade in the wine mixture for 30 minutes before baking.*

COLD FOOD ON THE GO

For many people, it's hard to feel satisfied after eating an ordinary sandwich. This is because many sandwiches (even ones that include vegetable-rich spreads) contain only a minimal amount of vegetables and proteins. A sandwich that is made up almost entirely of starch won't leave you feeling satisfied for a long time, since it's hard to be satisfied eating mostly starch. An excellent way to make your meals more satisfying, even when you are preparing them in the morning to take to work, is by enriching them with vegetables and proteins. A great way to do this is to replace sandwiches with salads that include whole grains, such as the one the next page. **With fewer carbohydrates than an ordinary sandwich, you can make a large salad that includes whole grains and vegetables and is much more satisfying.**

Salads that include whole grains travel very well if they are made with the right ingredients and stored properly. In fact, salads made with hard vegetables that aren't too watery will even improve over time. Stored in an airtight plastic container and refrigerated, they can be packed in the morning (or even the night before) and will stay fresh and flavorful until lunchtime.

When making salads that contain whole grains, be flexible with your substitutions. For example, the pearl barley used in the recipe on page 160 can be replaced with a leftover starch that was served at dinner the night before. It can also be replaced with easy-to-prepare starches such as bulgur or whole-wheat couscous. The cucumbers and mushrooms can be replaced with peppers, sautéed zucchini, broccoli, radishes, or any other vegetables that are eaten raw or were sautéed in advance. Add some fresh herbs and you have a delicious salad that is ideal for taking to work.

If you still feel like having a sandwich every now and again, bring along a vegetable salad from home. Eating salad alongside a sandwich will make your meal more attractive and more satisfying. Since you already have a sandwich, the salad you bring from home doesn't need to include starch, but do select hard vegetables that will stay crispy until lunchtime. Refrain from adding juicy vegetables such as tomatoes, since they can make your salad soggy over time.

Even if you purchase a sandwich at work, you can still enhance your meal by bringing from home a simple salad, such as the one on the next page. If you find the sandwiches sold at work are too big for a sensible single serving, split it (and your homemade salad) with a coworker. If this becomes a lunchtime ritual, you can even start sharing the salad duties with your coworker. This means enjoying healthier lunches at the office every day, and preparing salad only half of the time.

Cucumber and Parsley Root Salad

Cucumber and Parsley Root Salad

To my delight, root vegetables are becoming increasingly popular, both in hot dishes (see the Beef Shoulder in Fresh Oregano and Root Vegetable Sauce, page 77) and cold dishes such as this one. Raw root vegetables that are thinly sliced add a great flavor and slightly rough texture to salads. In the recipe below, the parsley root is chopped with a food processor, but you can also grate it, as in the Green Salad with Chickpea Seed Sprouts and Root Vegetables (page 169), or cut it into very small cubes. For variety, replace the parsley root with celery root, or the chives with dill.

Calories	42
Total fat	3 g
Calories as fat	22%
Saturated fat	1 g
Cholesterol	0 mg
Carbohydrates	3 g
Dietary fiber	1 g
Sodium	127 mg
Protein	0 mg
Carbohydrate choices	**None**

Exchanges: ½ fat

INGREDIENTS

Serves 5 / Serving size: ½ cup

- 1 medium parsley root, peeled
- 2 cloves garlic, crushed
- 8 tablespoons coarsely chopped chives
- 3 medium Lebanese cucumbers, peeled, seeded, and cut into small cubes
- 1 tablespoon fresh lemon juice

- 1 tablespoon extra-virgin olive oil
- 1 teaspoon seeded and chopped red hot chili pepper
- Pinch Atlantic sea salt
- Pinch ground black pepper

PREPARATION

1. In a food processor, process parsley root, garlic, and chives until finely chopped. Transfer to a large bowl.

2. Add cucumbers, lemon juice, oil, and chili pepper, and mix to combine. Let sit for a few minutes, to allow flavors to blend.

3. Season with salt and pepper before serving.

Avocado and Pearl Barley Salad

This salad requires a couple of small hard cucumbers that do not contain much liquid. If they are liquidy, slice them in half lengthwise and remove the seeds with a teaspoon. Cut the crispy flesh into cubes and add these to your salad. The cucumber's flavor will be retained and the texture of the salad will stay crispy. For variation, replace the pearl barley with leftover brown rice, or make fresh bulgur or whole-wheat couscous.

INGREDIENTS

Serves 8 / Serving size: ¾ cup

- 1 cup pearl barley, rinsed and drained
- 2 tablespoons vegetable stock (page 63), optional
- 2 cups water
- Pinch Atlantic sea salt, or to taste
- 2 medium Lebanese cucumbers, seeded and cut into cubes
- 1 cup diced button mushrooms
- 1 medium avocado, ripe but firm, peeled, pitted, and cut into ½-inch cubes
- 3 tablespoons chopped fresh thyme
- ½ cup chopped fresh parsley
- 4 tablespoons extra-virgin olive oil
- 4 tablespoons fresh lemon juice
- 1 clove garlic, crushed
- 1 teaspoon honey
- Pinch ground black pepper

Calories	198
Total fat	11 g
Calories as fat	50%
Saturated fat	2 g
Cholesterol	0 mg
Carbohydrates	23 g
Dietary fiber	6 g
Sodium	80 mg
Protein	4 g
Carbohydrate choices	**1½**

Exchanges: 1½ starch, 2 fat

PREPARATION

1. In a small pot over high heat, bring pearl barley, stock, water, and salt to a boil. Reduce heat to low and cook for 20 minutes, or until liquid is absorbed. Rinse with cold water, drain, and transfer to a medium bowl.
2. Add cucumbers, mushrooms, avocado, thyme, and parsley, and toss together until combined. Add oil, lemon juice, garlic, and honey, and mix until combined. Let sit for 30 minutes for flavors to blend. Season with salt and pepper before serving.

USING FROZEN INGREDIENTS

To make your kitchen conducive to quick cooking, I suggest keeping a variety of essential ingredients in your freezer. You may not have thought of the two suggestions below, which can help make your cooking easier, tastier, and healthier.

Fruit

Frozen vegetables have been a freezer staple for years, but another item I recommend keeping in your freezer is fruit. Stocking your freezer with fruit is simple: when you have some extra room in your freezer, or when your favorite fruit is in season, simply wash or peel the fruit (as required), place it in a freezer-safe storage bag, and freeze it for up to three months. Frozen fruit can be used to make chilled beverages and desserts. Put frozen fruit in a blender with water or milk to make a refreshing shake; combine it with yogurt to make a satisfying fruit smoothie. You can also process frozen fruit in a blender to make chilled fruit soups (see Cherry Minestrone, page 123) or mash it with a fork to make granita (see Melon Salad with Plum Granita and Mint page 225).

Pureed frozen bananas make a deliciously creamy frozen dessert. Ripe bananas are an excellent fruit to freeze. Process frozen bananas in a food processor, without any added cream or sugar, and you'll have a creamy, airy dish with a texture similar to ice cream. Peel the bananas, cut them into quarters, and then place the quarters in a freezer-safe storage bag. Bananas can be frozen for up to two months. When you want a sweet treat or simple dessert, just process them in a food processor until smooth and serve. If the frozen bananas are too hard to process, let them thaw on the counter for a minute or two only before putting them in the food processor. If your food processor is unable to process the bananas, add 1 or 2 tablespoons of boiling water.

Tofu

The texture of some products changes when frozen, and tofu is one of them. Frozen and thawed tofu is spongier and more absorbent than fresh tofu, so it really absorbs flavors. This change is an advantage if you plan to cook the tofu with sauce or as a stew. It's not recommended for tofu you want to sauté or to use in creams or spreads.

Keep cubes of frozen tofu in your freezer, and add them to dishes with sauce. When you want to make a dish that contains tofu with sauce, simply defrost the tofu before using it. Its texture will be more absorbent and its taste richer. To reduce the thawing time, cut the tofu into cubes before freezing it.

Tofu isn't just for vegetarians—add it to meat dishes! Tofu is high in protein, so it is often considered a meat replacement in Western kitchens. In Asian cuisine, tofu is often used in combination with meat. It absorbs the meat's flavors, enhancing the taste of the dish. To discover this for yourself, try the Beef and Tofu with Asian Sauce on facing page.

I recommend adding tofu to any red meat dish that contains liquids. You'll increase the amount of calcium in the dish, and often reduce energy density as well. Many recipes in this book are perfect for adding tofu. These include the Beef Stew with String Beans in Beer and Dried Fruit (page 87), the Beef Shoulder in Fresh Oregano and Root Vegetable Sauce (page 77), and even the Whole-Wheat Spaghetti with Roasted Vegetable Bolognaise (page 196).

Beef and Tofu with Asian Sauce

Though soft tofu is recommended for making sauces, hard tofu is generally best for sautéing. But even hard tofu is relatively soft, so be careful when you mix it into this dish, and try to handle it as little as possible. Try mixing the dish by simply rotating the wok or pan, since stirring them with a spoon might break the tofu into smaller pieces.

INGREDIENTS

Serves 8 / Serving size: ¾ cup

- 2 tablespoons unrefined canola oil
- 1 clove garlic, crushed
- ½ teaspoon peeled and chopped fresh ginger
- ½ pound lean ground round
- Pinch Atlantic sea salt, or to taste
- Pinch ground black pepper, or to taste
- ½ teaspoon seeded and chopped red hot chili pepper
- 2 tablespoons low-sodium soy sauce
- 1 tablespoon mirin
- 1 tablespoon vegetable stock (page 63), optional
- 1 cup water
- ½ pound firm tofu, frozen and thawed, cut into ½-inch cubes
- 1 teaspoon unrefined sesame oil
- 2 tablespoons finely chopped scallions

Calories	130
Total fat	9 g
Calories as fat	62%
Saturated fat	2 g
Cholesterol	19 mg
Carbohydrates	2 g
Dietary fiber	1 g
Sodium	229 mg
Protein	10 g
Carbohydrate choices	**None**

Exchanges: 1 lean meat, 1 fat

PREPARATION

1. Place wok over medium heat, and add canola oil, swirling to coat. When oil is hot, add garlic and ginger and sauté for 3 minutes, until brown. Add beef, salt, and pepper. Sauté over medium-high heat for 3 minutes. Reduce heat to medium-low, and cook, stirring occasionally, for 15 minutes, to allow liquid to evaporate. Add hot pepper, soy sauce, and mirin, and cook for 3 minutes, until mixed.

2. Add stock, water, and tofu, and cook for about 10 minutes, until liquid evaporates almost completely and mixture is almost dry. Add salt and pepper, to taste. Drizzle with sesame oil, and sprinkle scallions over top. Serve with a starch such as brown rice.

Banana Granita with Grape Chips

Grapes contain a relatively large amount of sugar, so they won't freeze completely and can be eaten directly from the freezer without any defrosting. Use grapes sparingly, or serve them to children as a naturally sweet snack. To prepare grapes for freezing, just remove the stems, wash and dry them, and place them in a freezer-safe storage bag. Frozen grapes can be stored from one summer to the next.

Calories	78
Total fat	0 g
Calories as fat	0%
Saturated fat	0 g
Cholesterol	0 mg
Carbohydrates	18 g
Dietary fiber	2 g
Sodium	1 mg
Protein	1 g
Carbohydrate choices	**1**
Exchanges: 1 fruit	

INGREDIENTS

Serves 8 / Serving size: 2 scoops

- **6 small bananas, peeled, quartered, and frozen**
- **1 tablespoon unsweetened date honey**
- **4 seedless grapes, frozen**

PREPARATION

1. Remove bananas from freezer and let sit at room temperature for 1 to 2 minutes. Transfer to a food processor, add date honey, and process until smooth.

2. Remove grapes from freezer and cut into halves, then slice thinly. To serve, scoop pureed bananas with a small ice cream scoop and top with grape slices.

Banana Granita with Grape Chips

FREEZING MEALS

Be resourceful and freeze the food you cook—vegetable bakes, stews, and more. You can put a hot meal on the table just minutes after you come home from work, or you can leave defrosting and heating instructions for your kids or spouse. Try to keep one or two containers of homemade food in your freezer at all times.

Use frozen stews to upgrade the food you bring to work

Another excellent way to use frozen dishes is to bring them to work. Many offices have a small refrigerator and microwave. Bring frozen soup, stew, or a vegetable bake to work with you, store it in the refrigerator until lunchtime, and heat it up when you're hungry. You can prepare dishes especially for this purpose or simply use leftovers from previous meals. All you have to do in the morning is remove the plastic container from the freezer and bring it with you to work.

The best dishes for bringing to work are those that have a relatively large quantity of liquids, like the stew on the facing page, so that heating them up in the microwave doesn't cause them to dry out. If you don't have a refrigerator at work, bring your frozen foods in an insulated lunch bag. If the frozen dish you bring doesn't contain starch, add a starchy ingredient to your meal. For example, if you have frozen vegetable soup, bring along a piece of whole-wheat bread. If you have frozen vegetable stew, bring along cooked brown rice or whole-wheat pasta, and heat up the starch by mixing it with the hot vegetable stew. You can also keep a bag of bulgur or whole-wheat couscous at work. All you need to prepare these starches is some boiling water and a bowl with a lid (see page 20).

Persian Beef Stew with Quince and Pomegranate Seeds

I particularly like this recipe, since it includes quince and black lemons. If you have trouble finding these ingredients, you can use apples instead of quince or regular lemons instead of black lemons. Black lemons are a distinctive spice in Persian cuisine, and any new spice on your spice rack is a cause for celebration. Made by drying them underground using coals, black lemons have a delicately sour taste that is especially suited to meat, vegetable, poultry, and fish dishes. Crack open whole black lemons or grind them. Remove the seeds before grinding to prevent a bitter flavor.

INGREDIENTS

Serves 10 / Serving size: 1 cup

- 2 pounds lean beef round cubes
- Pinch Atlantic sea salt, or to taste
- ¼ teaspoon ground black pepper, or to taste
- 2 tablespoons unrefined canola oil
- 1 medium onion, finely chopped
- 3 cloves garlic, crushed
- 2 medium tomatoes, chopped
- 2 tablespoons vegetable stock (page 63), optional
- 2 cups water
- 4 prunes, pitted
- 2 medium quinces, peeled, seeded, and cut into quarters
- 2 tablespoons fresh lemon juice
- ¼ teaspoon sweet paprika
- Pinch ground nutmeg
- 2 black lemons, cracked open
- 1 tablespoon unsweetened pomegranate juice concentrate
- 1 tablespoon pomegranate seeds, for garnish

TIP *In this recipe, quince is cooked in a covered pot with a relatively small amount of liquid. If the flavor of the dish isn't rich enough at the end of the cooking period, remove the lid and simmer for a few more minutes.*

Calories	178
Total fat	8 g
Calories as fat	40%
Saturated fat	2 g
Cholesterol	45 mg
Carbohydrates	10 g
Dietary fiber	2 g
Sodium	113 mg
Protein	10 g
Carbohydrate choices	½

Exchanges:
2 lean meat, 2 vegetable, ½ fat

PREPARATION

1. Season beef with salt and pepper. In a large pot, heat oil over medium-high heat until hot enough for frying. Add beef and sear on all sides. Add onion and garlic and sauté for 3 minutes. Add tomatoes and cook for another minute.

2. Add stock, water, and prunes and bring to a boil. Reduce heat to simmer, cover, and cook for 45 minutes. Add quince, lemon juice, paprika, nutmeg, black lemons, and pomegranate juice concentrate, cover and cook for another 45 minutes. Add salt and pepper to taste, and mix in pomegranate seeds just before serving.

USING SEED SPROUTS FOR QUICK COOKING

Seed sprouts are legumes that have undergone a short sprouting process. Seed sprouts can be found in the vegetable section of many grocery stores and are easy to grow at home using a wide variety of legumes. The next time you soak raw chickpeas overnight for cooking, increase the quantity and use some for making seed sprouts. Chickpea been sprouts are convenient to use and excellent for upgrading salads and cooked dishes. The sprouting process changes the nutritional content of legumes, and they take on the value of vegetables. Seed sprouts contain more vitamins than legumes and less protein and carbohydrates. Their caloric content is also considerably lower.

Make a salad without using a knife

Unlike legumes, seed sprouts don't need to be cooked. With a handful of seed sprouts and some baby salad greens, you can make a salad without using a knife. This means you can prepare salad in very little time and won't have any mess to clean up afterward. Seed sprouts can also be added to any dish that ordinarily contains legumes. They have a more delicate texture and shorter preparation time than legume, and are easier to digest.

How to make seed sprouts

All you need is some room in your pantry and some legumes. Every type of raw legume can sprout as long as it is in its natural form and hasn't been cut or split. The process is simple: let the legumes soak for 10 to 24 hours, then spread them in a layer on a large plate, tray, or colander. Make sure the layer is no more than a couple of legumes thick. Cover the legumes with a damp kitchen towel or with a plastic wrap that is pierced in a few spots with a fork, and place them in a dark place. Moisten the legumes twice a day, once in the morning and once in the evening, for the next two or three days. You'll know the seed sprouts are ready when a tiny sprout appears on each legume. At this stage, the seed sprouts are ready to eat. They can be eaten immediately or stored in the refrigerator for several days.

How to make seed sprouting a routine

Even if you aren't soaking legumes for cooking, it doesn't take very much time to fill a bowl with water, soak a few legumes such as chickpeas or lentils, and spread them on a tray. This is all it really takes to prepare seed sprouts, and once you do it a few times, you'll easily get into the routine. Some stores even sell special containers for storing legumes during the sprouting process.

Green Salad with Chickpea Seed Sprouts and Root Vegetables

I like making this salad with chickpea seed sprouts, but you can use any type of seed sprout you like. If you buy seed sprouts at the supermarket, look for a package with a mixed selection. If the texture of uncooked seed sprouts is too crunchy for you, try blanching the sprouts briefly, or steam them for 1 minute before adding them to the salad.

Calories	77
Total fat	7 g
Calories as fat	22%
Saturated fat	1 g
Cholesterol	0 mg
Carbohydrates	4 g
Dietary fiber	1 g
Sodium	61 mg
Protein	1 g
Carbohydrate choices	**None**

Exchanges: 1 vegetable, 1½ fat

INGREDIENTS

Serves 12 / Serving size: ¾ cup

Salad

- ½ pound chickpea seed sprouts
- 2 medium carrots, coarsely grated
- 1 medium kohlrabi, peeled and coarsely grated
- 5 ounces (about 5 cups) baby salad greens

- 1 tablespoon honey
- ½ teaspoon ground cumin
- ¼ teaspoon Atlantic sea salt
- ½ teaspoon ground black pepper
- 4 tablespoons chopped chives

Dressing

- 6 tablespoons extra-virgin olive oil
- 6 tablespoons white wine vinegar

PREPARATION

1. Prepare salad: In a large salad bowl, combine seed sprouts, carrots, kohlrabi, and baby salad greens.

2. Prepare dressing: In a mixing jar, mix together oil, vinegar, honey, cumin, salt, pepper, and chives and mix well. Pour dressing over salad and toss to coat before serving.

Family Meals

Try to incorporate family meals into your schedule as often as possible. Even if those occur only on the weekend, meals are an excellent opportunity to spend quality time with your family and friends. Family meals are also the best way to set a healthy example for your children. Studies show that children learn many food habits from watching their parents. Children who don't like to eat vegetables may gradually change their ways if they see the adults at the table relishing a tasty salad or veggie side dish.

In Europe, a traditional family meal can last two hours or longer. This may be a bit too long for you, but you should still try to extend your family meal if possible, chatting with the people around the table. You'll likely find that this is an excellent time to relax after a busy day. During a leisurely meal such as this, you may even discover that you require less food to be satisfied. In this chapter, you'll find ideas and examples of recipes to help you build family meals.

Family meals, especially when they are held on the weekend, are an excellent opportunity to prepare dishes that require a bit more preparation time, such as cooking wheat grains or roasting lean beef. These meals are often planned in advance; this means you have the chance to go shopping for specific ingredients and do some of the preparation in advance, like soaking legumes or brown rice.

When shopping for family meals, buy vegetables that will stay fresh for the following week. While cooking, take advantage of the fact that you are already in the kitchen to make sauces, spreads, and other dishes that can be used as bases for meals in the coming days. Select bases that don't require a lot of attention (roasted eggplants or peppers, vegetable stock) and can be prepared while other food is cooling. Here are a few ideas to get you started:

- When you buy fresh fish for the Sea Bass Ceviche with Bermuda Onion and Sumac (page 174), buy a few extra fish fillets. Put the extra fish in a baking pan with a bit of lemon juice, white wine, and fresh herbs, or wrap it in parchment paper and aluminum foil. Bake it in the oven (which will already be on) for about 10 minutes, and you'll have baked fish that can be served during the week (for more ideas see page 155).

- Make a double batch of the Indian-Style Chilled Yogurt Soup (page 173) and refrigerate half, which you can eat throughout the week as a satisfying breakfast or with whole-grain bread and salad for a quick lunch. You can also use this dish as a marinade for the additional fish you purchased for the ceviche. Let the fish marinate in the mixture for about 30 minutes before baking.

- Make a double portion of millet when preparing Mediterranean Ratatouille with Millet (page 177) and store it in the refrigerator. Later in the week, mix the millet into cold salads, which you can bring to work, or use it as the starch for a stir-fry.

- You can also double the ratatouille only in this recipe. Because ratatouille is moist, it is ideal for freezing and can be used later as a side dish, a sauce for fish or chicken, the base for a hearty omelet, or a crepe filling (see page 203).

- Prepare extra Grilled Eggplant Moussaka with Roasted Pepper Cream (page 178). It can be stored in plastic containers in your refrigerator or freezer and served during the week with millet or a salad. You can also bring moussaka to work and heat it in the microwave at lunchtime. Moussaka has enough liquid to keep it from drying out when reheated.

- Make extra cookies and sauce when you make the Almond Cookies in Apricot Sauce (page 184). The cookies can be eaten during the week instead of store-bought cookies or other sweets. Use the extra sauce to add a sweet touch to many other dishes, as recommended on page 182.

These are just a few of many, many options. Just remember that the goal isn't to eat the same food all week, but to use the dishes you prepare for family meals as a base for future meals. With just a little extra work when you're already in the kitchen, you can prepare delicious and healthy food for an entire week.

APPETIZERS AND SOUPS

Starting with an appetizer can help you eat less and feel satisfied

Appetizers are excellent for people who find it hard to be satisfied with a meal if they don't fill their plates. When making family meals, try to add interesting vegetarian appetizers that don't contain starches, or serve dishes that contain a combination of vegetables along with lean meats, poultry, or fish (unless you are restricted in the amount of protein you can eat for health reasons). For example, try serving the Chicken Medallions Stuffed with Pumpkin and Spinach with Tomato and Basil Sauce (page 40), the Swiss Chard Dim Sum with Sea Bass and Water Chestnuts (page 104), or the Spinach Pastry with Goat Cheese and Smoked Salmon (page 103). All of these dishes are excellent and unique appetizers that will upgrade your meal and help people at the table feel satisfied with fewer calories and less carbohydrate. See recipe on page 174 for another recommended appetizer.

Serve soup as a satisfying appetizer

The meal will be more enjoyable, last longer, and provide greater satisfaction with fewer calories and carbohydrates.

There is a technique that can significantly reduce the time you spend preparing meals with several courses. It is taught in every cooking school but rarely used in home kitchens. Before you start cooking, take a few minutes to organize your work. Think about the order in which dishes need to cook and bake to maximize your use of the stove and oven (which can become a bottleneck in your workflow). Check each recipe in advance. Some may use the same ingredients. For example, if you need chopped onions in more than one recipe, figure out how many chopped onions you'll need altogether, and prepare all the onions at once.

You'll be amazed to discover how much time you can save by spending just a couple of minutes looking over the recipes in advance. In fact, it may turn out that most of the ingredients you need for an appetizer can be prepared as you are preparing the main course. If this allows you to add an appetizer to every family meal, you'll savor the results, as will the people who are dining with you.

Indian-Style Chilled Yogurt Soup

This recipe demonstrates how to use yogurt as a base for soup. It is inspired by a classic French recipe, and the use of Indian spices makes it an interesting variation. I highly recommend giving this soup your own twist. The combination of yogurt, herbs, garlic, lemon, stock, and spices imbues the soup with a particularly rich flavor, so very little salt is necessary. Goat cheese and goat yogurt, both of which are used in this recipe, have rather strong flavors. If you prefer milder flavors, use yogurt and cheese made with lamb's or cow's milk.

Calories	164
Total fat	8 g
Calories as fat	44%
Saturated fat	5 g
Cholesterol	31 mg
Carbohydrates	8 g
Dietary fiber	0 g
Sodium	407 mg
Protein	15 g
Carbohydrate choices	½

Exchanges: 1 milk, 1½ fat

INGREDIENTS

Serves 6 / Serving size: 1 cup

- 1 cup water
- 1 tablespoon vegetable stock (page 63), optional
- 17 ounces plain, low-fat goat yogurt
- 8½ ounces soft (spreadable), low-fat goat cheese
- 2 teaspoons cumin seeds, toasted and ground (page 64)
- 2 teaspoons coriander seeds, toasted and ground (page 64)
- 2 tablespoons fresh lemon juice
- 2 medium Lebanese cucumbers, grated
- 4 cloves garlic, crushed
- 4 tablespoons chopped fresh mint
- Pinch Atlantic sea salt
- Pinch ground black pepper

PREPARATION

1. In a medium bowl, mix together water, stock, yogurt, and cheese. Add cumin, coriander, lemon juice, cucumbers, garlic, and mint.

2. Cover and refrigerate for at least 1 hour, to allow flavors to blend. Season with salt and pepper and serve.

Sea Bass Ceviche with Bermuda Onion and Sumac

Ceviche is a Central American dish that involves cutting fish into small pieces and "cooking" it with vinegar rather than heat. Because cooking in vinegar is a delicate process, only fresh, high-quality fish should be used to make ceviche. For variety, you can replace the sea bass with another white fish fillet, such as corvina, or non-white varieties, like salmon and tuna. In this recipe, lemon juice is used as vinegar.

Calories	116
Total fat	2 g
Calories as fat	16%
Saturated fat	1 g
Cholesterol	45 mg
Carbohydrates	3 g
Dietary fiber	0 g
Sodium	77 mg
Protein	20 g
Carbohydrate choices	**None**

Exchanges: 2 lean meat

INGREDIENTS

Serves 8 / Serving size: ½ cup

- 10 ounces fresh sea bass fillet, skinless and cut into thin slices or ½-inch squares
- 4 tablespoons finely chopped Bermuda onion
- 6 tablespoons fresh lemon juice
- 1 tablespoon seeded and finely chopped green chili pepper
- 4 tablespoons chopped fresh cilantro
- 2 tomatoes, seeded and finely cubed
- ¼ teaspoon Atlantic sea salt
- ¼ teaspoon ground black pepper
- ½ teaspoon sumac

PREPARATION

1. In a large non-reactive bowl, place fish, onion, lemon juice, hot pepper, and cilantro. Carefully mix to coat, then cover with plastic wrap and refrigerate for 2 hours.

2. Add tomatoes, then season with salt and pepper. Arrange mixture on a serving dish, sprinkle with sumac, and serve.

Sea Bass Ceviche with Bermuda Onion and Sumac

TIP *Balsamic vinegar can be used as vinegar for a Mediterranean touch, or use rice vinegar for an Asian flavor. The herbs can be replaced with your favorite variety, and the vegetables can be replaced with roasted zucchini, kohlrabi, turnip, or any vegetables that complement a sour flavor. If you plan to add vegetables that contain a lot of water such as tomatoes, do so just before serving. Try serving ceviche on a bed of Turnip and Kohlrabi Cubes with Olive Oil and Sumac (page 228), Grilled Zucchini in Mint Vinaigrette (page 230), or on bean or beet sprouts.*

THE MAIN COURSE

Serving Protein

Family meals are an excellent time for making recipes that take a bit more time to prepare and contain more vegetables and less carbohydrate, salt, and fat. Take lasagna, for example, a dish loved by children and adults alike. Moussaka (see recipe on page 178) is a Greek dish that resembles lasagna but contains roasted vegetables rather than lasagna noodles. Just as roasted eggplant can be used instead of pasta to make ravioli (page 102), roasted vegetables can replace lasagna noodles to make a dish that is very rich in vegetables. The preparation may take a bit longer, but the result is delicious and contains fewer calories and carbohydrates. In fact, one serving of moussaka contains two vegetable servings. Served with a salad and the ratatouille it fulfills almost all your vegetable requirements for the day in a single meal. Take advantage of your time in the kitchen to prepare meat, poultry, seafood, or fish dishes that take a bit more time, but are rich in vegetables.

Warm side dishes

Variety is important when it comes to enjoying food. Quick-cooking whole grains such as bulgur and whole-wheat couscous are excellent, but if you rely only on these when you cook, you and your family may grow bored. Whole grains that require longer cooking times don't necessarily require a lot of attention; they just spend more time in the pot. When you cook a family meal, you are already in the kitchen for a relatively long time, so this is an excellent time to prepare whole-grains starches that need longer to cook, such as brown rice or millet. All you have to do is put the starch in a pot with water, bring it to a boil, and let it cook while you go about preparing the rest of the meal (which will, hopefully, include a warm vegetable side dish).

Salads

Green salads don't have to be based on lettuce. In fact, you can make a delightful green salad based on fresh herbs. Herb leaves used to make salads should be as fresh as possible, and you should add them to the list when you shop for family meals. Note that not all refrigerated vegetables stay fresh for the same lengths of time. While baby salad leaves and lettuce can be kept for a couple of days and retain their freshness, fresh herbs wilt quickly and lose flavor, making them less useful as a main salad ingredient. Parsley that is four days old can be chopped and added to salad or used to cook sauces or soups, but it isn't fresh enough to serve as whole sprigs in a salad. If you only go shopping once a week, use the ingredients you buy wisely.

Mediterranean Ratatouille with Millet

The principle of this dish is simple: a variety of seasonal vegetables with crispy skin are cut into cubes, then cooked with fresh herbs and spices. The classic recipe recommends sautéing the vegetables in a pan first, then transferring them to a pot. In this version, I roast the vegetables instead of sautéing them, since excellent results can be achieved in less time (page 89).

INGREDIENTS

Serves 10 / Serving size: 1 cup

Ratatouille

- 1 medium unpeeled eggplant, cut into ½-inch cubes
- 2 firm medium zucchini, cut into ½-inch cubes
- ¼ teaspoon Atlantic sea salt
- ¼ teaspoon ground black pepper
- 5 tablespoons extra-virgin olive oil
- ½ medium onion, finely chopped
- 1 clove garlic, crushed
- 1 medium red bell pepper, seeded and cut into ½-inch cubes
- 2 medium tomatoes, seeded and finely chopped
- 3 tablespoons fresh chopped thyme
- ½ teaspoon honey
- 1 tablespoon fresh chopped basil

Millet

- 1 cup millet
- 1½ cups water
- 2 tablespoons vegetable stock (page 63), optional
- ¼ teaspoon Atlantic sea salt

TIP *The taste of ratatouille can be altered by taking a journey through different cultures. Take a tip from the Balkan kitchen by replacing the basil and thyme with celery and paprika. Opt for an Indian touch by replacing these herbs with curry, garam masala, and a bit of turmeric. You can also vary the vegetables, or augment them with parsley root, celery root, carrots, or your own choices.*

Calories	164
Total fat	8 g
Calories as fat	44%
Saturated fat	1 g
Cholesterol	0 mg
Carbohydrates	21 g
Dietary fiber	4 g
Sodium	67 mg
Protein	3 g
Carbohydrate choices	**1½**

Exchanges:
1 starch, 1 vegetable, 1½ fat

PREPARATION

1. Prepare ratatouille: Preheat oven to 350°F. In a medium bowl, combine eggplant and zucchini. Mix with salt and pepper, then toss with 3 tablespoons olive oil to coat. Transfer to a baking dish and roast for about 30 minutes, stirring occasionally until soft and brown. Remove from oven and set aside.

2. In a large pot, heat 2 tablespoons oil over medium-high heat. Add onion and garlic and sauté for 5 minutes, until onion is golden brown. Add red pepper and tomatoes, and cook over medium heat for 5 minutes.

3. Add roasted eggplant, zucchini, thyme, and honey, and mix well. Cook for 10 minutes over low heat. Add basil and cook for another 30 seconds, then remove from heat. Add salt and pepper to taste.

4. Prepare millet: In the meantime, combine millet with water, stock, and salt in a small pot. Bring to a boil over medium-high heat, then reduce heat to low and cook for about 30 minutes, until liquid is absorbed. Serve warm, with ratatouille on top.

Grilled Eggplant Moussaka with Roasted Pepper Cream

For variety in this recipe, replace the eggplant with grilled zucchini slices (page 47), or replace the eggplant with 1 pound roasted pumpkin slices, and tomatoes with 3 pounds of Swiss chard, chopped and sautéed with 1 tablespoon of olive oil in a wok over medium heat. The ground turkey can be replaced with lean ground beef or ground chicken breast. Make sure you don't cook the turkey for more than 20 minutes, so that it stays moist and has a texture suitable for lasagna.

INGREDIENTS

Serves 10 / Serving size: 2 x 5-inch piece

Cream

- 1½ ounces soft silken tofu
- 1 tablespoon extra-virgin olive oil
- 1 tablespoon fresh lemon juice
- 2 medium red bell peppers, roasted, peeled and seeded (page 39), and cut into strips
- 2 tablespoons chopped fresh oregano
- Pinch ground black pepper
- Pinch Atlantic sea salt

Moussaka

- 3 large eggplants, cut into ¼-inch lengthwise slices
- ½ teaspoon ground black pepper, or to taste
- ¼ teaspoon Atlantic sea salt, or to taste
- 2 tablespoons extra-virgin olive oil, plus more for greasing
- 1 medium onion, finely chopped
- 1 clove garlic, crushed

- 2 pounds ground lean turkey
- 1 cinnamon stick
- 3 bay leaves
- 2 large tomatoes, sliced into thin rounds

Calories	212
Total fat	9 g
Calories as fat	38%
Saturated fat	2 g
Cholesterol	69 mg
Carbohydrates	11 g
Dietary fiber	6 g
Sodium	141 mg
Protein	22 g
Carbohydrate choices	**1**

Exchanges:
2 lean meat, 2 vegetable, ½ fat

PREPARATION

1. Prepare cream: In a food processor, process tofu, oil, and lemon juice, for 3-5 minutes, until smooth. Add red peppers and oregano and process until smooth. Add salt and pepper to taste; then set aside.

2. Prepare moussaka: Season eggplant slices with salt and pepper. Heat a lined grill pan over high heat and grill eggplant in batches for about 5 minutes on each side, until ready.

3. In a large frying pan, heat oil over medium-high heat. Add onion and garlic and sauté for 3 minutes, until onion is golden brown. Add turkey, cinnamon stick, bay leaves, salt, and pepper. Cook over high

Grilled Eggplant Moussaka with Roasted Pepper Cream

heat until turkey whitens. Reduce heat to low-medium and cook for 20 minutes. Remove cinnamon stick and bay leaves.

4. Preheat oven to 350°F. Grease a 10 x 15-inch baking pan. Arrange one-third of eggplant slices in an even layer on bottom of pan. Spoon half the turkey mixture on top, and arrange half the tomato slices top. Arrange a second layer of eggplant slices on, turkey mixture, and tomato slices. Top with a final layer of eggplant slices. Using a rubber spatula, top with a ¼-inch layer of cream, then bake for 30 minutes, until cream begins to brown. Let cool for about 10 minutes before serving.

Fresh Herb Salad with Lemon Juice and Toasted Cashews

With most fresh herbs, if you don't have the patience to separate the leaves from the stem, you can chop coarsely the stem with leaves. The exception to this is mint, since its stem is quite coarse and must be removed before adding the leaves to salads. Herb salads are best without the addition of vegetables. For variety, try adding nuts or cubes of low-fat, semi-soft, white cheese and a pinch of sumac. Sumac adds bright color and a slightly sour flavor to this salad; it is an excellent addition to your spice rack.

Calories	63
Total fat	5 g
Calories as fat	71%
Saturated fat	1 g
Cholesterol	0 mg
Carbohydrates	4 g
Dietary fiber	1 g
Sodium	87 mg
Protein	1 g
Carbohydrate choices	**None**

Exchanges: 1 vegetable, 1 fat

INGREDIENTS

Serves 8 / Serving size: ¾ cup

- 1½ ounces (1 bunch) fresh parsley, leaves picked, rinsed, and patted dry
- 1 ounce (½ bunch) fresh mint, leaves picked, rinsed, and patted dry
- 1 ounce (½ bunch) fresh cilantro, leaves picked, rinsed, and patted dry

- 3 ounces (about 3 cups) fresh arugula, leaves picked, rinsed, patted dry, and coarsely chopped
- 3 ounces (about 3 cups) baby arugula
- 2 tablespoons extra-virgin olive oil
- 6 tablespoons fresh lemon juice
- Pinch Atlantic sea salt
- 1 ounce unsalted cashews, toasted (page 57) and coarsely chopped

PREPARATION

1. In a medium bowl, mix together parsley, mint, cilantro, and arugula.
2. Add oil, lemon juice, and salt, tossing until evenly coated. Sprinkle with cashews, and serve.

Fresh Herb Salad with Lemon Juice and Toasted Cashews

DESSERTS

When making desserts for family meals, choose a recipe that will leave you with leftovers that can be enjoyed during the rest of the week. If you prepare a larger quantity of apricot sauce in the following recipe, the only extra preparation time you'll require is the amount of time it takes to grate a bit more orange peel. Leftover sauce can be stored in the refrigerator for several weeks; just be sure to use a clean spoon each time you remove some from the jar. Use it to ease and upgrade your cooking in a variety of ways. At breakfast, for example, it can be a spread on whole-wheat toast or used to fill crepes (page 203). It can also be added to milk with granola or mixed into plain yogurt as a substitute for the fruited varieties that contain sugar or sugar substitutes.

The texture of this sauce is relatively thick, but if you thin it with a bit of water, it can be used to top various desserts. To do this, heat ½ cup sauce with ½ cup water over medium heat, mixing constantly until the sauce and water combine thoroughly. Pour over baked goods such as the Apple-filled Phyllo Pastry (page 143), the Ricotta and Pear Dim Sum (page 144), or any other baked dish you prepare. The sauce can also be used as a replacement for honey in the Carrot Cake with Pears and Honey Almond Glaze (page 138). To make a delicious frozen treat, mix 1 cup of apricot topping with 1 cup of yogurt in a food processor, then transfer to the freezer. Remove mixture from freezer and process once more before serving. See instructions for making sorbet on page 126 for more guidelines.

Note how many options are possible from a single sauce made in a large quantity. If you prepare any fruit sauce in a double batch, you'll find it easy to upgrade your cooking. You can also serve the almond cookies with another sauce in this book, such as the Pomegranate and Red Wine Sauce (page 143) or the Pistachio and Apple Sauce (page 144).

Almond Cookies in Apricot Sauce

Almond Cookies in Apricot Sauce

In this recipe, the cookies are sweetened only by the almonds, and most of the dessert's sweetness actually comes from the apricot sauce served on the side. See pages 110–125 for more tips on sweetening. For variations to the sauce, try adding a clove or cardamom pod while it cooks. You can also replace the dried apricots with a favorite fruit such as dried figs. You can also vary the recipe by replacing the ground almonds with ground walnuts, pecans, pistachios, cashews, or any other nut you like. Remember that some nuts, such as almonds, are sweeter than others. (See page 57 on choosing nuts.)

INGREDIENTS

Makes 20 cookies / Serving size:
2 cookies + 1 tablespoon sauce

Cookies
- **2 large egg whites**
- **Pinch Atlantic sea salt**
- **5 ounces blanched almonds, finely ground**

Sauce
- **7 unsweetened dried apricots, cut into quarters**
- **1 teaspoon grated orange rind**
- **Pinch Atlantic sea salt**
- **⅓ cup water**
- **1 teaspoon honey**

PREPARATION

1. Prepare cookies: Preheat oven to 325°F and line a baking sheet with parchment paper. In the bowl of an electric mixer, whip egg whites and salt until stiff and shiny peaks form. Using a rubber spatula, fold almonds into egg whites, one tablespoon at a time, just until evenly combined.

2. Using 2 teaspoons, drop batter onto baking sheet, leaving space between each cookie. Bake for 12 to 15 minutes, until golden brown. Transfer to a wire rack to cool.

3. Prepare sauce: In the meantime, combine dried apricots, orange rind, salt, and water in a small saucepan and bring to a boil over medium-high heat. Reduce heat to low and cook for 20 minutes, until sauce reduces by about two-thirds. Remove from heat and let cool slightly.

4. Use a fork to remove a few pieces of orange rind from the apricot mixture, for garnish, and transfer the rest to a food processor. Add honey and process until smooth. Serve cookies with orange rind as garnish, and apricot sauce on the side.

TIP *If you want a crunchier cookie, add 1 or 2 tablespoons of whole-wheat flour with the ground almonds. The more flour you add, the crispier the cookies will be. Don't replace the ground almonds with almond flour since almond flour absorbs more liquids and will produce a batter that is too dry.*

Calories	92
Total fat	7 g
Calories as fat	68%
Saturated fat	1 g
Cholesterol	0 mg
Carbohydrates	4 g
Dietary fiber	2 g
Sodium	73 mg
Protein	4 g
Carbohydrate choices	**None**

Exchanges: 1 lean meat, 1 fat

Cooking For Kids

The earlier you instill healthy eating habits in your children, the greater the chance they will maintain them as adults. For example, children who are used to the texture of whole grains will tend to prefer them to white grains. Those who enjoy healthy snacks may never develop a taste for saltier alternatives or sweetened soft drinks.

One of the best ways to help children develop healthier eating habits is to set a personal example. You don't need to make a big deal out of eating healthier food. Just make sure there are healthy foods served at family meals, and fill your own plate with them. After seeing you eat these foods on a regular basis, there's a good chance your children will start doing the same, even if at a later stage.

In today's environment, it's hard to maintain a healthy lifestyle. Try to maintain a "protected environment" at home by keeping plenty of healthy foods in your pantry and eating less healthy items only outside of home. For example, if you go out for ice cream with your kids every now and then, all of you will eat a lot less than if you keep it in the freezer.

If your children have already less-than-desirable eating habits, your task may be a bit more complicated. Children may be hesitant to try new foods that have unfamiliar tastes or textures. Even if you prepare excellent brown rice, kids who are used to other starches may not want to try it because of its different color or texture. One solution for drawing children to healthier foods is encouraging them to participate in the preparation, since many children will be happy to try foods that they have helped prepare. Another solution is to camouflage healthier foods, so that children get used to the taste and texture of these foods without actually knowing that they are trying something new.

Throughout this chapter, you'll find a selection of tips for cooking for kids. These include ideas on how to introduce whole grains to your children, how to increase their vegetable consumption, and how to prepare foods children like, such as pizza and hamburger, using healthier ingredients and techniques. When it comes to dessert, you'll find suggestions on how to deal with sweets. And just to make sure adults don't feel neglected, most recipes includes recommended adjustments for adults.

THE FIRST TRICK: USING HEALTHIER TECHNIQUES

Many kids love eating fish and chips. They like the dish's golden color and relish the crispy coating that contrasts nicely with the soft inside. The challenge of healthy cooking is how to achieve these colors and textures using a technique that is healthier than deep-frying. Your oven is the solution, but a bit more attention is required.

Baking: for a golden finish and crispy coating

When it comes to achieving a golden finish, the following recipe demonstrates how to prepare delicious and thick French fries by brushing chunks of potato with a thin layer of oil, baking them in the oven, then broiling them for a few minutes. As for a crispy coating, this can also be achieved in the oven, as long as one understands an important difference between deep-frying and baking. When foods are deep-fried, the cooking time is very short and the heat is very high, therefore ingredients must be made of tiny pieces such as breadcrumbs. In the oven, the heating process takes more time. To achieve a good crispy coating in the oven, the coating must be made up of thicker pieces that won't dry. Fish covered in a breadcrumb coating won't turn out properly when baked in the oven because breadcrumbs aren't suited to this type of baking.

One coating suitable for oven baking (and used in the following recipe) is coarsely ground puffed rice. For best results, make sure you don't grind the puffed rice too finely. If you do, the oven's heat will cause the coating to dry out. Other coatings suitable for oven baking are coarsely ground almonds, sesame seeds, and nigella seeds.

If you are making this dish for adults, or for children who won't mind seeing a few green flakes on their baked fish, try adding dried herbs to the coating (see Sesame and Herb Chicken Fingers, page 215). If you'd like a delicious coating that's not crispy, chop up mixed Portobello, Porcini, and button mushrooms, and dip the fish pieces in the mushroom mixture before baking.

Fish and Chips

Fish and Chips

If you're preparing this dish for adults, or if you are cooking for children who like to try new foods, replace the egg with pure tahini, mustard, or almond butter. All of these ingredients will help the coating stick to the fish, while giving the dish an interesting flavor (see Sesame and Herb Chicken Fingers, page 215).

INGREDIENTS

Serves 8 / Serving size: 4 pieces of fish + 1 cup chips

Chips
- 16 baby potatoes, halved
- ¼ teaspoon ground black pepper
- ¼ teaspoon Atlantic sea salt
- 2 tablespoons extra-virgin olive oil

Fish
- 1 cup unsweetened and unsalted puffed rice cereal
- 1 large egg, beaten
- ¼ teaspoon ground black pepper
- ¼ teaspoon Atlantic sea salt
- Eight 4-ounce tilapia fillets, skinless
- 4 tablespoons fresh lemon juice

PREPARATION

1. Prepare potatoes: Preheat oven to 450°F and line a baking sheet with parchment paper. Place potatoes in a large bowl and season with salt and pepper. Add oil and toss gently to coat.

2. Arrange potatoes, skin-side up, on baking sheet. Bake for 30 minutes, or until soft. Remove from oven and reduce oven temperature to 350°F.

3. While potatoes are baking, prepare fish: Place puffed rice cereal in a food processor and process until crushed. Transfer to a flat plate. In a small bowl, mix egg with salt and pepper.

4. Cut each fish fillet into quarters and season with salt and pepper. Sprinkle a few drops of lemon juice on each fillet. One by one, dip fillets in beaten egg then in crushed rice cereal, to coat on both sides. Line a baking sheet with parchment paper. Arrange fish on baking sheet.

5. Bake fish for 6 minutes. Then set oven to broil, and return potatoes to oven. Broil potatoes and fish for 2 minutes, turning over fish after 1 minute, until crispy.

Calories	247
Total fat	6 g
Calories as fat	22%
Saturated fat	1 g
Cholesterol	69 mg
Carbohydrates	30 g
Dietary fiber	4 g
Sodium	546 mg
Protein	21 g
Carbohydrate choices	**2**

Exchanges: 2 lean meat, 2 starch

THE SECOND TRICK: USING HEALTHIER INGREDIENTS

Pizza, another kids' favorite, doesn't really deserve its unhealthy reputation. Its basic ingredients, after all, are starch, protein, and vegetables. If you stick to healthy ingredients for the crust and toppings as well, pizza can be a delicious and nutritious dish. The well-respected chef at a new pizzeria I visited uses white flour for the dough but heaps on fresh vegetables and high-quality, low-fat cheeses, transforming the finished products into healthy culinary treats. The list of vegetable topping choices is as long as the line of customers waiting to order.

Hamburgers are another favorite, and they, too, can be made with healthier ingredients. First of all, I recommend preparing them yourself, to reduce the amount of processed meat. In fact, why not use freshly ground, lean beef? Choose your own cut at the butcher, and ask to have the fat trimmed before grinding.

The role of fat in hamburgers is to provide a juicy and light texture. Hamburgers made with only lean beef may be too dry or dense to be tasty. An excellent way of adding juiciness to hamburgers made with lean ground beef is to add vegetables to the mixture. Not only will the vegetables upgrade the taste and texture of the hamburgers, but they will also increase consumption of vegetables. As you'll see in the recipe on page 194, roasted eggplant is an excellent vegetable for adding to hamburgers. Although roasting the eggplant does take a bit of time, the result is worth it. You can also add grated zucchini or blanched spinach to the lean ground beef for a faster variation. If you want to reduce the amount of beef your family consumes, try making hamburgers using lean ground turkey.

The previous recipe demonstrated how a standard recipe can be made healthier by simply changing the technique. The recipes on the following pages use the same techniques with higher quality ingredients. Think of these two principles the next time you want to make a favorite recipe and are looking for ways to make it healthier. This can help you come up with solutions that are creative and tasty.

Mini Pizzas with Meat and Tahini Sauce or Tomato Sauce with Cheese and Mushrooms

Mini Pizzas—Dough

The dough in this recipe is easy to make, and can definitely be prepared with kids. In order to avoid making it too different from standard pizza dough made with white flour, use a combination of 50% white flour and 50% whole-wheat flour the first few times you make it. If you don't have time to make pizza dough, use a day-old whole-wheat bread slice for crust. If your kids are likely to notice this pizza's darker crust, make an effort to spread sauce right up to the edges of the dough, so that no crust is visible.

INGREDIENTS

Makes 20 3-inch pizza crusts

- 4½ ounces (about 1 cup) whole-wheat flour, plus more for dusting
- 4½ ounces (about 1 cup) all-purpose white flour
- 1 teaspoon thin Atlantic sea salt
- ½ teaspoon dry active yeast
- ⅔ cup lukewarm water
- 1 tablespoon extra-virgin olive oil

PREPARATION

1. In a medium bowl, mix together flours and salt. Add yeast and mix until combined. Add water and mix until dough forms. Add oil and knead until incorporated. Cover dough with a clean kitchen towel and set aside to rise in a warm place for 40 minutes. In the meantime, prepare sauce (see pages 192 and 193).

2. Preheat oven to 350°F and line a baking sheet with parchment paper. When dough has risen, punch down and transfer to a lightly floured surface. Roll out dough to about ½-inch thick, and use an upside-down glass to cut 3-inch rounds. Arrange rounds on baking sheet and spread with about 1 tablespoon of Meat and Tahini Sauce (page 192) or Tomato Sauce with Cheese and Mushrooms (page 193) right up to the edges of the dough. Bake for 30 minutes, or until crust browns.

Mini Pizza—Meat and Tahini Sauce

If you want to take advantage of this pizza for increasing your children's consumption of vegetables, try replacing ⅓ of the meat in the recipe below with roasted eggplant using the technique demonstrated on page 194. If you want to enhance the sauce's flavor, replace the tahini with almond butter.

Calories	65
Total fat	2 g
Calories as fat	28%
Saturated fat	1 g
Cholesterol	6 mg
Carbohydrates	9 g
Dietary fiber	1 g
Sodium	153 mg
Protein	3 g
Carbohydrate choices	**½**

Exchanges: ½ starch, ½ fat

INGREDIENTS

Makes 20 tablespoons / Serving size: One 3-inch pizza crust + 1 tablespoon sauce

- ½ **pound lean ground round**
- ½ **large onion, finely chopped**
- **1 tablespoon pure tahini**
- **2 tablespoons fresh lemon juice**
- ½ **teaspoon ground allspice**
- **1 clove garlic, crushed**
- **1 tablespoon finely chopped parsley**
- ¼ **teaspoon Atlantic sea salt**
- ¼ **teaspoon ground black pepper**
- **1 tablespoon raw pine nuts**

PREPARATION

1. Mix together beef, onion, tahini, lemon juice, allspice, garlic, parsley, salt, and pepper.
2. Spread 1 tablespoon of sauce on each round of dough, and sprinkle with pine nuts. Bake as instructed.

Mini Pizza—Tomato Sauce with Cheese and Mushrooms

When making tomato sauce for pizza, make sure to reduce it so that it doesn't have too much liquid. Excess liquid in the sauce is likely to damage the dough underneath it. If you are preparing pizza for adults, try adding strips of grilled yellow peppers or dots of pesto to this sauce. For a completely different look, replace the tomato sauce with Pumpkin and Caraway Seed Spread (page 107).

Calories	61
Total fat	2 g
Calories as fat	30%
Saturated fat	1 g
Cholesterol	1 mg
Carbohydrates	9 g
Dietary fiber	1 g
Sodium	190 mg
Protein	2 g
Carbohydrate choices	½
Exchanges: ½ starch, ½ fat	

INGREDIENTS

Makes 20 tablespoons / Serving size: One 3-inch pizza crust + 1 tablespoon sauce

- **4 medium tomatoes, halved**
- **1 teaspoon extra-virgin olive oil**
- **2 cloves garlic, peeled and thinly sliced**
- **1 tablespoon vegetable stock (page 63)**
- **½ cup water**
- **½ teaspoon Atlantic sea salt**
- **½ teaspoon ground black pepper**
- **1½ ounces low-fat, semi-soft white cheese, such as feta, cut into ½-inch cubes**
- **3 tablespoons sliced button mushrooms**

PREPARATION

1. Scoop out tomato seeds, and discard. Transfer tomatoes to a food processor and process until smooth.
2. In a saucepan, heat oil over medium-high heat. Add garlic and sauté until brown, about 3 minutes. Add tomatoes, water, and stock and bring to a boil. Reduce heat to low and simmer for about 15 minutes, until sauce thickens and reduces by about half. Add salt and pepper to taste. Spread 1 tablespoon of sauce on each round of dough, and sprinkle with cheese and mushrooms. Bake as instructed.

Beef and Eggplant Hamburgers with Homemade Ketchup

Note that this hamburger recipe doesn't contain eggs. If you use beef and refrigerate the patties for about 30 minutes before cooking, the amino acids in the beef will work to bind the mixture. If you replace the beef with ground turkey, however, you will need to add an ingredient to keep the mixture together. To cut down on unnecessary fat, I suggest using soda water instead of eggs. Add ⅓ cup soda water for every 2 pounds of meat. The soda water helps bind the meat and make the burgers light and airy.

INGREDIENTS

Serves 12 / Serving size: 2 small patties + 1 tablespoon sauce

Hamburgers

- 2 pounds lean ground round
- 2 medium eggplants, roasted (page 39), peeled, and pureed
- 1 medium onion, finely chopped
- 4 tablespoons chopped fresh parsley
- 2 cloves garlic, crushed
- ¼ teaspoon Atlantic sea salt
- ¼ teaspoon ground black pepper
- 2 tablespoons unrefined canola oil, for frying

Ketchup

- 6 medium tomatoes, halved
- 1 tablespoon extra-virgin olive oil
- 2 cloves crushed garlic
- ½ cup water
- 1 tablespoon vegetable stock (page 63), optional
- ½ teaspoon Atlantic sea salt
- ½ teaspoon ground black pepper

TIP *You can also use soda water instead of eggs when making chicken or fish burgers (see the Swiss Chard Dim Sum with Sea Bass and Water Chestnuts, page 104).*

Calories	252
Total fat	11 g
Calories as fat	39%
Saturated fat	3 g
Cholesterol	75 mg
Carbohydrates	11 g
Dietary fiber	6 g
Sodium	83 mg
Protein	28 g
Carbohydrate choices	**1**
Exchanges: 3 lean meat, 2 vegetable	

PREPARATION

1. Prepare hamburgers: Mix together beef, eggplant, onion, parsley, garlic, salt, and pepper. Shape into 24 even patties and arrange on a large plate or baking sheet. Cover and refrigerate for 30 minutes, to let burgers solidify and flavors blend.

2. In a medium frying pan, heat oil over medium heat. Fry patties for about 2 minutes on each side for medium, or according to preference.

3. Prepare ketchup: Scoop out tomato seeds and discard. Transfer tomatoes to a food processor and process until smooth.

4. In a medium frying pan, heat oil over medium-high heat. Add garlic and sauté for 3 minutes, until golden brown. Add tomatoes, water, and stock, and bring to a boil, then reduce heat to low and simmer, stirring occasionally, for about 20 minutes, until mixture is thick. Add salt and pepper to taste.

INCREASING VEGETABLE CONSUMPTION

A considerable challenge when feeding young people is increasing their consumption of vegetables. Here are some tips to help.

Hide the vegetables

The hamburger recipe on the previous page is an excellent example of how to hide vegetables (in this case, eggplant) inside a hamburger. Using this same technique, you can add grated zucchini and tomatoes to ground beef in the Stuffed Peppers with Brown Rice in Tomato Sauce (page 30). Similarly, the Bolognaise sauce in the recipe on the following page is upgraded by adding roasted eggplant and red peppers to the ground beef that blend nicely with the sauce's red color. Adults like roasted peppers, and children usually like the color red. This sauce contains one vegetable serving per person, and served with a salad, the meal provides almost half a daily vegetable requirement! Try incorporating a variety of vegetables into your meat recipes. This is especially easy when preparing ground beef, since it is excellent at concealing other ingredients.

Increase the amount of sauce

Another way to increase kids' vegetable consumption is to use more spreads, such as those described in the Lots of Vegetables chapter (pages 106–109), and adding colorful sauces. Imagine a pasta dish in which you increase the ratio of sauce to pasta. The starches will disappear under a larger amount of sauce, and you'll be serving a dish that is tastier and provides more vegetables. (You might even be able to conceal some whole-wheat pasta in such a dish.) Remember that vegetable-based sauces, such as tomato sauce, that are prepared from fresh or frozen vegetables are counted as a vegetable serving.

Wrap vegetables in dough

Stuffed dough is also a favorite with kids, and a healthy way to prepare it is to use vegetables for the filling and keep the wrap thin. Rice paper is a good choice, since it contains a relatively small quantity of carbohydrate. All you have to do is soak the wrappers briefly in warm water, then wrap them around sliced vegetables. Serve them whole or slice them, as in the recipe for Cheese and Vegetable Spring Rolls with Mediterrenean Vinaigrette (page 198). Children will also like helping to prepare this dish by selecting the vegetables for the filling, perhaps choosing their favorite colors.

Whole-Wheat Spaghetti with Roasted Vegetable Bolognaise

Reduction is a technique that enhances the flavor of vegetable-based dishes and reduces the use of salt (see page 76). The ground beef in the recipe below can result in a lot of liquid, especially if the meat was frozen and thawed. For best taste, cook the beef patiently until the liquid evaporates and the beef is slightly singed. You can integrate the peppers in interesting ways, for both children and adults, by cutting them into cubes or processing them in a food processor, for instance.

INGREDIENTS

Serves 8 / Serving size: 1½ cups

- 1 tablespoon extra-virgin olive oil
- 1 medium onion, finely chopped
- 2 cloves garlic, chopped
- 1 pound lean ground round
- 1 medium carrot, cut into ¼-inch cubes
- ½ teaspoon Atlantic sea salt, or to taste
- ½ teaspoon ground black pepper, or to taste
- 4 medium tomatoes, cored and scored with an X at the bottom
- 2 medium red bell peppers, roasted (page 39)
- 1 medium eggplant, roasted (page 39)
- ½ pound whole-wheat durum spaghetti
- 1½ ounces (1 bunch) fresh basil, leaves picked, rinsed, patted dry, and chopped

PREPARATION

1. In a large frying pan, heat oil over medium-high heat. Add onion and garlic, and sauté for 3 minutes, until onion is golden brown. Add beef, salt, and pepper and sear. Add carrot and cook over low heat, stirring regularly, for about 45 minutes, until liquids evaporate and beef is dry.

2. Bring a small pot of water to a boil over high heat. Place tomatoes in boiling water and blanch for 10 to 15 seconds, until skins loosen.

3. Remove tomatoes with a slotted spoon and place them in an ice water bath. When tomatoes are cool enough to handle, remove skins with a paring knife and cut in halve. Remove and discard seeds, and cut flesh into cubes.

4. Place roasted peppers and eggplant in a food processor and process until smooth. Transfer pepper, eggplant, and tomatoes to the frying pan, and cook for 10 minutes. In the meantime, prepare spaghetti according to instructions, and drain.

5. Mix basil into beef mixture, and add salt and pepper to taste. To serve, distribute spaghetti among individual serving dishes, and pour sauce over top.

Calories	216
Total fat	5 g
Calories as fat	21 %
Saturated fat	1 g
Cholesterol	26 mg
Carbohydrates	31 g
Dietary fiber	4 g
Sodium	187 mg
Protein	15 g
Carbohydrate choices	**2**

Exchanges: 1 lean meat, 1½ starch, 1 vegetable, ½ fat

Whole-Wheat Spaghetti with Roasted Vegetable Bolognaise

Cheese and Vegetable Spring Rolls with Vinaigrette

The vegetables in this recipe can be replaced with any vegetables that you (or your kids) prefer. The coarsely grated carrots combine with the alfalfa sprouts and baby salad greens to make a dense filling. If you replace any of the vegetables, be sure to create the same texture. Sliced spring rolls are excellent for entertaining guests of any age and can be served with many of the sauces in this book.

INGREDIENTS

Serves 10 / Serving size: 3 pieces + 1 tablespoon sauce

Spring rolls

- Five 8½-inch rice paper wrappers
- 2 medium carrots, coarsely grated
- 3½ ounces low-fat, semi-soft, white cheese, such as feta, cut into thick strips
- ½ cup fresh mint leaves
- ½ cup fresh basil leaves
- 2 cups alfalfa sprouts
- ½ medium avocado, ripe but firm, peeled, pitted, and cut into strips
- 2 cups mixed baby salad greens
- 1 tablespoon black sesame seeds, for garnish

Sauce:

- 4 tablespoons fresh lemon juice
- 4 tablespoons extra-virgin olive oil
- 1 tablespoon Dijon-style mustard
- 1 tablespoon honey
- ¼ teaspoon Atlantic sea salt
- ¼ teaspoon ground black pepper

PREPARATION

1. Prepare spring rolls: Partially fill a large heatproof bowl with warm water by mixing together boiling water and tap water. Soak 1 wrapper for 10 to 20 seconds, until it softens. Remove wrapper, gently shake off excess water, and lay on work surface. Place another wrapper to soak.

2. Arrange ⅕ of carrots, cheese, mint, basil, alfalfa, avocado, and mixed baby greens in a horizontal mound below center of wrapper (see photo on facing page), using your fingers to press filling firmly inside, to form a tight cylinder. Repeat process with remaining wrappers and filling.

3. Prepare sauce: Mix together lemon juice and olive oil. Add mustard, honey, salt and pepper.

4. Cut spring rolls into 6 even pieces and arrange on a serving dish, with filling displayed on top. Sprinkle with sesame seeds and serve with sauce on the side.

Calories	63
Total fat	5 g
Calories as fat	71%
Saturated fat	1 g
Cholesterol	3 mg
Carbohydrates	4 g
Dietary fiber	1 g
Sodium	44 mg
Protein	2 g
Carbohydrate choices	**None**

Exchanges: 1 vegetable, 1 fat

Cheese and Vegetable Spring Rolls with Vinaigrette

TIP *For variety, replace the cheese with strips of grilled chicken breast and serve with Asian Salsa (page 43), or replace the cheese with strips of tofu or fruit and serve with Ginger and Lemon Sauce (page 210). You can alter the vinaigrette by replacing the mustard and honey with 5 tablespoons of thinly grated beet, and sprinkling nigella seeds on the plate before serving.*

CHICKEN DISHES FOR THE WHOLE WEEK

You don't have to be a child to enjoy eating food with your hands. That's often the preferred method for eating chicken drumsticks, and is ideal for the recipe that appears on the facing page. You can replace the red vegetables in the sauce with any type of vegetable, or even with a fruit, nut, or herb. I recommend doubling, or even tripling, this recipe since cooked drumsticks can be refrigerated up to 4 days and frozen for several months. Since the dish is relatively moist, it can be defrosted in the microwave. It's also very easy to prepare. Just mix the drumsticks with the other ingredients and place them in the oven.

To make the chicken even easier to eat with your hands, try the following trick: cut around the bone of the drumstick, near the smaller end where there isn't any meat. This cut releases the tendons and gathers the meat at the other end of the drumstick while cooking, leaving a bare area of bone that is perfect for holding.

Chicken Drumsticks with Peppers and Cherry Tomatoes

Chicken Drumsticks with Peppers and Cherry Tomatoes

Pierce a hole in each cherry tomato using a toothpick or fork. This will prevent the tomatoes from exploding from steam pressure inside as they cook. If you are preparing this recipe for adults and want to make it a bit more interesting, replace the regular paprika with smoked paprika and add a bit of chopped scallion for garnish. Smoked paprika imbues foods with a lovely flavor, and is an excellent addition to any spice rack.

Calories	164
Total fat	11 g
Calories as fat	60%
Saturated fat	2 g
Cholesterol	24 mg
Carbohydrates	9 g
Dietary fiber	3 g
Sodium	224 mg
Protein	8 g
Carbohydrate choices	½

Exchanges:
1 lean meat, 2 vegetable, 1½ fat

INGREDIENTS

Serves 6 / Serving size:
2 drumsticks + 2 tablespoons
vegetables

- 2 tablespoons extra-virgin olive oil
- 2 tablespoons sweet paprika
- 1 teaspoon ground turmeric
- ¼ teaspoon Atlantic sea salt, or to taste
- ¼ teaspoon ground black pepper, or to taste
- Twelve 4-ounce chicken drumsticks, skinless
- 2 medium red bell peppers, seeded, stems removed, and sliced into strips
- 1 cup cherry tomatoes, pierced
- 1 medium onion, cut into rings

PREPARATION

1. Preheat the oven to 425°F. In a medium bowl, mix together olive oil, paprika, turmeric, salt, and pepper. Add chicken drumsticks, peppers, cherry tomatoes, and onion, and stir to coat.

2. Transfer mixture to a baking dish and bake for 40 minutes, stirring occasionally, until chicken is golden brown. Add salt and pepper to taste, and serve.

DESSERTS KIDS LIKE

Many kids love desserts that come out of the freezer, even if they aren't very sweet. In the Sweetening without Sugar chapter there is a recipe for fruity frozen sorbet (page 126), and in the Healthy Entertaining chapter you'll find a recipe for frozen granita (page 164), a dessert similar to ices. Children will delight in both. Try both recipes with seasonal fruit, and turn to the Quick Meals chapter (page 161) for tips on this.

Another dessert kids like is crepes. In the Baked Goods chapter (page 131), you'll find an example of how to mix vegetable or fruit puree with dough destined for sweet baked goods. A similar technique can be used to make batter as shown in the recipe on the facing page, in which mashed bananas are incorporated into the batter. You can increase the amount of banana in this recipe to achieve a more delicate texture. This will make the banana flavor quite dominant, but it's a flavor most children like. You can also grate apples, pears, or any other solid fruit you like into the batter to give it an airy texture. Fill the crepe dough, or other suitable dough, with seasonal fruits that your kids like, to make a variety of delicious desserts.

Crepes for dinner

Served with a savory rather than sweet filling, crepes can make a delicious dinner. In the following recipe, simply replace the mashed banana with a vegetable puree or two eggs. Bolognaise sauce (page 196) is an excellent filling for savory crepes, just heat and reduce it beforehand to remove some of the liquid. Ratatouille (page 177) is also an excellent savory filling for crepes, and tastes great when served along with sauce.

If you have leftover crepe batter, or if you made extra batter to begin with, refrigerate it overnight and use it to prepare a delicious breakfast. Add a bit of water to the chilled batter if necessary, since chilling the batter will cause it to thicken. Crepes served for breakfast can be filled with spreadable goat cheese or, for a sweet version, with Strawberries in Lemon Verbena and Thyme, with Ricotta (page 122).

Spelt Banana Crepes with Pears

When purchasing soy milk, read the label on the package carefully and make sure you buy an unsweetened and unsalted variety. "All Natural Ingredients" doesn't necessarily mean there is no added sugar, oil, or salt. To prevent your trip to the store from becoming an academic exercise, try focusing on a different product every week, reading the labels for that product until you find the brand that is most suitable for you.

INGREDIENTS

Serves 12 / Serving size: 1 crepe + 2 tablespoons pears

Crepes

- ½ medium banana, cut into chunks
- 1½ ounces unsweetened and unsalted soy milk
- 5 ounces (1 cup) spelt flour
- 2 ounces (½ cup) all-purpose white flour
- Pinch Atlantic sea salt
- ¼ cup plus 1 tablespoon water
- 2 tablespoons unrefined canola oil

Filling

- 4 tablespoons dry red wine
- 1 teaspoon honey
- 8 tablespoons balsamic vinegar
- 4 Anjou pears, cored and cut into ½-inch cubes

PREPARATION

1. Prepare crepes: In a food processor, combine banana and soy milk and process until smooth.

2. In a medium bowl, mix together flours and salt. Mix banana mixture into flour mixture, then gradually add ¼ cup water, stirring until smooth and desired consistency is reached. Pour mixture through a fine-mesh strainer to eliminate chunks. Cover bowl with plastic wrap, and chill for 30 minutes.

3. In the meantime, prepare filling: In a small saucepan over medium heat, bring wine, honey, and vinegar to a boil. Add pears and cook over medium heat for 15 minutes, until pears soften and liquids evaporate.

4. Remove crepe batter from refrigerator and mix in remaining tablespoon water, if necessary, and oil. Heat a non-stick crepe pan over medium-high heat and pour in half a ladle of batter. Swirl batter around until bottom of pan is covered. Cook until bubbles start appearing on top. Flip crepe over and cook on other side for about 30 seconds. Transfer to a plate. Repeat process with remaining batter.

5. To serve, spoon equal amounts of pears along middle of each crepe and roll. Pour remaining sauce over top and serve.

TIP The soy milk in this recipe can be replaced with cow's milk or rice milk. Just take note that soy milk is thicker than these alternatives. Consider the thickness you want to achieve and adjust the quantity you add, according to the type of milk.

Calories	143
Total fat	3 g
Calories as fat	19%
Saturated fat	0 g
Cholesterol	0 mg
Carbohydrates	24 g
Dietary fiber	3 g
Sodium	54 mg
Protein	3 g
Carbohydrate choices	**1½**

Exchanges: 1 starch, ½ fruit, ½ fat

Healthy Entertaining

When people entertain, they want to treat their guests to good food and show off their own culinary skills and generosity. They often heap on the food, much of which is high in fat and calories. Many guests, however, would be pleased to be served attractive, tasty food that is also healthy. They can then enjoy your event without having to worry about what they eat.

Many of the recipes in this book are perfectly suited to entertaining, particularly those in the Baked Goods chapter (pages 129–145) and the Snacks chapter (pages 226–238). Still, I decided to dedicate a whole chapter to this subject in order to share with you ten principles that will, I hope, help you transform your event into an enjoyable occasion that does not compromise on either taste or health. After your guests have gone home and you've finished cleaning up, go over the principles again, since they are the essence of this entire book.

ENRICH FOODS WITH VEGETABLES

As I hope you've already discovered, serving vegetables can be a lot more interesting than just celery and carrot sticks with dip. Vegetables can be served in attractive and interesting ways that inspire curiosity and ignite the appetite. Imagine, for example, a table full of vegetable-based antipasti in a variety of different colors and tastes. If you do decide to serve fresh vegetable sticks and dip, choose surprising vegetables, such as raw beets and raw pumpkin. Cut them into very thin sticks (no more than $\frac{1}{10}$ of an inch) and serve with a distinctly flavored dip.

The following recipe uses lettuce leaves rather than tortillas as wrappers. When you're not entertaining, wrap the lettuce roll in plastic wrap rather than slicing it into rounds, and you'll have a delicious, refreshing breakfast or lunchtime snack.

Lettuce Rolls with Goat Cheese, Raw Beets, and Bean Sprouts

Use the attractive outer leaves of the lettuce for this recipe, saving the more delicate inner leaves for a salad. For variation, fill the lettuce leaves with virtually any type of filling you like, including sliced chicken breast, pastrami, or smoked salmon. Spreading cheese or another sticky food to the leaf before adding the filling helps keep everything together when sliced. You can also use the Tofu and Sautéed Zucchini Spread (page 221) or the Red Tahini Spread (page 108). Mashed avocado can also be used, although its color is less suitable.

INGREDIENTS

Makes about twenty 1½-inch pieces / Serving size: 4 pieces

- 4 large romaine lettuce leaves
- 4 tablespoons low-fat, soft (spreadable) goat cheese
- 1 cup bean sprouts
- 5 chives
- 1½ ounces beet, cut julienne-style
- Pinch Atlantic sea salt
- Pinch ground black pepper
- Black sesame or nigella seeds, for garnish

Calories	33
Total fat	1 g
Calories as fat	27%
Saturated fat	1 g
Cholesterol	2 mg
Carbohydrates	4 g
Dietary fiber	1 g
Sodium	166 mg
Protein	2 g
Carbohydrate choices	None

Exchanges: 1 vegetable

PREPARATION

1. Remove the hard bottom of the lettuce leaves and cut each leaf into a rectangle.

2. Place 1 leaf on your work surface, and spread evenly with a thin layer of cheese. Arrange ¼ of the bean sprouts, chives, and beets in a row along bottom of rectangle. Add salt and pepper to taste. Roll up leaf, using your fingers to press filling firmly inside, to form a cylinder. Repeat process with remaining leaves and filling.

3. Cut each cylinder into four or five 1½-inch pieces. Arrange pieces on serving dish, and garnish with black sesame seeds.

REDUCE THE QUANTITY OF BAKED GOODS

At parties, people usually eat while standing, sometimes with their hands, and without paying a lot of attention to their food. Since ideal party food is easy to handle and not too complicated in terms of taste and appearance, it often consists of baked goods.

However, you can reduce the quantity of baked goods at your parties and still make food that is tasty, healthy, and easy to hold and eat. One method is to make vegetable sandwiches or rolls (like those in the previous recipe). You can also use skewers to serve foods such as Roasted Mushrooms and Leeks in Balsamic Vinaigrette (page 231), or single serving dishes for salads and soups. Cocotte dishes, for example, are prefect for savory salads such as the Thai Beef Salad with Onion and Lemongrass (page 213). Martini glasses are lovely for serving sweet salads such as the Melon Salad with Plum Granita and Mint (page 225), espresso cups are a unique way to serve hot soup, and highball glasses are ideal for cold soups, as demonstrated in the next recipe

Varying your serving dishes means a bigger clean-up job after the event, and you may opt for renting dishes or hiring someone to help out with the washing and drying. The increased cost can be balanced by cutting down on other expenses, suggested later in this chapter (see page 222).

Gazpacho with Raw Beets

Gazpacho with Raw Beets

The following recipe is my take on this classic Spanish soup, but you can use almost any combination of vegetables you like. Keep a bottle or two of unsalted pure tomato juice in your pantry. Tomato juice is an excellent base for many types of soup. Make sure it is 100% juice, with no added salt. You can always add salt after cooking, though the fresh herbs and aromatic vegetables you use will probably suffice.

INGREDIENTS

Serves 20 / Serving size: ⅔ cup

- **2 small tomatoes, coarsely chopped**
- **1 medium red bell pepper, seeded and coarsely chopped**
- **1 medium onion, coarsely chopped**
- **1 small beet, peeled and coarsely chopped**
- **½ small green chili pepper, seeded**
- **4 medium Lebanese cucumbers, seeded and coarsely chopped**
- **4 cups tomato juice containing no added salt**
- **2 tablespoons fresh lemon juice**
- **2 cloves garlic, peeled**
- **½ cup fresh cilantro leaves**
- **1 medium green bell pepper, seeded and coarsely chopped**
- **Pinch Atlantic sea salt, or to taste**
- **Pinch ground black pepper, or to taste**
- **1 medium Bermuda onion, cut into small cubes, for garnish**
- **1½ ounces (1 bunch) parsley, finely chopped, for garnish**

Calories	22
Total fat	0 g
Calories as fat	0%
Saturated fat	0 g
Cholesterol	0 mg
Carbohydrates	5 g
Dietary fiber	1 g
Sodium	38 mg
Protein	3 g
Carbohydrate choices	**None**

Exchanges: 1 vegetable

PREPARATION

1. In a food processor, process tomatoes, red bell pepper, onion, beet, chili pepper, and 3 cucumbers until smooth. Add tomato juice, lemon juice, garlic, and cilantro, and puree until smooth. Add remaining cucumber, and the green bell pepper, and process until soup is desired texture.

2. Refrigerate for at least 2 hours before serving. Add salt and pepper to taste, and garnish with Bermuda onion and parsley.

TIP *Some people like gazpacho that is finely processed, almost the texture of juice; others prefer it to be a bit chunky. My favorite texture is a combination of both. First, I put most of the ingredients into a food processor and puree them until smooth. Then I add the remaining ingredients and process the mixture just a bit, so that these ingredients have a coarser texture.*

USE HEALTHY DOUGH

If you do decide to serve baked goods when you entertain, use healthy dough to make them. For example, try the eggplant pastry on page 135 for single-serving pies, or the Pumpkin Dinner Rolls with Flakes of Thyme (page 132) for bite-size sandwiches. Another method for making individual-size servings is to slice a loaf of Beer and Almond Bread (page 131) and toast it for crostini, which you can top with Dried Tomato Spread (page 109), spreadable low-fat goat cheese, and baby arugula, or Red Tahini Spread (page 108) and slices of grilled beef (see Roast Sirloin with Thick Mushroom sauce, page 54). Crostini can also be served sweet, with ricotta, marinated fruit slices, and mint leaves (see Strawberries in Lemon Verbena and Thyme, with Ricotta, page 122). The following recipe uses rice paper wrappers for dough and is inspired by Vietnamese cooking.

Vietnamese Shrimp Dim Sum in Ginger and Lemon Sauce

Vietnamese cuisine has its own version of dim sum, one which is served without cooking. To succeed in filling this delicate pastry, slice the ingredients very thin. Make sure the carrot and cucumber sticks aren't too long or thick, and that the shrimp aren't too big. A filling that is too coarse will make the folding and rolling more difficult and the final product less attractive.

INGREDIENTS

Serves 20 / Serving size: 1 dim sum + 1 tablespoon sauce

Dim sum

- **7 ounces shrimp, peeled and deveined**
- **½ teaspoon Atlantic sea salt**
- **Twenty 8½-inch rice paper wrappers**
- **1 medium carrot, cut julienne-style**
- **2 cups bean sprouts**
- **1 cup chopped scallions**
- **3 medium Lebanese cucumbers, seeded and cut julienne-style**
- **¼ cup chopped fresh cilantro**
- **¼ cup chopped fresh mint**
- **½ teaspoon ground black pepper**
- **2 cups baby beet greens**

Sauce

- **¼ cup low-sodium soy sauce**
- **2 tablespoons fresh lemon juice**
- **3 tablespoons water**
- **1 small clove garlic, crushed**
- **1 small red hot pepper, seeded and chopped**
- **1 tablespoon mirin**
- **3 tablespoons peeled and chopped fresh ginger**
- **1 ounce coarsely chopped raw cashews**

PREPARATION

1. Prepare dim sum: In a medium pot over high heat, bring water with a pinch of salt to a boil. Add shrimp and cook for 2 minutes, until shrimp are orangey red. Drain shrimp and set aside. Partially fill a large heatproof bowl with warm water by mixing together boiling water and tap water. Soak one wrapper for 10 to 20 seconds, until it softens. Remove wrapper, gently shake off excess water, and lay on work surface. Place another wrapper to soak.

2. In a medium bowl, combine carrots, bean sprouts, scallions, shrimp, cucumbers, cilantro, mint, salt and pepper. Arrange $\frac{1}{20}$ of mixture along bottom edge of wrapper, leaving sides bare. Fold in sides and roll up wrapper, using your fingers to press filling firmly inside, to form a tight cylinder (see page 44). Repeat process with remaining wrappers and filling.

3. Prepare sauce: In a small bowl, mix together soy sauce, lemon juice, and water. Add garlic, pepper, mirin, ginger, and cashews, stirring until blended.

4. Arrange beet greens on a serving dish and place dim sum on top. Serve dim sum whole, with sauce on the side.

Calories	142
Total fat	8 g
Calories as fat	51%
Saturated fat	1 g
Cholesterol	110 mg
Carbohydrates	4 g
Dietary fiber	2 g
Sodium	284 mg
Protein	13 g
Carbohydrate choices	**None**

Exchanges: 2 lean meat, ½ fat

Vietnamese Shrimp Dim Sum in Ginger and Lemon Sauce, shown with grilled chiken

TIP *Vary this recipe by replacing the vegetables with any others you like. You can also replace the shrimp with 1 thinly sliced grilled chicken breast. To make the chicken suitably thin, pound it with a kitchen hammer to a thickness of about 1 inch, then grill it on a grill pan for 2 to 3 minutes on each side over medium heat. You can also cook the chicken breast in a small pot, a technique used in the Schezuan Chicken and Brown Rice Noodle Salad (page 153). If you like, add chopped shitake mushrooms to the filling and serve with a soy-based sauce.*

STRIVE FOR QUALITY, NOT QUANTITY

An excellent way of demonstrating your generosity as a host is to prepare high-quality food that gives your guests a culinary experience to remember. When determining the menu for an event, reduce the number of dishes you prepare, and select dishes with high-quality ingredients. This way you can invest more in every dish, without increasing your overall budget and preparation time. Your guests will be impressed and feel pampered, and I'm sure they won't go home hungry.

For example, try serving the Grilled Marinated Bass Fingers Wrapped in Swiss Chard (page 48) made with fresh grouper, or the Mango Sorbet (page 126) made with pure fruit, or serve the following salad, made with high-quality beef tenderloin. Guests will appreciate the high-quality food you are serving, and if there are no leftovers at the end of the party, you'll know you succeeded.

Thai Beef Salad with Onion and Lemongrass

Thai Beef Salad with Onion and Lemongrass

Lemongrass is an herb with a distinctly sour flavor that is often used in Thai cuisine. Various parts of the plant can be used for different purposes: the leaves can be used to make hot or cold beverages, granita (page 125), marinades, or soup. The stalk can be chopped and added to cooked dishes and salads (as in this recipe), or it can be used as a skewer for fish kabobs, imbuing the fish with a sour taste and interesting appearance.

Calories	138
Total fat	8 g
Calories as fat	52%
Saturated fat	2 g
Cholesterol	36 mg
Carbohydrates	3 g
Dietary fiber	0 g
Sodium	164 mg
Protein	12 g
Carbohydrate choices	**None**

Exchanges:
1 lean meat, 1 vegetable, 1 fat

INGREDIENTS

Serves 8 / Serving size: ¾ cup

- **Two ½-pound aged beef tenderloin steaks**
- **Pinch Atlantic sea salt, or to taste**
- **Pinch ground black pepper, or to taste**
- **2 tablespoons unrefined canola oil**
- **1 lemongrass stalk, finely chopped**
- **1 medium Bermuda onion, halved lengthwise then thinly sliced**
- **4 tablespoons chopped scallions**
- **6 tablespoons fresh lemon juice**
- **1 teaspoon fish sauce**
- **1 tablespoon low-sodium soy sauce**
- **1 tablespoon lemon zest, for garnish**

PREPARATION

1. Season beef with salt and pepper. In a large frying pan, heat oil over medium-high heat. Add beef and sear for 4 minutes on each side, or until medium-rare. Remove beef from pan and set aside to cool for about 15 minutes, then slice into very thin strips, slicing against the fibers of the meat. Transfer to a large bowl.

2. Add lemongrass, onion, scallions, lemon juice, fish sauce, and soy sauce, and mix until combined. Cover with plastic wrap and refrigerate for at least 1 hour, allowing flavors to absorb and meat to soften. Add salt and pepper to taste, garnish with lemon zest, and serve.

USE YOUR OVEN

Fried, crisp-crusted foods, convenient for serving and eating, are a popular choice for events. However, as discussed earlier (pages 39 and 186), baking is an excellent alternative to frying that can achieve the same texture with a lot less oil, even for dishes that people think can only be fried. Baking or roasting has another advantage over frying, especially when it comes to entertaining, since it is easy to bake large batches of food with relatively little effort. Imagine two baking sheets full of vegetables destined for roasting and antipasto. Think how much more time and effort it would take to fry these same vegetables.

One thing to remember is that foods baked in the oven won't change color the same way they do when fried. This can make it difficult to know when they are ready. By cutting the food into relatively large pieces, you reduce the likelihood of their drying out in the oven (even if you leave them in for a bit too long). The larger pieces are also easier for guests to handle. For the recipe on the facing page, select chicken breasts that are especially thick, and cut them into relatively large pieces.

Sesame and Herb Chicken Fingers

The flaky coating in this dish contains lots of dry herbs and very little salt. You can replace the herbs listed below with your own favorite selection; see page 70 for tips on how to do this. The Dijon-style mustard helps the herbs adhere to the chicken. Note that some types of this mustard have a grainy texture that is suitable for sauces but not recommended for this recipe which works best with a smooth variety.

Calories	76
Total fat	3 g
Calories as fat	37%
Saturated fat	1 g
Cholesterol	23 mg
Carbohydrates	2 g
Dietary fiber	1 g
Sodium	380 mg
Protein	11 g
Carbohydrate choices	**None**

Exchanges: 1 lean meat

INGREDIENTS

Serves 8 / Serving size: 3 pieces

- **10 tablespoons dried parsley**
- **2 tablespoons dried basil**
- **1 tablespoon nigella seeds**
- **1 tablespoon whole sesame seeds**
- **Four 4-ounce chicken breasts, cut widthwise into 1-inch strips**
- **¼ teaspoon Atlantic sea salt**
- **¼ teaspoon ground black pepper**
- **2 tablespoons smooth Dijon-style mustard**

PREPARATION

1. Preheat oven to 350°F and line a baking sheet with parchment paper. On a small plate, mix together parsley, basil, nigella, and sesame seeds.

2. Season chicken strips with salt and pepper; then brush each strip with a thin layer of mustard. Dredge chicken strips in mixed herb coating to cover both sides. Transfer to baking sheet and bake for 10 minutes, until ready.

SURPRISE YOUR GUESTS

In addition to serving interesting and high-quality foods when you entertain, try serving dishes that will surprise your guests. This will help you create an unforgettable experience. The Spinach Pastry with Goat Cheese and Smoked Salmon (page 103) is a dish that is sure to surprise, as is the following recipe. Who won't be impressed if you serve homemade red crackers that are unusual, attractive, and made from healthy ingredients.

Beet and Sesame Crackers

Beet and Sesame Crackers

This recipe uses boiling water, a technique that allows water and oil to partially mix, and results in the formation of dough that has the flakiness of pastry dough and the strength of simple dough. Because boiling water is critical in this recipe, use an electric mixer, or spoon, to mix the dough. Remember that dough made with vegetables doesn't keep for very long, though I doubt you'll have any of these crackers left at the end of your event!

INGREDIENTS

Makes about 100 small crackers /
Serving size: 3 crackers

- 5½ ounces beet, roasted (page 39)
- 12⅓ ounces (about 3 cups) whole-wheat flour
- 1 tablespoon Atlantic sea salt
- ½ cup white sesame seeds
- ½ cup extra-virgin olive oil
- ½ cup boiling water
- ½ beaten egg, for brushing
- 4 tablespoons black sesame, for garnish
- Canola oil, for greasing

TIP *When rolling out the dough for these crackers, save time by using the back of a baking pan for the final stage of rolling. This allows you to roll out the dough to the desired thinness, cut it directly on the pan, and not have to worry about transferring it to the baking pan. After you cut the dough into triangles, you can simply place the inverted pan into the oven and bake.*

Calories	81
Total fat	5 g
Calories as fat	56%
Saturated fat	1 g
Cholesterol	3 mg
Carbohydrates	9 g
Dietary fiber	3 g
Sodium	6 mg
Protein	3 g
Carbohydrate choices	½
Exchanges: ½ starch, 1 fat	

PREPARATION

1. Preheat oven to 325°F. Grease the backs of 3 large baking sheets with oil. Place roasted beets in a food processor and puree until smooth. If puree doesn't reach the desired texture, add some of the oil, and puree until smooth.

2. In a large bowl, mix together flour, salt, and sesame seeds. Add beet puree and mix until combined. Add remaining oil and mix lightly. Pour in boiling water and mix with spoon until dough is uniform.

3. Divide dough into three even parts, and roll out one part until it is about ½-inch thick. Transfer dough to back of 1 baking sheet and roll it out until it is about ¼-inch thick.

Brush top with beaten egg, and sprinkle with black sesame seeds. Cut into squares or triangles, and bake for 10 minutes, or until tops are golden brown. Repeat for each portion of dough.

4. Transfer crackers to a wire rack and cool completely before serving. Store in a dry container with a tight-fitting lid.

MAKE IT AN ACTIVE EVENT

Usually, by the time guests arrive at an event, all the food is prepared and ready to eat. Have you ever considered actively involving your guests in the food preparation?

Imagine that your guests are greeted by cooked brown rice, thinly sliced vegetables, and sheets of nori (seaweed used in sushi). Everyone can prepare sushi the way they like before sitting down to enjoy it together. Another idea for an active event is to prepare a variety of dim sum fillings and sauces, and have guests prepare their own dinner. These ideas save you preparation time, ensure that the food you serve is fresh, and help your guests break the ice.

Even if an active event doesn't suit your style, sushi is still an excellent dish to serve at parties, as demonstrated in the following recipe.

Sushi

Sushi

Though sushi is often made with white rice, brown rice is a delicious alternative. Brown rice is less sticky than white rice, and stickiness is essential when making sushi. But this challenge is easy to overcome. When mixing the mirin and rice vinegar into the rice, mash the rice grains with your spoon; this will break the brown rice kernels, releasing the starch and making the rice sticky. After just 20 or 30 seconds of mixing and mashing, the rice will be perfect for rolling into sushi.

INGREDIENTS

Makes 18 rolls / Serving size: 1 roll

Rice

- **2 cups brown round basmati rice, soaked overnight and drained**
- **Water**
- **½ cup rice vinegar**
- **1 tablespoon mirin**
- **½ teaspoon Atlantic sea salt**

Sushi rolls

- **18 sheets nori**
- **1 pound vegetables (such as cucumber, carrot, bean sprouts, radishes), cut julienne-style**
- **7 ounces naturally smoked or fresh salmon, or fresh tuna, sliced thin**
- **3½ ounces avocado, ripe but firm, cut julienne-style**
- **Black sesame seeds, for garnish**
- **Pickled ginger, optional**
- **Wasabi sauce mixed with water, optional**
- **Low-sodium soy sauce, optional**

Calories	127
Total fat	2 g
Calories as fat	14%
Saturated fat	1 g
Cholesterol	3 mg
Carbohydrates	21 g
Dietary fiber	3 g
Sodium	170 g
Protein	6 g
Carbohydrate choices	**1½**
Exchanges: 1½ starch	

PREPARATION

1. Prepare rice: Place rice in a medium pot, and add enough water to cover rice with ½ inch of water. Cover, bring to a boil, and cook over low heat until liquids are absorbed, about 30 minutes. Remove from heat and let sit, covered, for 15 minutes.

2. In a small saucepan, mix together rice vinegar, mirin, and salt. Heat gently over low heat to combine.

3. Transfer rice to a large wooden bowl and pour vinegar mixture over top. Mix with a wooden spoon, mashing the rice as you mix, until liquid is absorbed and rice sticky. Spread out rice on a baking sheet and let cool to room temperature.

(continued on page 220)

(continued from page 219)

4. Prepare sushi rolls: Lay 1 nori sheet on a bamboo sushi roller. Wet your hands so that rice doesn't stick, then spread 2 heaping tablespoons of rice, equal to ⅓ cup, in a thin layer that covers bottom ⅔ of sheet.

5. Arrange a row of vegetables and fish along bottom edge of nori. Roll nori upwards until top ⅓ of nori remains flat on the sushi roller. Wet this area with a bit of water, then press it onto the roll to seal. Press the roll firmly inside the bamboo roller to secure, then transfer to a plate. Repeat process with remaining nori, rice, and vegetables.

6. Wet blade of a sharp knife and cut each sushi roll into 6 even pieces. Arrange sushi on a serving dish and sprinkle black sesame seeds over top. Serve with ginger, wasabi, and a small bowl of soy sauce.

TIP *Preparing sushi is an excellent way of understanding what constitutes a single starch serving. It demonstrates how one serving can be used to make a satisfying meal. Measure ⅓ cup of rice and use it to cover the bottom two thirds of the nori sheet. You'll have to make the rice layer quite thin to succeed. This leaves lots of room for the vegetables and fish and is the best way to make high-quality, tasty sushi.*

SERVE VEGETABLE-RICH SAUCES AND SPREADS

Filling the tables at your event with vegetable-rich sauces and spreads doesn't just reduce the energy density you serve; it also adds color and attractiveness. Consider the tofu spread in the following recipe. It can be used as a dip with beet sticks or crackers (page 217), or to replace the goat cheese in the Lettuce Rolls with Goat Cheese, Raw Beets, and Bean Sprouts (page 205). This spread can also be used when making sushi by spreading it on the rice before adding the vegetables and rolling. Add 1 or 2 tablespoons of water to the spread to make a lovely dressing that is perfect for serving with dim sum (see pages 43, 104, and 210) or with the Sesame and Herb Chicken Fingers (page 215).

Throughout this book you'll find recipes for a variety of vegetable-based sauces and spreads. Serve as many of them as you like to upgrade your event with ease.

Tofu and Sautéed Zucchini Spread

To succeed with tofu-based spreads and dips, keep the following tips in mind. Choose soft tofu since it has the smooth texture you want when making dips. Process the tofu with lemon juice and olive oil in a food processor for 3 to 5 minutes, until the tofu is a soft paste. Make sure you wait until the texture is really smooth before adding ingredients such as herbs or vegetables; otherwise, the tofu won't achieve its maximum smoothness, since the other ingredients will interfere with the blending process.

Calories	17
Total fat	1 g
Calories as fat	53%
Saturated fat	0 g
Cholesterol	0 mg
Carbohydrates	2 g
Dietary fiber	1 g
Sodium	36 mg
Protein	1 g
Carbohydrate choices	**None**
Exchanges: free food	

INGREDIENTS

Makes 20 tablespoons / Serving size: 1 tablespoon

Zucchini

- 1 tablespoon extra-virgin olive oil
- 2 cloves garlic, crushed
- 6 medium zucchini, sliced into rounds
- Pinch ground black pepper
- Pinch Atlantic sea salt
- 1 tablespoon dry white wine

Tofu

- 3½ ounces soft silken tofu
- 1 tablespoon extra-virgin olive oil
- 1 tablespoon fresh lemon juice
- 1 ounce (½ bunch) fresh basil
- 3 tablespoons chopped fresh parsley
- 3 tablespoons chopped scallions
- Pinch Atlantic sea salt
- ¼ teaspoon of ground black pepper

PREPARATION

1. Prepare zucchini: In a large frying pan, heat oil over medium-high heat, and lightly sauté garlic until brown, about 2 minutes. Add zucchini, salt, and pepper, and sauté until zucchini browns, about 5 minutes. Add wine, and stir-fry until liquid evaporates, about 2 minutes. Set aside.

2. Prepare tofu: In a food processor, process tofu, oil, and lemon juice for 3 to 5 minutes, until smooth. Add zucchini mixture, basil, parsley, and scallions, and puree until smooth. Add salt and pepper to taste.

TIP *The technique in this recipe can be used with any combination of vegetables and herbs you like. For example, replace the zucchini with 6 roasted red bell peppers, and the scallions and basil with ½ cup chopped thyme.*

CUT DOWN ON SWEETENED BEVERAGES

Choosing which beverages to serve at an event can be challenging. Should you buy diet or regular drinks, and how much should you buy? If you've ever checked your bills after a party, you might have found that soft drinks were a big expense. You might also have noticed that you were left with a variety of soft drinks that your guests didn't touch. Try to reduce the amount of soft drinks you purchase when you entertain, and prepare water-based drinks instead, such as the one described in the following recipe. You'll free up your party budget for other purchases that can upgrade your event, such as better wine and high quality ingredients. I'm sure your guests will appreciate the difference.

Orange, Cucumber, and Mint Drink

Orange, Cucumber, and Mint Drink

This recipe should be prepared a day in advance for best flavor. Soak slices of citrus fruit and fresh herbs in water for 24 hours to create a delicious drink just waiting to be enjoyed. For a completely different flavor, replace the mint and orange with sage and lemon. Serve both drinks at your event to make a delicious impact. Another fresh idea for adding flavor to water is to process 1 fresh or frozen fruit (page 161) in your food processor, and mix it with fresh herbs and 4 cups of cold water.

Calories	10
Total fat	0 g
Calories as fat	0%
Saturated fat	0 g
Cholesterol	0 g
Carbohydrates	2 g
Dietary fiber	0 g
Sodium	20 mg
Protein	0 g
Carbohydrate choices	**None**

Exchanges: free food

INGREDIENTS

Serves 8 / Serving size: 1 cup

- 1 medium orange, scrubbed, halved, and thinly sliced
- 1 medium cucumber, scrubbed and thinly sliced
- 1 ounce fresh mint
- 8 cups water

PREPARATION

1. Place oranges, cucumbers, and mint in a large jug. Add water and refrigerate for at least 24 hours, to allow flavors to blend.
2. Serve chilled.

ENRICH THE DESSERT MENU WITH FRUITY DISHES

There are more fruit-based desserts than baked desserts in the Sweetening without Sugar chapter (pages 110–128). You can maintain this ratio at your event by serving more fruit-based desserts and fewer pastries. Try making cold fruit-based desserts, such as the Mango Sorbet and Fruit Salad with Maple Tahini (page 126), which has the delightful and airy texture of ice cream.

Another deliciously cold dessert is granita. This frozen, grainy dish is so attractive that most people won't notice if it isn't very sweet. Making granita is simpler than making sorbet and requires less precision. Simply add water or yogurt to pureed fruit, and put it in the freezer. Granita, unlike sorbet, will freeze completely, so be sure to freeze it in a thin layer, no more than ½-inch thick, so that it can be broken up into very small pieces with a fork before serving.

Melon Salad with Plum Granita and Mint

Melon Salad with Plum Granita and Mint

Granita can be made with apricots, berries, nectarines, or any other seasonal fruit. Granita can also be made with fresh herbs. For example, blanch 5 sprigs of mint in 2 cups of boiling water and 1 tablespoon of unsweetened date honey for 3 minutes. Remove from heat and remove mint sprigs. Pour mixture into a pan so that it is about ½ inch thick. Cool to room temperature, then transfer to the freezer. After the liquid freezes, break it up with a fork, and serve in martini glasses on top of chopped fresh fruit. To upgrade this dish, add 1 tablespoon of vanilla vodka or anise-flavored liquid to the mixture before freezing.

Calories	70
Total fat	0 g
Calories as fat	0%
Saturated fat	0 g
Cholesterol	0 mg
Carbohydrates	17 g
Dietary fiber	2 g
Sodium	84 mg
Protein	1 g
Carbohydrate choices	**1**
Exchanges: 1 fruit	

INGREDIENTS

Serves 8 / Serving size: ½ cup salad + 1 tablespoon granita

- 1½ ounces pitted plums, halved
- ½ teaspoon unsweetened date honey
- 2 tablespoons water
- 1 medium honeydew, peeled, seeded, and cut into ½-inch cubes
- 1 medium cantaloupe, peeled, seeded, and cut into ½-inch cubes
- ¾ ounce (½ bunch) fresh mint, leaves only, coarsely chopped for garnish

PREPARATION

1. In a food processor, combine plums, date honey, and water, and process until smooth. Spread a ½-inch layer of mixture in a baking dish and freeze for about 1 hour.

2. Combine honeydew and cantaloupe in a medium bowl. To serve, spoon melon into serving dishes. Break up granita with a fork, and distribute evenly on top. Sprinkle with mint leaves and serve.

Snacks

When is the last time you wanted a snack—something in the refrigerator that's tasty but not so calorie-laden as to make you feel guilty? A few carrot sticks or lettuce leaves won't do the trick. You want something a lot more interesting and satisfying—but just as healthy.

Having healthy and satisfying snacks on hand is important. Foods that will satisfy cravings and stave off hunger between meals. Many foods can satisfy this type of craving, but I decided to present the following collection of vegetable-based recipes, known commonly as antipasti, tapas, or mezzas. These are dishes made from cooked vegetables and served at room temperature. In Italy, they are generally served before pasta, thus their Italian name, antipasti.

Really, all you need to do to make antipasti is cook some vegetables, season them as desired, and serve them at room temperature. If you want to serve them a day or two after you prepare them, the results will be even better, since the vegetables will absorb flavors while sitting in the refrigerator. Wondering when you'll find time to make these dishes? Many of them require no more effort than slicing vegetables and putting them in the oven. So take advantage of times when you are already in the kitchen and the oven is on in order to make snacks that can last an entire week. All of them are easy to eat, delicious, and won't cause you to feel guilty about snacking.

Read this chapter differently from the rest of the book
One of the most often-used words in this book is "variety", and this is particularly important in this chapter. Once you understand the principles of healthy cooking, you'll feel free and confident to alter and create recipes in your kitchen. If you use even some of the techniques described in this book, you'll find that buying and preparing food is a lot more fun—not just an exercise in counting calories and carbohydrates.

When it comes to antipasti, making variations is really quite easy. In addition to trying the individual recipes, I suggest reading this chapter to learn about the various techniques that can be used. Select a technique that seems right for you, prepare the vegetables you want, and season it as desired. I'm sure that you'll come up with lots of ideas.

I hope that after reading this chapter you'll fill your refrigerator with plastic containers of antipasti. In addition to Turnip and Kohlrabi Cubes with Olive Oil and Sumac (page 228), Grilled Zucchini in Mint Vinaigrette (page 230), and Asian Antipasto (page 238), I also hope you'll feel sufficiently confident to create recipes that integrate different ideas from this chapter, such as carpaccio with beets and a bit of rosemary, eggplant in pesto sauce, and roasted zucchini in beet vinaigrette. Imagine again that you really want a snack. You open your refrigerator and are faced with a colorful assortment of scents and flavors. Now imagine your table covered in a white tablecloth and laden with dozens of small ceramic dishes filled with antipasti—a pleasure for the eyes and the palate.

Turnip and Kohlrabi Cubes with Olive Oil and Sumac

The technique used in this recipe is the simplest one: roasting. Fill a pan with vegetables you like, mix them with olive oil, and roast. Store the roasted vegetables in the refrigerator, and serve them at room temperature. That's all there is to it. I like using aromatic root vegetables to achieve a rich flavor with no other ingredients. You can upgrade dishes made in this manner by mixing them with 1 tablespoon of pure tahini immediately after they come out of the oven, or seasoning them with an aromatic spice such as sumac before serving.

Calories	43
Total fat	3 g
Calories as fat	63%
Saturated fat	1 g
Cholesterol	0 mg
Carbohydrates	3 g
Dietary fiber	2 g
Sodium	90 mg
Protein	1 g
Carbohydrate choices	**None**

Exchanges: 1 vegetable, ½ fat

INGREDIENTS

Serves 8 / Serving size: ½ cup

- **2 medium kohlrabi, peeled and cut into ½-inch cubes**
- **2 medium turnips, peeled and cut into ½-inch cubes**
- **Pinch ground black pepper**
- **Pinch Atlantic sea salt**
- **2 tablespoons extra-virgin olive oil**
- **½ teaspoon sumac**

PREPARATION

1. Preheat oven to 350°F. In a medium bowl, combine kohlrabi and turnips. Mix with salt and pepper, then toss with oil to coat.

2. Arrange vegetables in a single layer on a large baking sheet and roast for 15 to 20 minutes, until soft. Adjust oven to broil and grill for 2 minutes, stirring occasionally, until golden brown.

3. Remove from oven and cool to room temperature. Sprinkle with sumac before serving.

Turnip and Kohlrabi Cubes with Olive Oil and Sumac

Grilled Zucchini in Mint Vinaigrette

Grilling vegetables on a lined grill pan requires no additional oil (page 47). This recipe can be altered by replacing the zucchini with eggplant or pumpkin slices. The vinaigrette can also be used to flavor roasted cubes of kohlrabi and turnip, and it, too, can be varied. For example, try replacing the mint with parsley or chives, and use another type of vinegar or flavored oil.

Calories	56
Total fat	4 g
Calories as fat	64%
Saturated fat	1 g
Cholesterol	0 mg
Carbohydrates	4 g
Dietary fiber	1 g
Sodium	71 mg
Protein	1 g
Carbohydrate choices	**None**

Exchanges: 1 vegetable, 1 fat

INGREDIENTS

Serves 10 / Serving size: ½ cup

Zucchini

- **6 firm medium zucchini, sliced diagonally into thin rounds**
- **Pinch Atlantic sea salt**
- **Pinch ground black pepper**

Vinaigrette

- **3 tablespoons extra-virgin olive oil**
- **6 tablespoons balsamic vinegar**
- **2 cloves garlic, chopped**
- **4 tablespoons chopped fresh mint**

PREPARATION

1. Prepare zucchini: Season zucchini rounds with salt and pepper. Heat a grill pan over medium-high heat. Working in batches, roast zucchini rounds for about 1 to 2 minutes on each side, until dark lines appear. Transfer to a large bowl.

2. In a small bowl, combine oil, vinegar, garlic, and mint. Pour over zucchini rounds, and mix to coat. Let sit at room temperature for at least 30 minutes before serving, to allow flavors to blend.

Roasted Mushrooms and Leeks in Balsamic Vinaigrette

Rather than adding flavor to vegetables after they have been roasted, vegetables can also be roasted with a marinade. With this technique, the marinade is reduced during the cooking process, wrapping each vegetable in aromatic liquid and imbuing it with flavor. This dish is particularly distinct due to the combination of crispy leeks and soft mushrooms, two vegetables with different textures that cook well together.

INGREDIENTS

Serves 10 / Serving size: ½ cup

- 1 leek, halved lengthwise and cut into 1-inch pieces
- 5 ounces button mushrooms
- Pinch Atlantic sea salt
- Pinch ground black pepper
- ½ cup balsamic vinegar
- 1 tablespoon extra-virgin olive oil
- 1 clove garlic, chopped

Calories	28
Total fat	1 g
Calories as fat	32%
Saturated fat	0 g
Cholesterol	0 mg
Carbohydrates	4 g
Dietary fiber	0 g
Sodium	60 mg
Protein	0 g
Carbohydrate choices	**None**

Exchanges: 1 vegetable

PREPARATION

1. Preheat oven to 350°F. In a large bowl, mix together leek and mushrooms. Season with salt and pepper, then toss with vinegar, oil, and garlic to coat.

2. Transfer mixture to a baking dish and bake for 30 minutes, mixing occasionally, until leek is soft. Let cool to room temperature before serving.

TIP *To alter this dish, you can roast the mushrooms and leeks in equal parts of soy sauce and balsamic vinegar, or oil rather than marinade, and serve them with any of the other sauces, spices, or vinaigrettes described in this chapter. This recipe opens the window to a host of options for roasting with marinades. For example, the kohlrabi and turnip cubes from page 228 can be roasted with balsamic vinaigrette, and so can slices of zucchini. When you make variations, make sure to keep the recipe simple. That's the beauty of antipasto.*

Pumpkin Carpaccio with Nigella

Another method for cooking vegetables doesn't involve heating at all. Instead, vegetables are cooked in vinegar, a technique similar to that used for Sea Bass Ceviche with Bermuda Onion and Sumac (page 174). The acid slowly softens the ingredients, "cooking" them enough for eating. This technique, usually used for fish and meat, also works with hard vegetables, such as pumpkin, that are generally cooked. The trick is to slice the vegetables very thinly, even with a peeler.

TIP   *The pumpkin in this recipe can be replaced with beets or zucchini. The lemon juice can be replaced with other acidic liquids such as balsamic vinegar, rice vinegar, or any other type of vinegar you like. In addition to giving this dish a different flavor, vinegars also have a lower acidity than lemon juice, so the vegetables will need to soak for a bit longer before reaching the desired result. However, since you are preparing food to last the entire week, that shouldn't be a problem.*

Calories	26
Total fat	2 g
Calories as fat	69%
Saturated fat	1 g
Cholesterol	0 g
Carbohydrates	1 g
Dietary fiber	0 g
Sodium	97 mg
Protein	0 g
Carbohydrate choices	**None**
Exchanges: ½ fat	

INGREDIENTS

Serves 6 / Serving size: ½ cup

- **3 ounces fresh pumpkin, peeled and seeded**
- **¼ teaspoon Atlantic sea salt**
- **¼ teaspoon ground black pepper**
- **1 tablespoon fresh lemon juice**
- **1 tablespoon extra-virgin olive oil**
- **1 teaspoon nigella seeds**
- **1 tablespoon pumpkin seeds**

PREPARATION

1. Cut pumpkin into very thin slices. (Use a vegetable peeler if you like.) Arrange a thin layer of pumpkin slices at the bottom of a deep, flat-bottomed dish. Season with salt and pepper, and sprinkle with lemon juice and olive oil.

2. Arrange another layer of pumpkin slices on top. Season with salt and pepper and sprinkle with juice and oil. Repeat process until all pumpkin slices have been stacked. Let sit for at least 30 minutes.

3. To serve, arrange pumpkin slices in a thin layer on a large plate, and sprinkle with nigella and pumpkin seeds.

Pumpkin Carpaccio with Nigella

Artichoke Hearts Stuffed with Swiss Chard

Steaming and sautéing, two techniques used in this recipe, can be used in many other recipes in this chapter. For example, the zucchini on page 230 can be sautéed with a little olive oil, and the turnip and kohlrabi cubes on page 228 can be steamed. In the recipe below, the artichoke hearts are steamed and the Swiss chard is sautéed. For best results, look for artichokes that are large and easy to fill, and make sure to press the filling in firmly. Artichoke hearts can be stuffed with a variety of fillings; see suggestions on facing page.

Calories	106
Total fat	7 g
Calories as fat	59%
Saturated fat	1 g
Cholesterol	0 mg
Carbohydrates	10 g
Dietary fiber	4 g
Sodium	223 mg
Protein	3 g
Carbohydrate choices	½
Exchanges: 2 vegetable, 1 fat	

INGREDIENTS

Serves 8 / Serving size: 1 stuffed artichoke heart

- **8 large, frozen, artichoke hearts, thawed**
- **4 tablespoons extra-virgin olive oil**
- **1 pound Swiss chard, thinly sliced**
- **Pinch Atlantic sea salt**
- **Pinch coarsely ground black pepper**
- **4 tablespoons fresh lemon juice**
- **3 cloves garlic, chopped**

PREPARATION

1. Heat water in a pot over medium heat. Place artichoke hearts in a steamer basket, and place basket on pot the size of the steamer basket. Cover basket and steam artichokes for 10 minutes, until soft. Add water to pot, if necessary.

2. In the meantime, in a medium frying pan, heat 1 tablespoon oil over medium-high heat. Add Swiss chard and sauté for 15 minutes, until chard is completed wilted. Add salt and pepper to taste.

3. Separately, in a non-reactive medium bowl, mix together lemon juice, remaining 3 tablespoons oil, and garlic.

4. Stuff artichoke hearts with Swiss chard, then place in bowl with lemon juice marinade. Cover and refrigerate for at least 3 hours before serving.

Artichoke Hearts Stuffed with Swiss Chard

TIP *Artichoke hearts can be stuffed with a variety of fillings, as long as the fillings are first processed coarsely in a food processor. For variety, replace the filling with Grilled Zucchini in Mint Vinaigrette (page 230), Turnip and Kohlrabi Cubes with Olive Oil and Sumac (page 228), or Roasted Mushrooms and Leeks in Balsamic Vinaigrette (page 231). The artichoke hearts can be sliced and grilled in a lined pan, baked in the oven and served with sumac, or marinated in Mint Vinaigrette (page 230). Artichoke hearts can also be cut into cubes and roasted with leeks and mushrooms.*

Baby Peppers Stuffed with Baby Arugula and Cheese

Another attractive filling for roasted vegetables are fresh vegetables, finely chopped into a salad. This is the only recipe in this chapter that uses cubes of low-fat, semi-soft, white cheese, but you can upgrade almost any antipasto with cubes of low-fat, semi-soft, white cheese. For example, try mixing them with the grilled zucchini in the Grilled Zucchini in Mint Marinade (page 230). You can also serve it on the Pumpkin Carpaccio with Nigella (page 232). The Swiss chard filling in the previous recipe can be enhanced by mixing it with a bit of spreadable goat cheese and lemon.

Calories	36
Total fat	2 g
Calories as fat	50%
Saturated fat	1 g
Cholesterol	2 mg
Carbohydrates	4 g
Dietary fiber	1 g
Sodium	101 mg
Protein	1 g
Carbohydrate choices	**None**

Exchanges: 1 vegetable, ½ fat

INGREDIENTS

Serves 8 / Serving size: 1 stuffed pepper

Peppers
- 4 red or yellow baby peppers, halved lengthwise, seeds removed
- Pinch Atlantic sea salt
- Pinch ground black pepper
- 1 tablespoon extra-virgin olive oil

Filling
- 5 tablespoons chopped baby arugula
- 2 tablespoons chopped fresh parsley
- 2 tablespoons cubed low-fat semi-soft cheese, such as feta
- 1 tablespoon balsamic vinegar
- Pinch Atlantic sea salt
- Pinch ground black pepper

PREPARATION

1. Prepare peppers: Preheat oven to 350°F. Season peppers with salt and pepper, and brush insides with oil. Place on a baking sheet and roast for 5 to 10 minutes, or until peppers brown. Set aside to cool.

2. Prepare filling: In a medium bowl, mix together baby arugula, parsley, cheese, vinegar, and salt and pepper to taste. Fill pepper halves with mixture, and serve.

Baby Peppers Stuffed with Baby Arugula and Cheese

TIP *The Swiss chard filling in the previous recipe can also be used for the baby peppers here, and the filling here can, in turn, be used for the artichoke hearts in the previous recipe. Create your own pepper fillings with grated root vegetables and lemon juice, or try the Taboule Salad (page 22) or the Thai Beef Salad with Onion and Lemongrass (page 213).*

Asian Antipasto

The final recipe in this chapter demonstrates a completely different approach to making antipasto. All of the techniques and ingredients used in the previous recipes come from the Mediterranean kitchen. The following recipe is a fusion of techniques from the Mediterranean and flavors from Asia—try it and see what wonderful flavor the antipasto receives thanks to this simple twist. With the same ease, you can fuse in Latin flavors by wrapping antipasto in a corn-flour tortilla and topping it with salsa, filling the baby pepper in the previous recipe with guacamole, or stuffing artichoke hearts with a bean mixture.

INGREDIENTS

Serves 15 / Serving size: ½ cup

Sauce

- 6 tablespoons extra-virgin olive oil
- 6 tablespoons low-sodium soy sauce
- 4 tablespoons balsamic vinegar
- 3 tablespoons yuzu juice
- 1 tablespoon honey
- 3 teaspoons peeled and grated fresh ginger
- 5 cloves garlic, crushed
- 3 tablespoons chopped fresh basil
- 3 tablespoons chopped fresh mint
- 1 tablespoon chopped and seeded red hot chili pepper

Vegetables

- 40 cherry tomatoes, pierced
- 1 medium fennel bulb, sliced
- 4 medium zucchini, yellow and green, thickly sliced
- 2 medium onions, quartered
- 1 head garlic, cloves separated and peeled
- 2 cups cauliflower florets

Calories	93
Total fat	6 g
Calories as fat	58%
Saturated fat	1 g
Cholesterol	0 mg
Carbohydrates	10 g
Dietary fiber	2 g
Sodium	234 mg
Protein	2 g
Carbohydrate choices	½
Exchanges: 2 vegetable, 1 fat	

PREPARATION

1. Prepare sauce: In a medium bowl, mix together oil, soy sauce, vinegar, and yuzu juice. Mix in honey, then add ginger, garlic, basil, mint, and chili pepper, mixing until thoroughly combined. Set aside.

2. Prepare vegetables: Preheat oven to 400°F. In a large bowl, mix together tomatoes, fennel, zucchini, onions, garlic, and cauliflower.

3. Pour sauce over vegetable mixture, tossing until thoroughly coated. Transfer mixture to a large shallow baking dish and roast for 30 minutes, until cauliflower softens. Serve at room temperature.

IN SUMMARY—SO WHERE DO I START?

This book contains a large amount of information, and you'll probably need some time to "digest" the healthy cooking techniques and abundant recipes. Here are a few suggestions to help you make these techniques and recipes part of your daily life.

For some people, the easiest way to make changes is simply to make a decision to change, wake up the next morning, and start everything anew. This might be called the cold turkey approach. For others, however, this method doesn't lead to long-term behavior change. This is specially true when it comes to eating habits, as these develop over the course of a lifetime and are complex and deeply rooted.

As a first step, I suggest that you break down the big change you'd like to make into a number of smaller changes. Start by choosing a few of the healthy suggestions in this book, and focus on them alone. After you feel comfortable with the new approaches and they become part of your shopping and cooking routine, you can try making a few more changes.

By the time you have reached this part of the book, you have likely already tried a few of the suggested changes. Some of them probably felt more comfortable than others. Start with the changes that best fit your lifestyle and food preferences and try adopting them. When you are comfortable with these changes, flip through the book again, and try out a couple more changes. Try out changes that include using different tools, ingredients, and cooking techniques. On the one hand, you don't want changes that are too complicated to carry out; on the other hand, you do want to make changes that are new and significant.

Even if these changes don't feel natural at the beginning, after a bit of time, I am sure that some of them will become habits, and you won't even notice you are doing them. This is the time to relax in your chair and feel good about yourself. Because you've succeeded. You've made healthy changes that are bound to help you feel better and stay healthier for years to come. It's also the time to choose a few more new healthy habits. I hope that you'll always find something new and interesting.

INDEX

EXCHANGE LISTS FOR DIABETES

THE FOOD LISTS

The following chart shows the amount of nutrients in 1 serving from each list.

Food List	Carbohydrate (grams)	Protein (grams)	Fat (grams)	Calories
Carbohydrates Starch: breads, cereals and grains, starchy vegetables, crackers, snacks and beans, peas, and lentils	15	0-3	0-1	80
Fruits	15	-	-	60
Milk				
Fat-free low-fat, 1%	12	8	0-3	100
Reduced-fat, 2%	12	8	5	120
Whole	12	8	8	160
Sweets, Desserts and Other Carbohydrates	15	varies	varies	varies
Nonstarchy vegetables	5	2	-	25
Meat and Meat Substitutes				
Lean	-	7	0-3	45
Medium-fat	-	7	4 7	75
High-fat	-	7	8+	100
Plant-based proteins	-	7	varies	varies
Fats	-	-	5	45
Alcohol	varies	-	-	100

STARCH

BREAD

Food	Serving Size
Bagel, large (about 4 oz)	¼ (1oz)
☹ Biscuit, 2½ inches across	1
Bread	
☺ reduced-calorie	2 slice (1½ oz)
white, whole grain, pumpernickel, rye, unfrosted raisin	1 slice (1 oz)
Chapatti, small 6 inches across	1
☹ Cornbread, 1¾ inch cube	1 (1½ oz)
English muffin	½
Hot dog bun or hamburger bun	½ (1 oz)
Naan, 8 inches by 2 inches	¼
Pancake, 4 inches across, ¼ inch thick	1
Pita, 6 inches across	½
Roll, plain, small	1 (1½ oz)
☹ Stuffing, bread	⅓ cup
☹ Taco shell, 5 inches across	2
Tortilla, corn, 6 inches across	1
Tortilla, flour, 6 inches across	1
Tortilla, flour, 10 inches across	⅓ tortilla
☹ Waffe, 4-inch square or 4 inches acroos	1

CEREALS AND GRAINS

Food	Serving Size
Barley, cooked	⅓ cup
Bran, dry	
☺ oat	¼ cup
☺ wheat	½ cup
☺ Burgul (cooked)	½ cup
Cereals	
☺ bran	½ cup
cooked (outs, oatmeal)	½ cup
puffed	1½ cup
shredded wheat, plain	½ cup
sugar-coated	½ cup
unsweetend	¾ cup
Couscous	⅓ cup
Granola	
low-fat	¼ cup
☹ regular	¼ cup
Grits, cooked	½ cup
Kasha	½ cup
Miller, cooked	⅓ cup
Muesli	¼ cup
Pasta, cooked	⅓ cup
Polenta, cooked	⅓ cup
Quinoa, cooked	⅓ cup
Rice, white or brown, cooked	⅓ cup
Taboule, prepared	½ cup
Wheat germ, dry	3 Tabiespoons
Wild rice, cooked	½ cup

☺ **More than 3 grams dietary fiber per serving**

☹ **Extra fat, or prepared with added fat. (Count as 1 starch + 1 fat.)**

480 milligrams or more of sodium per servng

STARCHY VEGETABLES

Food List	Serving size
Cassava	⅓ cup
Corn	½ cup
on cob, large	½ cob (5 oz)
☺ Hominy, canned	¾ cup
☺ Mixed vegetables	1 cup
with corn, peas, or pasta	
☺ Parsnips	½ cup
☺ Peas, green	½ cup
Plantain, ripe	⅓ cup
Potato	
baked with skin	¼ large (3 oz)
boiled, all kinds	½ cup or ½ medium (3 oz)
☹ mashed, with milk and fat	½ cup
French-fried (oven baked)	1 cup (2 oz)
☺ Pumpkin, canned,	1 cup
no sugar added	
Spaghetti/pasta sauce	½ cup
☺ Squash, winter (acorn, butternut)	1 cup
☺ Succotash	½ cup
Yam, sweet potato, plain	½ cup

CRACKERS AND SNACKS

Food	Serving size
Animal crackers	8
Crackers	
☹ round-butter type	6
saltine-type	6
☹ sandwich-style, cheese or	3
peanut butter filling	
☹ whole-wheat regular	2-5 (¾ oz)
☺ whole-wheat lower fat or crispbreads	2-5 (¾ oz)
Graham cracker, 2 ½-inch square	3
Matzoh	¾ oz
Melba toast, about 2-inch by	4 pieces
4-inch piece	
Oyster crackers	20
Popcorn	3 cups
☹☺ with butter	3 cups
☺ no fat added	3 cups
☺ lower fat	3 cups
Pretzels	¾ oz
Rice cakes, 4 inches across	2
Snack chips	
fat-free or baked (tortilla, potato),	15-20 (¾ oz)
baked pita chips	
☹ regular (tortilla, potato)	9-13 (¾ oz)

BEANS, PEAS, AND LENTILS
The choices on this list count as 1 starch + 1 lean meat

Food	Serving size
☺ Baked beans	⅓ cup
☺ Beans, cooked (black, garbanzo,	½ cup
kidney, lima, navy, pinto, white)	
☺ Lentils, cooked (brown, green, yellow)	½ cup
☺ Peas, cooked (black-eyed, split)	½ cup
✎ ☺ Refried beans, canned	½ cup

Note: Beans, peas, and lentils are also found on the Meat and Meat Substitutes list, page 251.

FRUIT
The weight listed includes skin, core, seeds, and rind.

Food	Serving size
Apple, unpeeled, small	1 (4 oz)
Apples, dried	4 rings
Applesauce, unsweetened	½ cup
Apricots	
canned	½ cup
dried	8 halves
☺ fresh	4 whole (5½ oz)
Banana, extra small	1 (4 oz)
☺ Blackberries	¾ cup

FRUIT (continued) The weight listed includes skin, core, seeds, and rind.

Food	Serving size
Blueberries	¾ cup
Cantaloupe, small	⅓ melon or 1 cup cubed (11 oz)
Cherries	
sweet, canned	½ cup
sweet fresh	12 (3 oz)
Dates	3
Dried fruits (blueberries, cherries, cranberries, mixed fruits, raisins)	2 Tablespoons
Figs	
dried	1½
☺ fresh	1½ large or 2 medium (3½ oz)
Fruit cocktail	½ cup
Grapefruit	
large	½ (11 oz)
sections, canned	¾ cup
Grapes	17 (3 oz)
Honeydew melon	1 slice or 1 cup cubed (10 oz)
☺ Kiwi	1 (3½ oz)
Mandarin oranges, canned	¾ cup
Mango, small	½ fruit (5½ oz) or ½ cup
Nectarine, small	1 (5 oz)
☺ Orange, small	1 (6½ oz)
Papaya	½ fruit or 1 cup cubed (8 oz)
Peaches	
canned	½ cup
fresh, medium	1 (6 oz)
Pears	
canned	½ cup
fresh, large	½ (4 oz)
Pineapple	
canned	½ cup
fresh	¾ cup
Plums	
canned	½ cup
dried (prunes)	3
small	2 (5 oz)

Food	Serving size
☺ Raspberries	1 cup
☺ Strawberries	1¼ cups whole berries
☺ Tangerines, small	2 (8 oz)
Watermelon	1 slice or 1¼ cups cubes (13 ½ oz)

FRUIT JUICE

Food	Serving size
Apple juice/cider	½ cup
Fruit juice blends, 100% juice	⅓ cup
Grape juice	⅓ cup
Grapefruit juice	½ cup
Orange juice	½ cup
Pineapple juice	½ cup
Prune juice	⅓ cup

☺ More than 3 grams dietary fiber per serving

☺ Extra fat, or prepared with added fat. (Count as 1 starch + 1 fat.)

🖊 480 milligrams or more of sodium per servng

MILK

Different types of milk and milk products are on this list. However, two types of milk products are found on other lists:
- Cheeses are on the Meat and Meat Substitutes list (because they are rich in protein).
- Cream and other dairy fats are on the Fats list.

Milk and yogurts are grouped in three categories (fat-free, low-fat, reduced-fat, or whole) based on the amount of fat they have. The following chart shows you what 1 milk choice contains:

	Carbohydrate (grams)	Protein (grams)	Fat (grams)	Calories
Fat-free (skim), low fat (1%)	12	8	0-3	100
Reduced-fat (2%)	12	8	5	120
Whole	12	8	8	160

Selection tips
- 1 cup equals 8 fluid oz or ½ pint.
- If you choose 2% or whole-milk foods, be aware of the extra fat.

MILKS AND YOGURTS

Food	Serving size	Count as
Fat-free or low-fat (1%)		
Milk, buttermilk, acidophilus milk, Lactaid	1 cup	1 fat-free milk
Evaporated milk	½ cup	1 fat-free milk
Yogurt, plain or flavored with an artificial sweetener	⅔ cup (6 oz)	1 fat-free milk
Reduced-fat (2%)		
Milk, acidophilus milk, kefir, Lactaid	1 cup	1 reduced-fat milk
Yogurt, plain	⅔ cup (6 oz)	1 reduced-fat milk
Whole		
Milk, buttermilk, goat's milk	1 cup	1 whole milk
Evaporated milk	½ cup	1 whole milk
Yogurt, plain	8 oz	1 whole milk

DAIRY-LIKE FOODS

Food	Serving size	Count as
Chocolate milk		
fat-free	1 cup	1 fat-free milk + 1 carbohydrate
whole	1 cup	1 whole milk + 1 carbohydrate
Eggnog, whole milk	½ cup	1 carbohydrate + 2 fats
Rice drink		
flavored, low-fat	1 cup	2 carbohydrates
plain, fat-free	1 cup	1 carbohydrate
Smoothies, flavored, regular	10 oz	1 fat-free milk + 2½ carbohydrates
Soy milk		
light	1 cup	1 carbohydrate + ½ fat
regular, plain	1 cup	1 carbohydrate + 1 fat
Yogurt		
and juice blends	1 cup	1 fat-free milk + 1 carbohydrate
low carbohydrate (less than 6 grams carbohydrate per choice)	⅔ cup (6 oz)	½ fat-free milk
with fruit, low-fat	⅔ cup (6 oz)	1 fat-free milk + 1 carbohydrate

NONSTARCHY VEGETABLES

Amaranth or Chinese Spinach	Cabbage (green, bok choy, Chinese)
Artichoke	Carrots
Artichoke hearts	Celery
Asparagus	☺ Chayote
Baby corn	Coleslaw, packaged, no dressing
Bamboo shoots	Cucumber
Beans (green, wax, Italian)	Eggplant
Bean sprouts	Gourds (bitter, bottle, luffa, bitter melon)
Beets	Green onions or scallions
🧂 Borscht	Greens (collard, kale, mustard, turnip)
Broccoli	Hearts of palm
☺ Brussels sprouts	Jicama

Kohlrabi	Soybean sprouts
Leeks	Spinach
Mixed vegetables (without corn, peas, or pasta)	Squash (summer, crookneck, zucchini)
Mung bean sprouts	Sugar pea snaps
Mushrooms, all kind, fresh	☺ Swiss chard
Okra	Tomato
Onions	Tomatoes, canned
Oriental radish or daikon	🧂 Tomato sauce
Pea Pods	🧂 Tomato, vegetable juice
Peppers (all varieties)	Turnips
Radishes	Water chestnuts
Rutabaga	Yard-long beans
🧂 Sauerkraut	

SPREADS, SWEETS, SWEETENERS, SYRUPS AND TOPPINGS

Food	Serving size	Count as
Fruit Spreads,100% fruit	1½ tablespoon	1 carbohydrate
Honey	1 tablespoon	1 carbohydrate
Jam or jelly, regular	1 tablespoon	1 carbohydrate
Sugar	1 tablespoon	1 carbohydrate

MEAT AND MEAT SUBSTITUTES

Meat and meat substitutes are rich in protein. Foods from this list are divided into 4 groups based on the amount of fat they contain. These groups are lean meat, medium-fat meat, high-fat meat, and plant-based proteins. The following chart shows you what one choice includes.

	Carbohydrate (grams)	Protein (grams)	Fat (grams)	Calories
Lean meat	-	7	0-3	100
Medium-fat meat	-	7	4-7	130
High-fat meat	-	7	8+	150
Plant-based protein	varies	7	varies	varies

LEAN MEATS AND MEAT SUBSTITUTES

Food	Amount
Beef: Select or Choice grades trimmed of fat: ground round, roast (chuck, rib, rump), round, sirloin, steak (cubed, flank, porterhouse, T-bone), tenderloin	1 oz
Beef jerky	1 oz
Cheeses with 3 grams of fat or less	1 oz
Cottage cheese	¼ cup
Egg substitutes, plain	¼ cup
Egg whites	2
Fish, fresh or frozen, plain: catfish, cod, flounder, haddock, halibut, orange roughy, salmon, tilapia, trout, tuna	1 oz
Fish, smoked: herring or salmon (lox)	1 oz
Game: buffalo, ostrich, rabbit, venison	1 oz
Hot dog with 3 grams of fat or less per oz (8 dogs per 14 oz per package) Note: May be high in carbohydrate.	1
Lamb: chop, leg, or roast	1 oz
Organ meats: heart, kidney, liver Note: May be high in cholesterol	1 oz
Oysters, fresh or frozen	6 medium
Pork, lean Canadian bacon rib or loin chop, roast, ham, tenderloin	1 oz 1 oz
Poultry, without skin: Cornish hen, chicken, domestic duck or goose (well-drained of fat), turkey	1 oz
Processed sandwich meats with 3 grams of fat or less per oz: chipped beef, deli thin-sliced meats, turkey ham, turkey kielbasa, turkey pastrami	1 oz
Salmon, canned	1 oz
Sardines, canned	1 oz
Sausage with 3 grams of fat or less per oz	1 oz
Shellfish: clams, crab, imitation shellfish, lobster, scallops, shrimp	1 oz
Tuna, canned in water or oil, drained	1 oz
Veal, lean chop, roast	1 oz

MEDIUM-FAT MEAT AND MEAT SUBSTITUTES

Food	Amount
Beef: corned beef, ground beef, meatloaf, Prime grads trimmed of fat (prime rib), short ribs, tongue	1 oz
Cheeses with 4-7 grams of fat per oz: feta, mozzarella, pasteurized processed cheese spread, reduced-fat cheeses, string	1 oz
Egg Note: High in cholesterol, so limit to 3 per week	1
Fish, any fried product	1 oz
Lamb: ground, rib roast	1 oz
Pork: cutlet, shoulder roast	1 oz
Poultry: chicken with skin; dove, pheasant, wild duck, or goose; fried chicken; ground turkey	1 oz
Ricotta cheese	2 oz or ¼ cup
Sausage with 4-7 grams of fat per oz	1 oz
Veal, cutlet (no breading)	1 oz

HIGH-FAT MEAT AND MEAT SUBSTITUTES
These foods are high in saturated fat, cholesterol, and calories and may raise blood cholesterol levels if eaten on a regular basis. Try to eat 3 or fewer servings from this group per week.

Food	Amount
Bacon pork	2 slices (16 slices per lb or 1 oz each, before cooking)
turkey	3 slices (½ oz each before cooking)
Cheese, regular: American, bleu, brie, cheddar, hard goat, Monterey jack, queso, and Swiss	1 oz
Hot dog: beef, pork, or combination (10 per lb-sized package)	1
Hot dog: turkey or chicken (10 per lb-sized package)	1
Pork: ground, sausage, spareribs	1 oz
Processed sandwich meats with 8 grams of fat or more per oz: bologna, pastrami, hard salami	1 oz
Sausage with 8 grams fat or more per oz: bratwurst, chorizo, Italian, knockwurst, Polish, smoked, summer	1 oz

PLANT-BASED PROTEINS

Because carbohydrate content varies among plant-based proteins, you should read the food label.

Food	Amount	Count as
"Bacon" strips, soy-based	3 strips	1 medium-fat meat
☺ Baked beans	⅓ cup	1 starch + 1 lean meat
☺ Beans, cooked: black, garbanzo, kidney, lima, navy, pinto, white	½ cup	1 starch + 1 lean meat
☺ "Beef" or "sausage" crumbles, soy-based	2 oz	½ carbohydrate + 1 lean meat
"Chicken" nuggets, soy-based	2 nuggets (1½ oz)	½ carbohydrate + 1 medium-fat meat
☺ Edamame	½ cup	½ carbohydrate + 1 lean meat
Falafel (spiced chickpea and wheat patties)	3 patties (about 2 inches across)	1 carbohydrate + 1 high-fat meat
Hot dog, soy-based	1 (1½ oz)	½ carbohydrate + 1 lean meat
☺ Hummus	⅓ cup	1 carbohydrate + 1 high-fat meat
☺ Lentils, brown, green, or yellow	½ cup	1 carbohydrate + 1 lean meat
☺ Meatless burger, soy-based	3 oz	½ carbohydrate + 2 lean meats
☺ Meatless burger, vegetable and starch-based	1 patty (about 2½ oz)	1 carbohydrate + 2 lean meats
Nut spreads: almond butter, cashew butter, peanut butter, soy nut butter	1 tablespoon	1 high-fat meat
☺ Peas, cooked: black-eyed and split peas	½ cup	1 starch + 1 lean meat
✎ ☺ Refried beans, canned	½ cup	1 starch + 1 lean meat
"Sausage" patties, soy-based	1 (1½ oz)	1 medium-fat meat
Soy nuts, unsalted	¾ oz	½ carbohydrate + 1 medium-fat meat
Tempeh	¼ cup	1 medium-fat meat
Tofu	4 oz (½ cup)	1 medium-fat meat
Tofu, light	4 oz (½ cup)	1 lean meat

FATS

Fats and oils have mixtures of unsaturated (polyunsaturated and monounsaturated) and saturated fats.
Foods on the Fats list are grouped together based on the major type of fat they contain. In general, 1 fat choice equals:
- 1 teaspoon of regular margarine, vegetable oil, or butter
- 1 tablespoon of regular salad dressing

UNSATURATED FATS – MONOUNSATURATED FATS

Food	Serving Size
Avocado, medium	2 tablespoons (1 oz)
Nut butters (*trans* fat-free): almond butter, cashew butter, peanut butter (smooth or crunchy)	1½ teaspoons
Nuts	
almonds	6 nuts
Brazil	2 nuts
cashews	6 nuts
filberts (hazelnuts)	5 nuts
macadamia	3 nuts
mixed (50% peanuts)	6 nuts
peanuts	10 nuts
pecans	4 halves
pistachios	16 nuts
Oil: canola, olive, peanut	1 teaspoon
Olives	
black (ripe)	8 large
green (stuffed)	10 large

POLYUNSATURATED FATS

Food	Serving Size
Margarine: lower-fat spread (30%-50% vegetable oil, *trans* fat-free)	1 tablespoon
Margarine: stick, tub (*trans* fat-free), or squeeze (*trans* fat-free)	1 teaspoon
Mayonnaise	
reduced-fat	1 tablespoon
regular	1 teaspoon
Mayonnaise-style salad dressing	
reduced-fat	1 tablespoon
regular	2 teaspoons
Nuts	
Pignolia (pine nuts)	1 tablespoon
walnuts, English	4 halves
Oil: corn, cottonseed, flaxseed, grape seed, safflower, soybean, sunflower	1 teaspoon
Oil: made from soybean and canola oil – Enova	1 teaspoon
Plant stanol esters	
light	1 tablespoon
regular	2 teaspoons
Salad dressing	
reduced-fat	2 tablespoons
Note: May be high in carbohydrate	1 tablespoon
regular	
Seeds	
flaxseed, whole	1 tablespoon
pumpkin, sunflower	1 tablespoon
sesame seeds	1 tablespoon
Tahini of sesame paste	2 tablespoons

SATURATED FATS

Food	Serving Size
Bacon, cooked, regular or turkey	1 slice
Butter	
reduced-fat	1 tablespoon
stick	1 teaspoon
whipped	2 teaspoons
Butter blends made with oil	
reduced-fat or light	1 tablespoon
regular	1½ teaspoons
Chitterlings, boiled	2 tablespoons (½ oz)
Coconut, sweetened, shredded	2 tablespoons
Coconut milk	
light	⅓ cup
regular	1½ tablespoons
Cream	
half and half	2 tablespoons
heavy	1 tablespoon
light	1½ tablespoons
whipped	2 tablespoons
whipped, pressurized	¼ cup
Cream cheese	
reduced-fat	1½ tablespoons (¾ oz)
regular	1 tablespoon (½ oz)
Lard	1 teaspoon
Oil: coconut, palm, palm kernel	1 teaspoon
Salt pork	¼ oz
Shortening, solid	1 teaspoon
Sour cream	
reduced-fat or light	3 tablespoons
regular	2 tablespoons

ACKNOWLEDGEMENTS

Thanks to Roni Kaufman and Amitai Rotem, for helping me realize a dream.

Thanks to the team of chefs comprised of Shani Mador, Batchen Yoffe, Ohad Alt, and Bat-Sheva Dori-Karlier, who were my sources of inspiration.

To my friends who are amazingly persistent and willing to try out my recipes. To Paula Payne for precisely calculating the recipes, to Hope Warshaw for reviewing, and to Danya for her marvelous photographs. To Ruth Moshe for her good advice, and to Shoshana for her English editing.

To Batchen Yoffe, thanks for the Rolled Apricot Fruit Leather with Goat Cheese and Basil recipe. To Ohad Alt, thanks for the Nectarines Roasted in Orange Juice and Date Honey, Wild Rice and Beet Salad, and Grilled Marinated Bass Fingers Wrapped in Swiss Chard recipes. To Bat Sheva Dori-Karlier, thanks for the Carrot Cake with Pears and Honey Almond Glaze, Beer and Almond Bread, and Almond Cookies in Apricot Sauce recipes.

Edited by Shoshana Brickman
Photography by Danya Weiner
Design by Michal & Dekel
Reviewed by Hope S. Warshaw, MMSc, RD, CDE, BC-ADM.
Nutrient analysis of recipes: Paula D. Payne, MS, LD, RD, President Piedmont Nutrition Associates, Inc.